SCIENCE QUESTIONS AND ANSWERS

Contents

Body Science	**5**
Body Science Quiz	34
Animal Science	**35**
Animal Science Quiz	64
Plant Science	**65**
Plant Science Quiz	94
Earth Science	**95**
Earth Science Quiz	124
Indoor Science	**125**
Indoor Science Quiz	154
Outdoor Science	**155**
Outdoor Science Quiz	184
Glossary	185
Index	188

Cloverleaf
An imprint of Evans Brothers Limited

Cloverleaf is an imprint of Evans Brothers Limited

First published in the UK by
Evans Brother Limited
2a Portman Mansions
Chiltern Street
London W1M 1LE

© in this edition Evans Brothers Limited 1998
© text Anita Ganeri 1992, 1993
© illustrations Evans Brothers Limited 1992, 1993

All rights reserved. No part of this publication may be reproduced, stored in a retrieval system or transmitted in any form or by any means, electronic, mechanical, photocopying, recording or otherwise, without prior permission of Evans Brothers Limited.

Printed by Wing King Tong

Acknowledgements

The author and publishers would like to thank the following people
for their valuable help and advice:
Dr Puran Ganeri MBBS, MRCGP, DCH
Sally Morgan MA, MSc, MIBiol
Nicky Tovey BA, MA

Illustrations: Virginia Gray and Jillian Luff
Editors: Catherine Chambers and Jean Coppendale
Design: Monica Chia
Production: Jenny Mulvanny and Peter Thompson

SCIENCE
QUESTIONS & ANSWERS

Body Science

Anita Ganeri

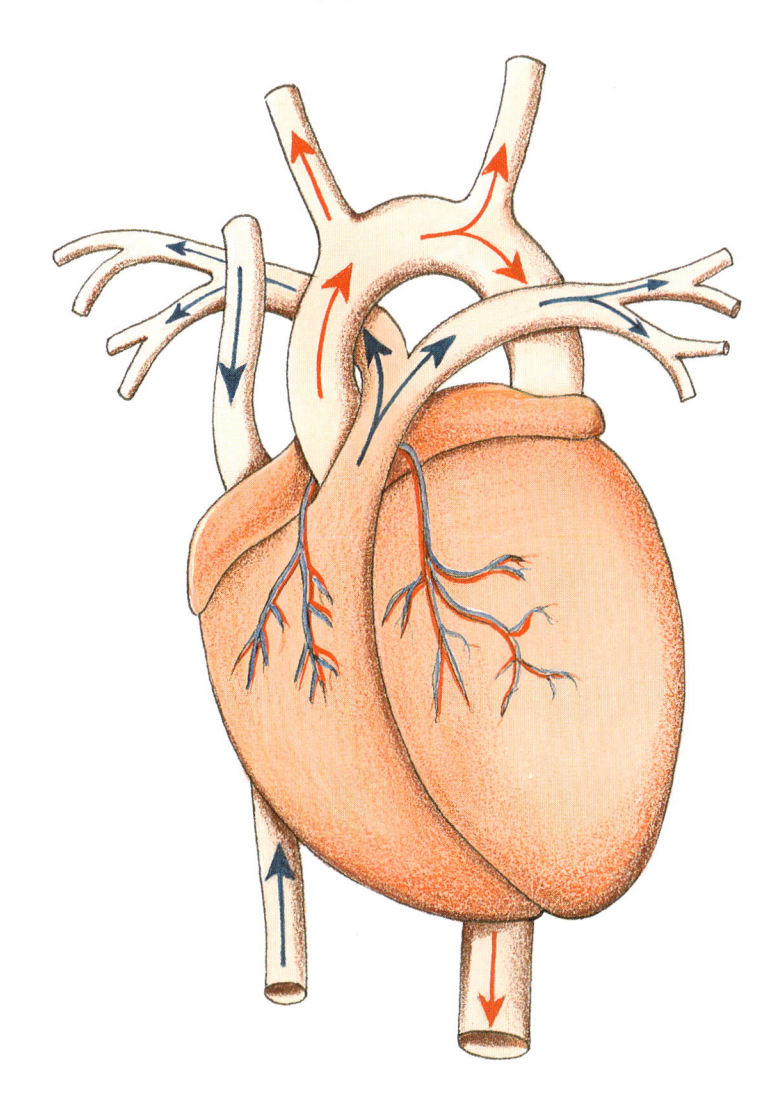

Acknowledgements

Page 8 - (top) Dr Manfred Kage, Bruce Coleman Limited, (bottom) Alfred Pasieka, Bruce Coleman Limited; page 10 - Dr Manfred Kage / Science Photo Library; page 12 - John Garrett, Bubbles; page 13 -(left) Hutchison Library, (right) David Campione / Science Photo Library; page 15 - (top) G & M David De Lossy, The Image Bank, (bottom) Hank Morgan / Science Photo Library, (inset) Lois Joy Thurston, Bubbles; page 18 - Robert Harding Picture Library; page 19 - Sally Morgan, Ecoscene; page 20 - Jacques Cochin, The Image Bank; page 23 - (top left) Philip Kretchmar, The Image Bank, (bottom left) Steve Niedorf, The Image Bank, (top right) Sally Morgan, Ecoscene, (middle) Adrien Duey, The Image Bank, (bottom right) Nino Mascardi, The Image Bank; page 24 - Petit Format, J D Dauple / Science Photo Library; page 25 - Sally Morgan, Ecoscene; page 27 - (left) Biophoto Associates, (right) Danny Brass / Science Photo Library; page 29 - Leo Mason, The Image Bank; page 31 - (top left) Sally Morgan, Ecoscene, (bottom left) Ian West, Bubbles, (top right) Hans Reinhard, Bruce Coleman Limited; page 32 - M I Walker / Science Photo Library.

Contents

What are you made of?	**8**
• What is a cell made of?	9
What are bones for?	**10**
What are muscles for?	**12**
Why does your heart beat?	**14**
How do you breathe?	**16**
• Why do you pant when you have been running?	17
• Why do you sneeze?	18
• What makes you cough?	18
• What causes hiccups?	19
• Why do you get a 'stitch'?	19
Why do you feel hungry?	**20**
• Where does your food go?	21
• What happens when food goes down 'the wrong way'?	22
• Why does your tummy rumble?	22
• Which foods are good for you?	23
What does your brain do?	**24**
• Why are people left or right-handed?	25
How do you see?	**26**
• Why do people have to wear glasses?	27
• Why are people's eyes different colours?	27
How do you hear sounds?	**28**
• Why do you feel dizzy?	29
How do you smell things?	**30**
• Why do people sniff at things?	31
How do you taste things?	**32**
How do you feel things?	**33**
Body Science Quiz	**34**

What are you made of?

Take a good, long look at yourself. How many parts of your body can you name? Bones, muscles, skin, nails, heart - these are just a few to start with. There are many more, all working together to make your body function properly.

So what are you made of? Your body is about two-thirds water. In an adult man, this is about 40 litres of water, enough to fill 120 fizzy drink cans. But your bones, muscles, skin and so on are made of tiny living things, called cells. You are made of about 50,000 million of these little building blocks.

Cells come in different shapes and sizes, and each type has a different job to do. For example, red blood cells are tiny, and shaped like doughnuts. Nerve cells have long, thin, trailing 'tails'.

Groups of the same types of cell make up **body tissue**. There are different kinds, such as muscle tissue and skin tissue. Groups of different types of tissue form organs, such as your heart or lungs. Each organ has its own special job to do in your body.

Most of your cells are repaired or replaced as they die or wear out. Bone cells last for years, but the cells lining part of your digestive tube, in your stomach, only live for two to three days. Red blood cells, however, live for about four months. The only cells which are not replaced when they die are those which make your nerves ... and your brain.

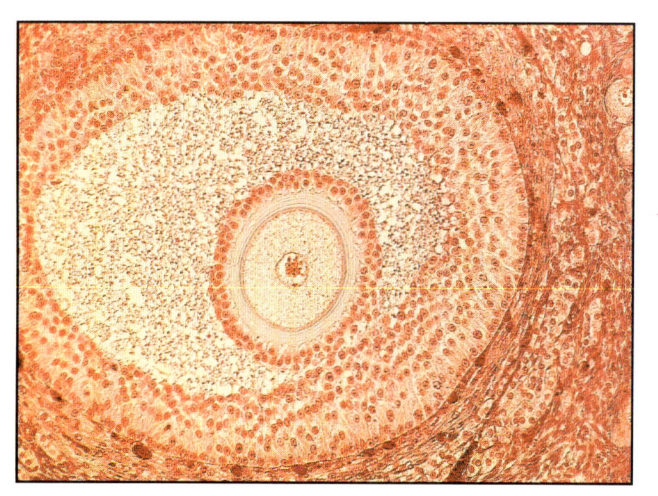

Female egg cells, or ova, are stored inside a woman's ovaries. They are about 0.1 - 0.2 millimetres wide.

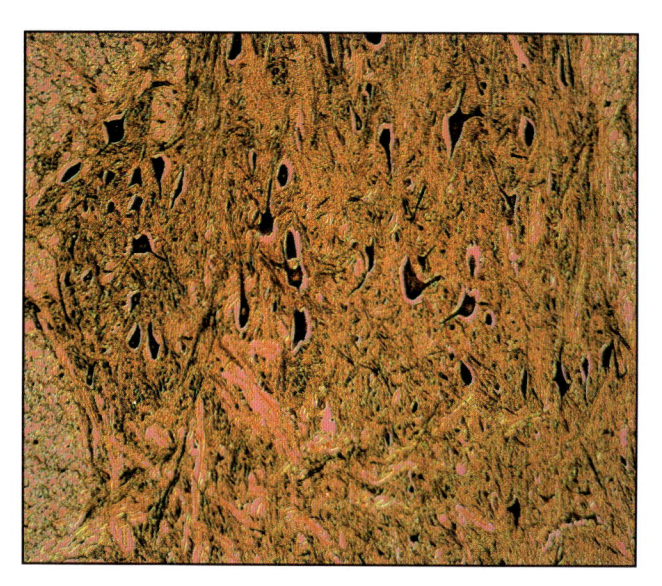

This photo shows nerve cells from the spinal cord. They help you to move. They are shown magnified by 64 times.

? Did you know?

Most cells are too small to be seen except under a microscope. The biggest cells are female egg cells. They can just be seen with the naked eye. Some of the smallest cells are in your brain. They are just 0.005 millimetres across. Hundreds would fit on this full stop.

What is a cell made of?

cell membrane
The cell's outer layer; it keeps the cell's shape and lets oxygen and **nutrients** in, and **waste products** out.

cytoplasm
This is the jelly-like main part of the cell; it is about two-thirds water, with some protein.

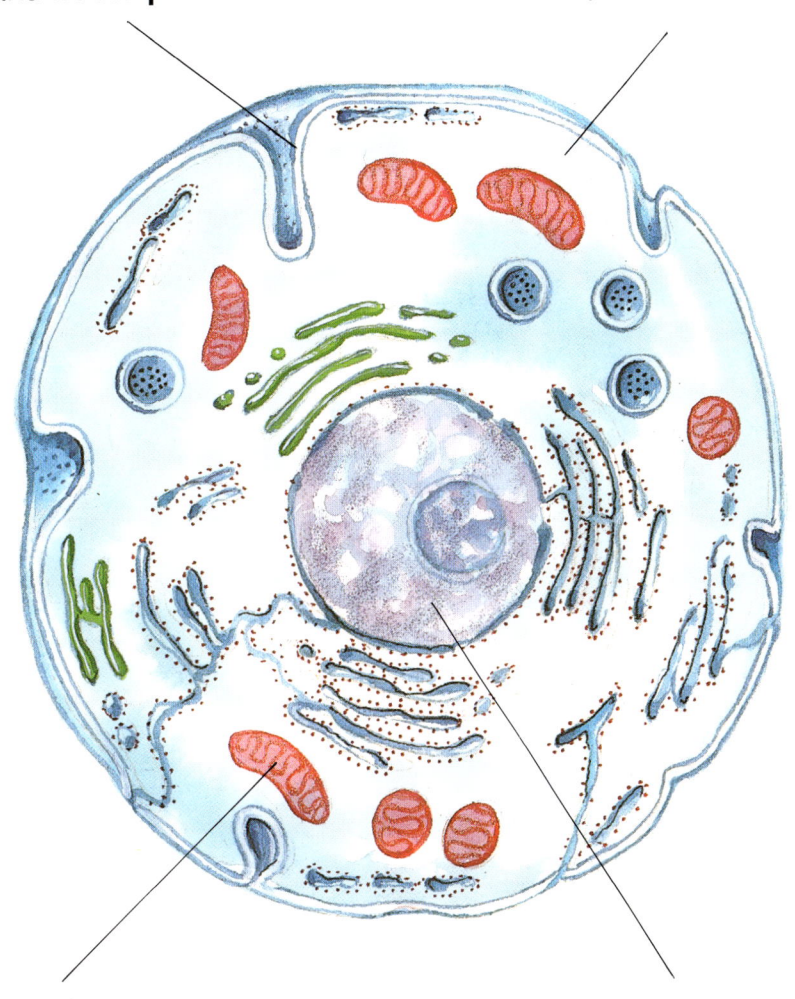

There are lots of other small particles which cannot be seen underneath an ordinary microscope. They have many different jobs to do. This particle is a mitochondrion (mitochondria). Mitochondria are the cell's power stores. They make energy that helps to keep the cell working.

nucleus
The centre of the cell's body and its controller; it contains special threads, called chromosomes. These carry coded instructions, called genes, which tell the cell how to work.

What are bones for?

There are lots of bones inside your body. They make up your skeleton. Bones are tough and strong. But they can also bend slightly so that they do not break too easily. Your skeleton holds your body up and keeps its shape. Without it, you would collapse in a floppy heap on the floor.

Some bones help to protect the soft, delicate parts of your body. The spine, or backbone, protects your main nerves. The skull protects your brain, and the ribs protect your heart and your lungs.

Bones also help you to move. They cannot bend very much, so your body has joints where it can twist and turn. There are joints at your knees, ankles, elbows and shoulders. Your knee and elbow joints act a bit like hinges on a door, so that you can bend your legs and arms.

In a joint, two bones meet and are held in place by strong, stretchy straps, called ligaments. The ends of each bone are covered in tough, shiny cartilage, a kind of cushion which stops bones from rubbing or wearing out. The joint is kept well oiled by a liquid, called synovial fluid.

> **? Did you know?**
>
> Your biggest bones are in your thighs. Your smallest bones are in your ears. An adult has about 206 bones in the body, but a baby has over 300. Some of these bones join together as the baby gets older.

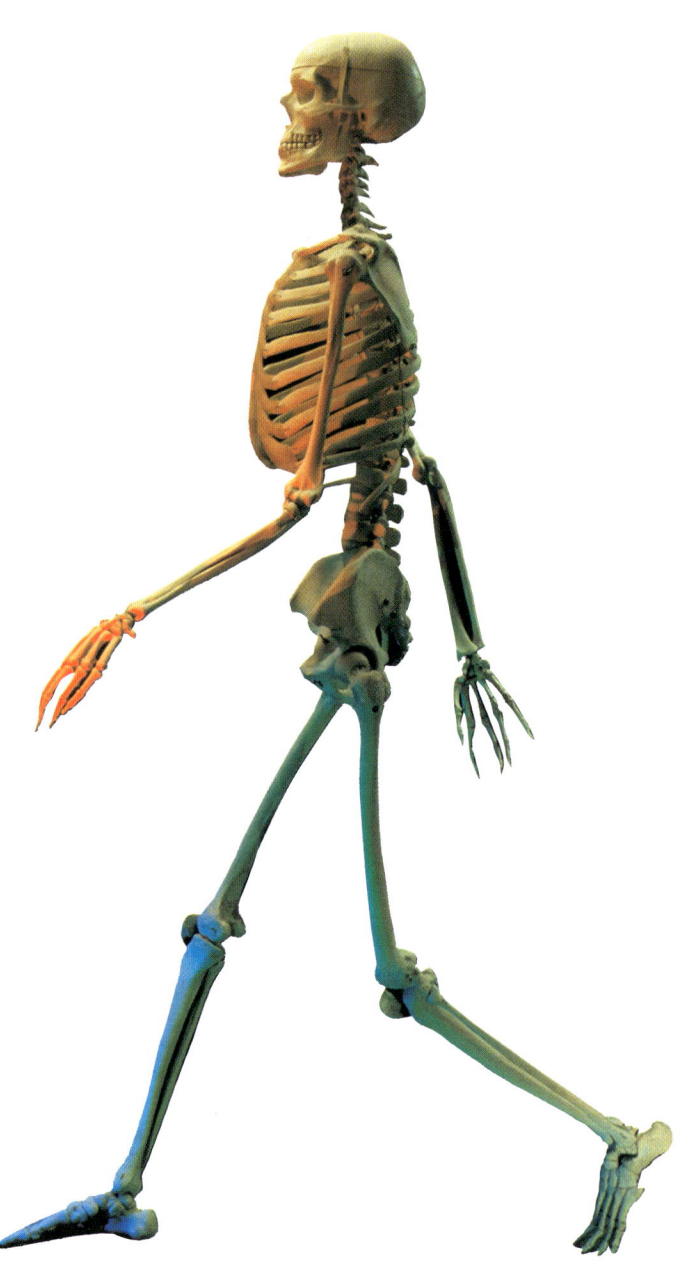

Your skeleton provides a tough framework for your body. The bones hold you up, rather like scaffolding around a building. They also protect the soft organs inside your body from injury. The joints between your bones and the muscles attached to them allow you to move freely.

Here you can see some of the main bones in your skeleton. They all have scientific names. But many also have common names which you might know already.

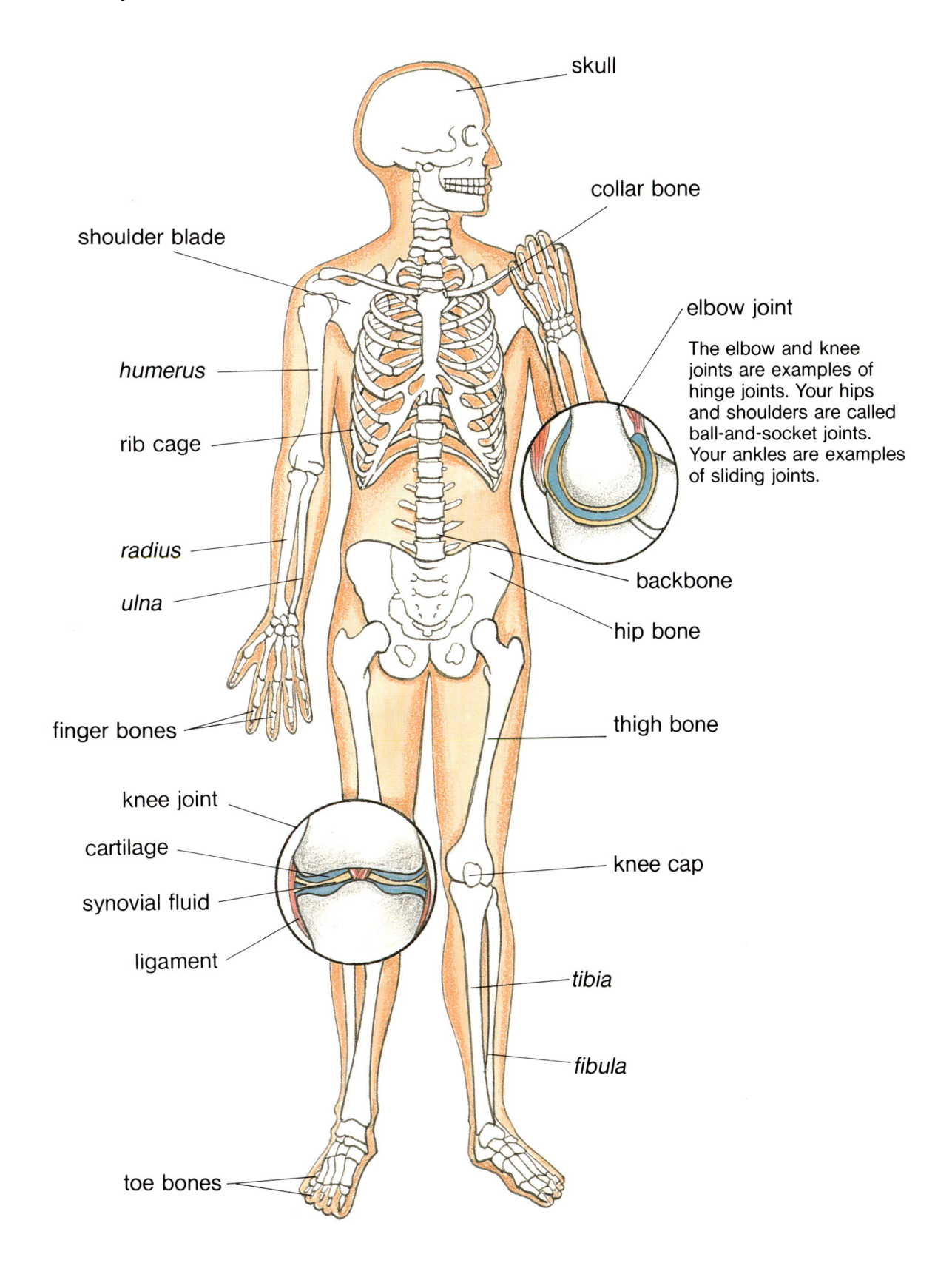

- skull
- collar bone
- shoulder blade
- elbow joint

  The elbow and knee joints are examples of hinge joints. Your hips and shoulders are called ball-and-socket joints. Your ankles are examples of sliding joints.

- *humerus*
- rib cage
- *radius*
- *ulna*
- backbone
- hip bone
- finger bones
- thigh bone
- knee joint
- cartilage
- synovial fluid
- knee cap
- ligament
- *tibia*
- *fibula*
- toe bones

What are muscles for?

Muscles work with bones, so that you can move. Muscles are **supple** and strong. They have long strips at each end which fix them to bones. These are called tendons. There is a big tendon at the back of your heel. Can you feel it? It is called your Achilles tendon.

When you want to move, your brain sends a message to your muscles. It tells them to get shorter, or contract. As they contract, they pull on the bone and move it. This is how your elbow bends, or your head nods.

You have hundreds of muscles under your skin. They often work in pairs to move different parts of your body. To move your elbow one way, one muscle gets shorter and the other relaxes. To move it the other way, the muscles change jobs.

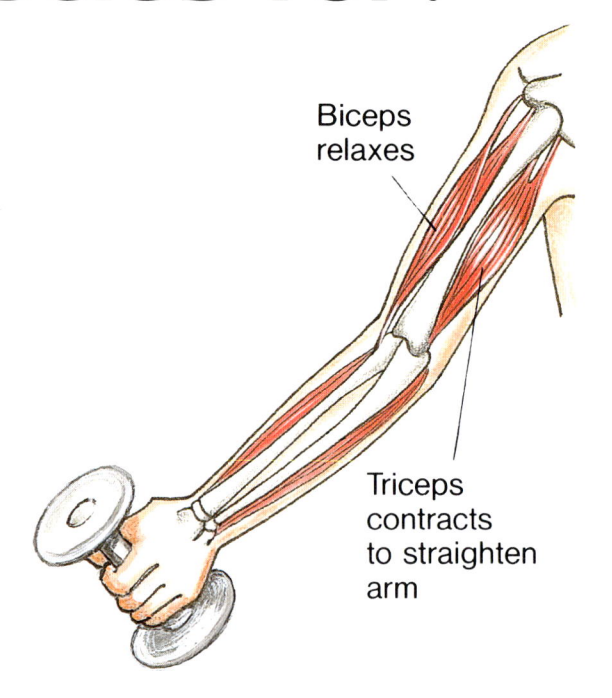

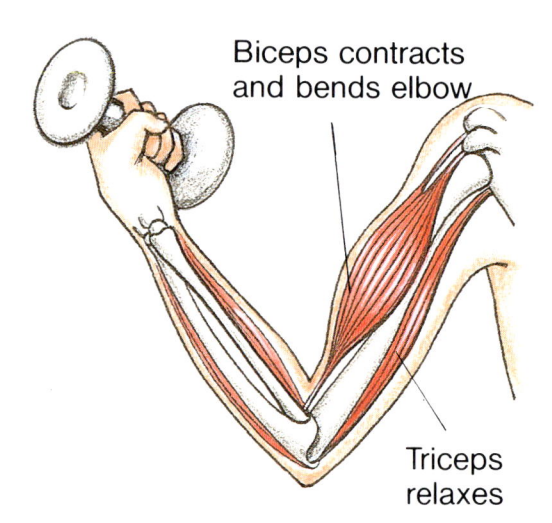

These upper arm muscles work in pairs to move the lower arm up or down. When one muscle contracts, the other relaxes.

You use hundreds of different muscles when you play football.

❓ Did you know?

You have about 650 muscles in your body. The biggest are in your bottom and the smallest are in your ear. You use an amazing 200 muscles when you walk.

shoulder muscles

chest muscles
pectoral muscles

triceps ⎤ upper
             arm
biceps ⎦ muscles

muscles in bottom
gluteus maximus

thigh muscles

hamstring muscles
(in the back of the leg)

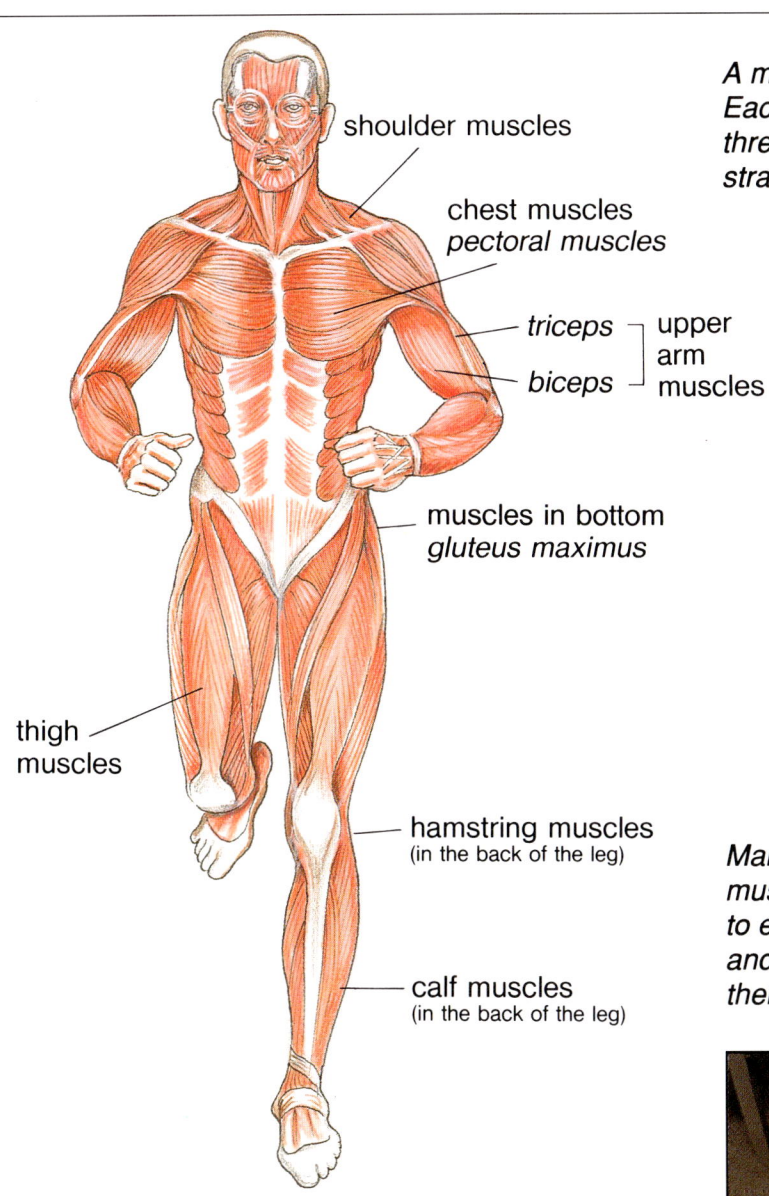

calf muscles
(in the back of the leg)

A muscle is made up of bundles of muscle fibres. Each fibre, in turn, is made up of even tinier threads called myofibrils. They are made up of strands of **protein.**

Inside a muscle

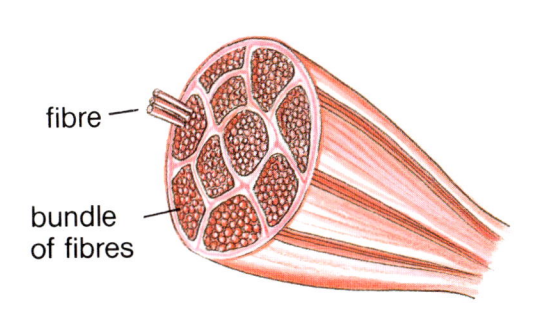

fibre

bundle of fibres

Many people work very hard to keep their muscles in good shape. Some people lift weights to exercise their muscles and make them bigger and stronger. Athletes have to train hard to keep their muscles strong.

Most muscles are only known by their scientific names. Some also have common names. Muscles lie in layers all over your body just under your skin.

Why does your heart beat?

Your body needs **nutrients** from food, and oxygen from the air to make it work properly. These are carried to all parts of the body by your blood. The blood also takes away **waste products**, such as carbon dioxide gas, which could poison your cells. Blood has to be pushed around your body all the time, and this is where your heart comes in. It acts like a muscly pump, sending blood around your body with every beat.

Your heart beats about 80 to 90 times a minute. With each beat, the left side of your heart pumps blood from your lungs, where it collects a store of oxygen, to the rest of your body. The right side pumps stale blood from your body to your lungs, for more oxygen. Special flap-like valves in your heart snap shut after the blood has gone through. This stops it flowing backwards. They make a 'lub dub' sound as they close. This is your heartbeat.

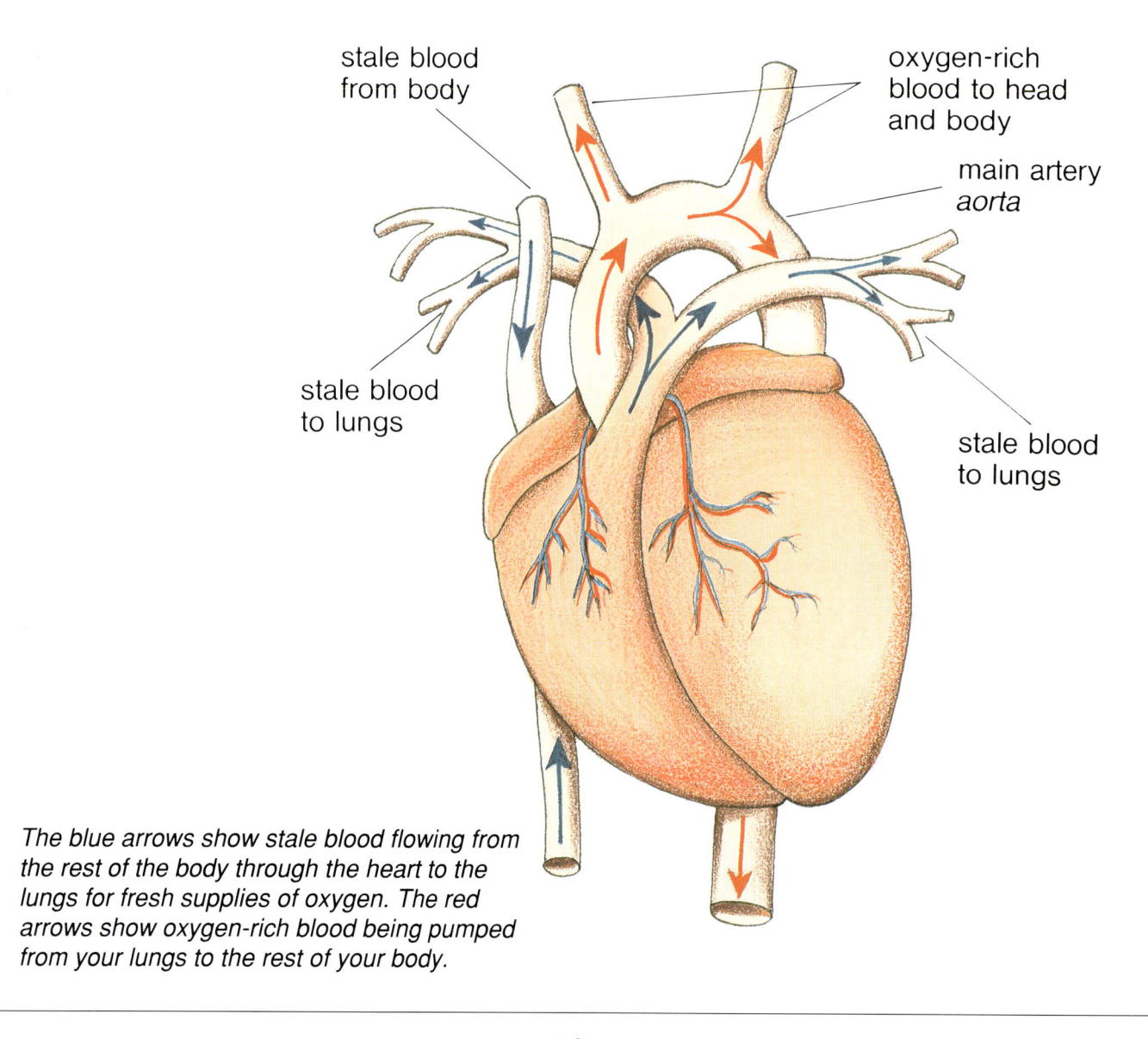

stale blood from body

oxygen-rich blood to head and body

main artery *aorta*

stale blood to lungs

stale blood to lungs

The blue arrows show stale blood flowing from the rest of the body through the heart to the lungs for fresh supplies of oxygen. The red arrows show oxygen-rich blood being pumped from your lungs to the rest of your body.

Jogging or cycling helps to make your heart and lungs stronger and improve your blood circulation. They are called aerobic forms of exercise. They increase your ability to get oxygen around your body.

? Did you know?

Your clenched fist is about the size of an adult's heart. The heart is made of a special type of muscle, called cardiac muscle. Unlike the type of muscle in your arms and legs, it never stops working while you are alive.

? Did you know?

When you are resting, about one cupful of blood is pumped around your body with every three beats of your heart. When you exercise, about two cupfuls are pumped with just one beat.

! See for yourself

Each time your heart beats, blood surges or rushes through your body. You can feel this surge when you take your pulse. This measures how often your heart beats each minute. Press the inside of one wrist with the middle fingers of your other hand. Can you feel a gentle throbbing? This is your blood surging through your wrist. Use a watch to count the number of surges in one minute. The number of surges you count is called your pulse rate. Do this twice: first after you have been sitting quietly for a while, and then after you have been running around. You should have quite different pulse rates.

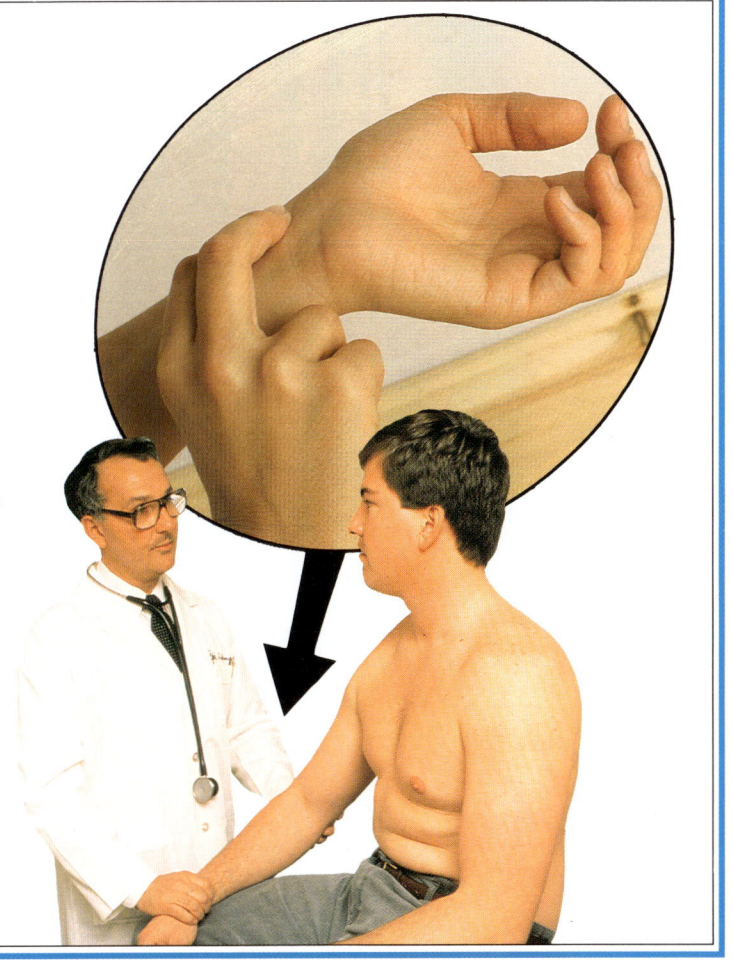

How do you breathe?

Just as a car needs petrol, your body needs oxygen, a gas from the air, to make it work properly. Without oxygen, your cells would die in a few minutes. Cells also make a waste gas called carbon dioxide. The cells need to get rid of this waste gas so that it does not poison them. This is why you breathe - to supply your cells with oxygen and take away waste.

You breathe all the time, automatically. Air goes in through your nose or mouth, down your windpipe (trachea), then down two tubes (bronchi) into your lungs. In each lung, these tubes branch again and again, rather like a tree. At the end of each branch is a tiny bubble-like structure, called an air sac or **alveolus**.

The air sacs (alveoli) are covered with fine **blood vessels**. Oxygen passes from the alveoli into your blood and is then carried around your body. Waste carbon dioxide passes the other way, to be breathed out.

When you breathe in, your ribs move up and out to give your lungs room to expand as you suck air in. Your diaphragm (the sheet of muscle across your chest, under your lungs) also moves down to make more space. When you breathe out, your ribs move in and down, and your diaphragm moves upwards. This makes the space in your chest smaller, and helps to squeeze air out.

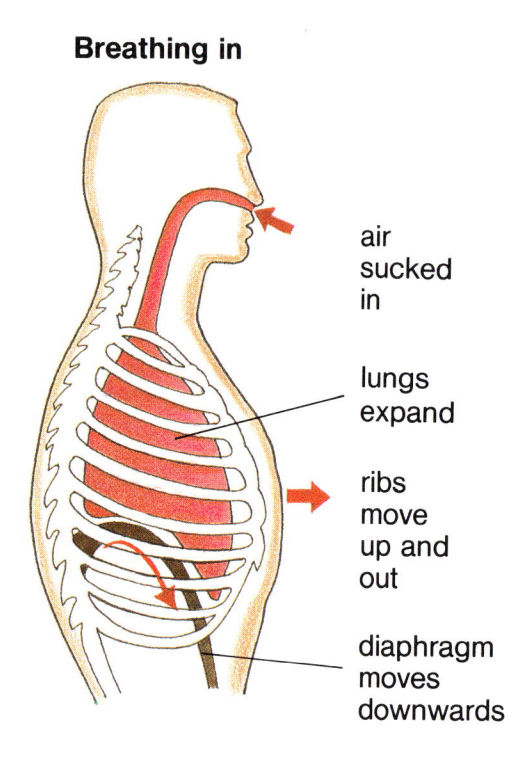

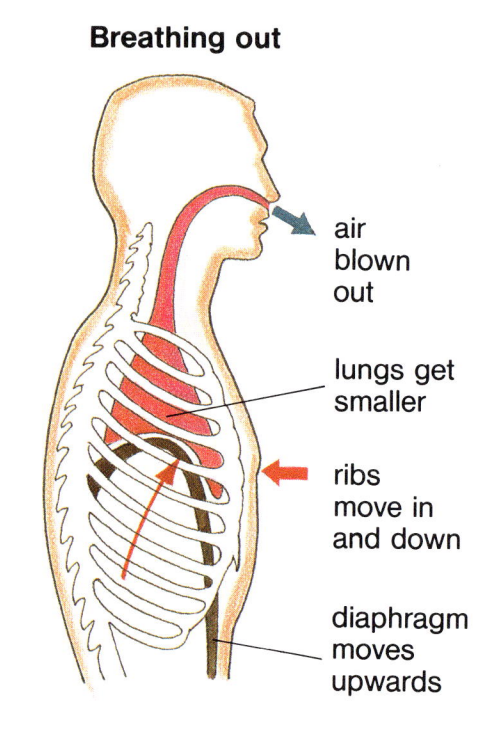

Breathing in

- air sucked in
- lungs expand
- ribs move up and out
- diaphragm moves downwards

Breathing out

- air blown out
- lungs get smaller
- ribs move in and down
- diaphragm moves upwards

Why do you pant when you have been running?

When you exercise, your muscles work harder and need more oxygen than usual. Your brain tells you to breathe quicker to get enough oxygen to your muscles. Panting helps you to take more air in.

Did you know?

Alveoli give your lungs a huge surface for taking in oxygen. You have about 6 million alveoli. If they could all be flattened out, they would cover a tennis court.

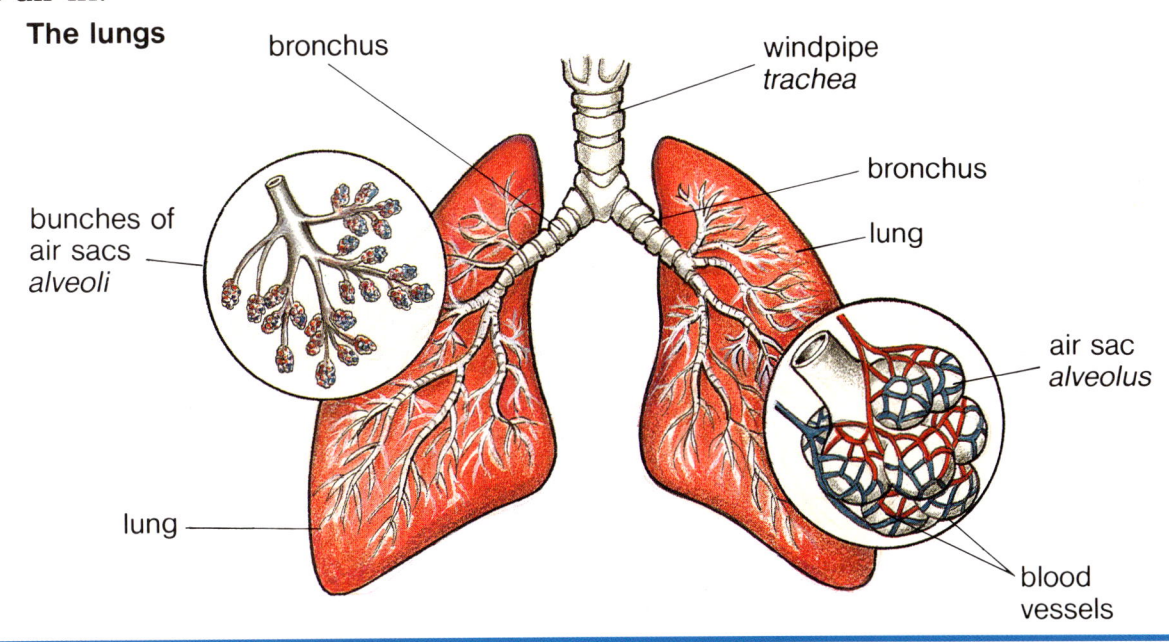

The lungs

- bronchus
- windpipe *trachea*
- bronchus
- lung
- bunches of air sacs *alveoli*
- air sac *alveolus*
- lung
- blood vessels

See for yourself

To see how big your breaths are, you will need a big plastic milk container and a length of plastic tubing. Fill the container up by holding it in a sink full of water. Then tip it upside-down quickly, in the sink, without lifting it out of the water. Make sure that the container stays full. Put one end of the tube under it and breathe out through the other end. Your breaths will force some of the water out of the container. Do this 10 times, then mark the level of water on the container with a ball-point pen.

Now you can see how the air in each breath replaced a certain volume, or amount of water in the container. Empty the container and fill it up to the mark you made with more water from the tap. The water represents the air that you breathed out. Now you can pour that water into a measuring jug to see how many millilitres of air you breathed out. Divide the number of millilitres by 10 to give you the volume of each breath. Now you know how big each breath is.

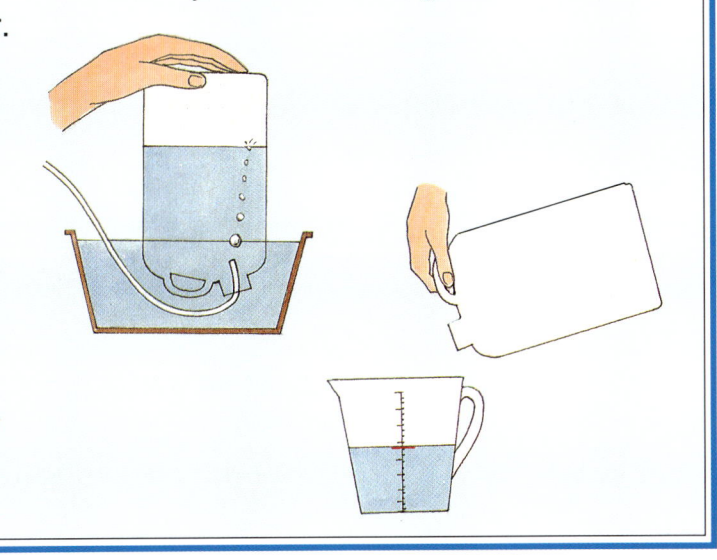

Why do you sneeze?

You sneeze when you have a cold or if you are allergic, or react badly, to dust or flower pollen in the air. Sometimes you seem to sneeze for no reason at all. But sneezing does have a useful purpose. You sneeze to blow irritating dust or mucus (a slimy substance produced when you have a cold) out of your nose and to clear your breathing passages. Have you ever tried to stop yourself sneezing? It is very difficult to do because sneezing is an **automatic reaction**. When you sneeze, your throat closes and air builds up in your lungs. Suddenly, the air explodes out of your nose.

What makes you cough?

Coughing also helps to clear blockages in your throat, lungs and breathing tubes. When you cough, your vocal cords close and the muscles in your chest squeeze, building up the pressure of air in your lungs. When the pressure is too great, your vocal cords open and the air rushes out of your mouth. It carries with it any irritating bits of dust or mucus, and hopefully allows you to breathe more easily again.

[?] Did you know?

The longest sneezing fit lasted over 2.5 years. The person sneezed about 1 million times in the first year, that is about 2,740 times a day.

[?] Did you know?

Coughs and sneezes travel at high speed. You normally breathe air out at about 8 kilometres per hour. In a cough, the air travels at about 100 kilometres per hour. In a sneeze, the air is forced out at up to 160 kilometres per hour.

[!] See for yourself

Coughs and sneezes can spread diseases when you have a cold. A sneeze contains about 100,000 tiny droplets of mucus, full of cold germs. When the germs are exploded into the air, other people can easily breathe them in if you do not catch them in a handkerchief. To see how a sneeze spreads germs, you will need a large sheet of paper, a drinking straw and a cup of water that has been coloured with food dye. Make sure that you, and everything around you, are well covered.

Suck up some water through the straw. Stand about a metre away from the paper and blow the water hard at the paper. The splatters of colour are like the mucus drops in a sneeze. How far have they spread over the paper?

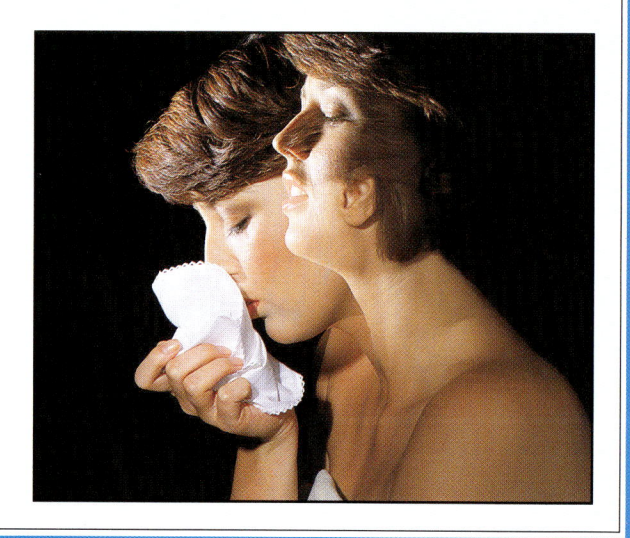

What causes hiccups?

Your diaphragm is the flat sheet of muscle under your ribs, which you use for breathing. You get hiccups when it contracts, or squeezes, more violently than normal. This causes you to breathe in with short gasps of air. Your vocal cords close suddenly and make the 'hic' sound you hear.

No one knows exactly why hiccups start. But even unborn babies get them. You may get hiccups if you have eaten or drunk too quickly, or too much.

The hiccups usually stop quite quickly, but people have thought up plenty of weird and wonderful cures. They include holding your breath, giving the person with hiccups a fright, or trying to drink a glass of water from the wrong side of the glass. This may not cure your hiccups, but you might forget about them for a while.

This is one of the ways that people try to cure their hiccups. Do you think it will work or will you just get a wet face?

Why do you get a 'stitch'?

Do you ever get a sharp, stabbing pain in your side when you are running or doing exercise? This is known as a 'stitch'. It is caused when your diaphragm gets cramp, or tightens up. This happens when you suddenly begin doing hard exercise, and so you start breathing more quickly. Your diaphragm suddenly has to work much harder than normal and you may get a stitch.

The pain usually goes away after a few minutes. If it does not go, bend down and touch your toes to stretch and relax your diaphragm. You may get a stitch if you exercise too soon after eating a meal. Always wait at least two hours after eating before you do any hard exercise.

? Did you know?

The longest attack of hiccuping on record began in 1922 ... and lasted for 70 years! The sufferer led a normal life, but could not wear false teeth as they would have jumped up and down in his mouth. He hiccuped about 25 times a minute, 1,500 times an hour, 36,000 times a day.

Why do you feel hungry?

Everything you do uses up energy. Running and swimming use up lots of energy, but breathing and even blinking use energy too. You get your energy from the food that you eat. You also get nutrients from food. These help you to grow and to mend worn-out or injured parts of your body.

You get hungry because your supplies of energy and nutrients are running low. A special part of your brain, called the appetite centre, detects this. It makes you think that you should eat something, so you feel hungry.

Some foods contain lots of energy. Others contain very little. You could run a 2 kilometre race on the amount of energy in a chocolate bar. But you could only run 50 metres on the energy contained in a lettuce leaf.

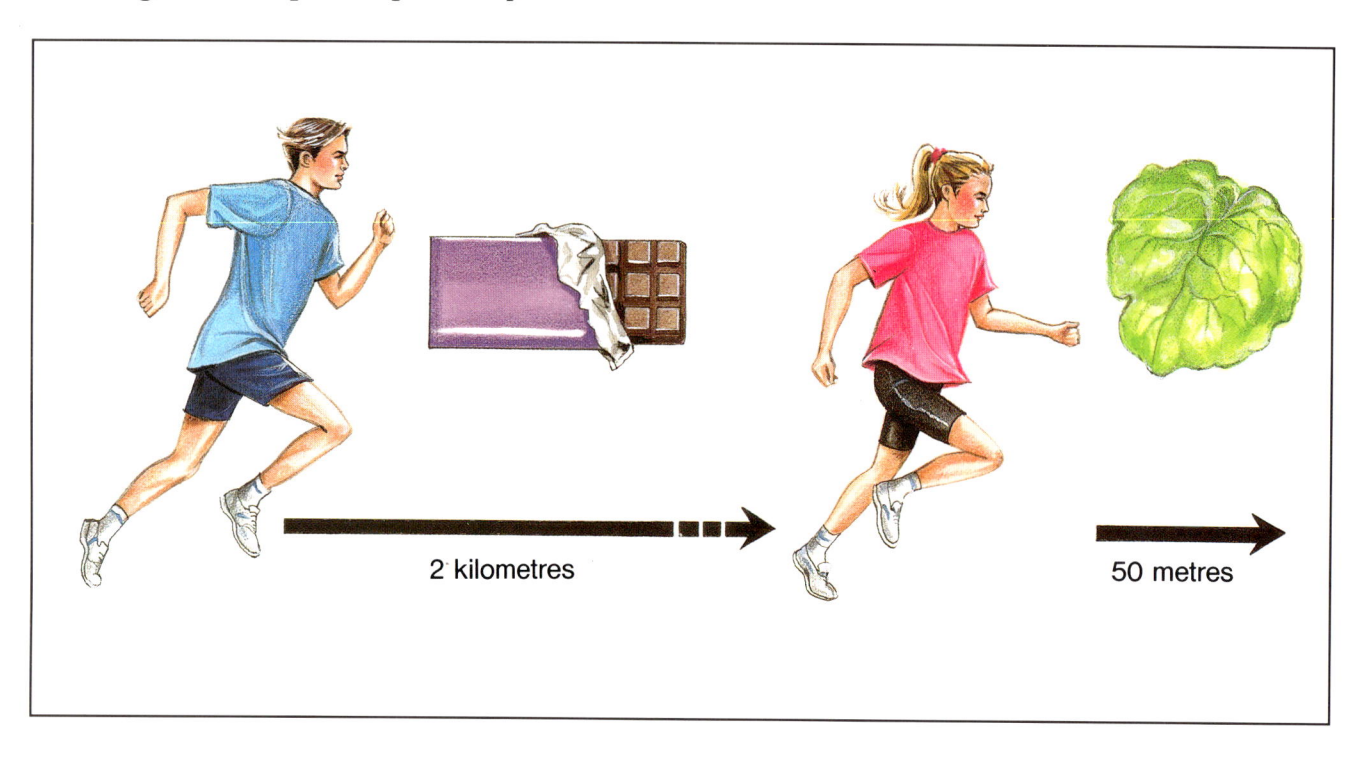

2 kilometres

50 metres

Sudden spurts of intense activity use up a lot of energy. Athletes have to follow special diets which are high in protein to build up their muscles and carbohydrates to give them energy. Protein is found in foods such as fish, meat and beans. Carbohydrates are found in foods such as bread, rice and potatoes.

Where does your food go?

When you are enjoying munching an apple or a chocolate bar, you do not stop to think where the food is going, or what will happen to it. The food starts a long journey through your body, through a long system of tubes, called your digestive system. As it travels, it is broken down into tiny particles, small enough to be absorbed by your blood and carried around your body to your cells.

From your mouth, your food travels down a long tube, called the oesophagus. It does not just slide down, but is pushed by muscles in the oesophagus. This pushing is called peristalsis. The power of the muscles means that food can still go down even if you are standing on your head.

The food is pushed into your stomach where it is mixed with juices and broken down into a soup-like mash. It stays in your stomach for about four hours. Then it travels through your small intestine, where more juices are added. Most of the food is **digested** here, passing through the walls of the intestine and into your bloodstream.

Any undigested, or unwanted food goes into the next part of your digestive system, the large intestine. This waste is turned into brown faeces, which are squeezed out of your bottom when you go to the toilet.

Your digestive system is about 9 metres long, from beginning to end. A meal may take about three days to pass right through you. It stays in your stomach for only about four hours.

The digestive system

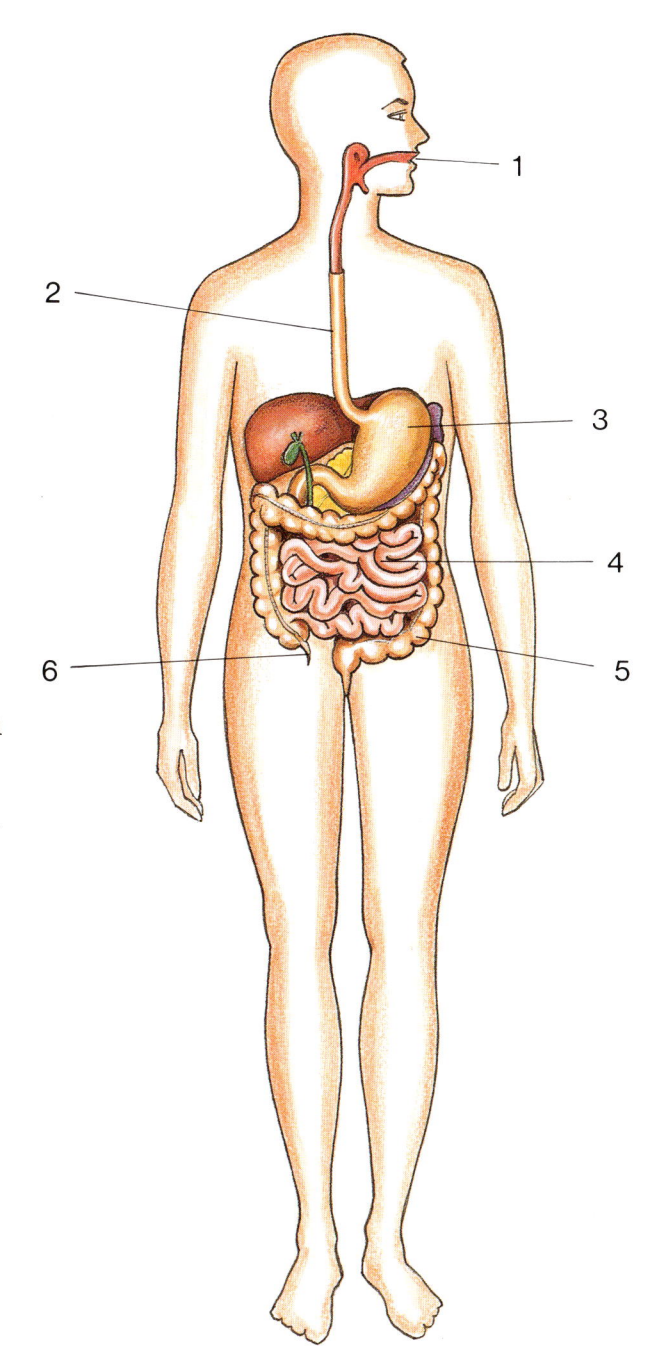

1. mouth
2. oesophagus
3. stomach
4. small intestine
5. large intestine
6. appendix (see page 27)

What happens when food goes down 'the wrong way'?

When you swallow a piece of food, a flap called the epiglottis covers the top of your windpipe, and the food goes down your oesophagus and into your digestive system. But this process can go wrong. If you accidentally breathe in as you swallow the food, the epiglottis opens up. Then the food gets into your windpipe. You may choke on it and have difficulty in breathing properly. This is when food goes down 'the wrong way'.

Why does your tummy rumble?

Your tummy sometimes rumbles when you are hungry. But not always. It may also rumble as food and air are squeezed through your body, along your digestive tubes.

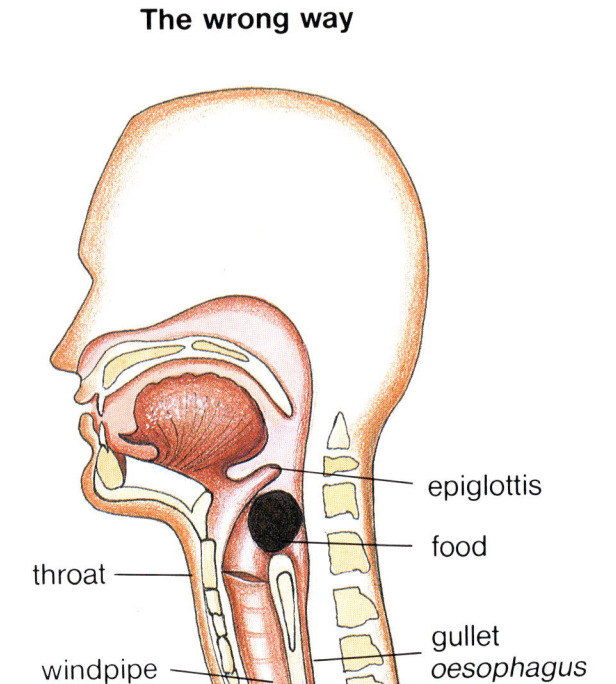

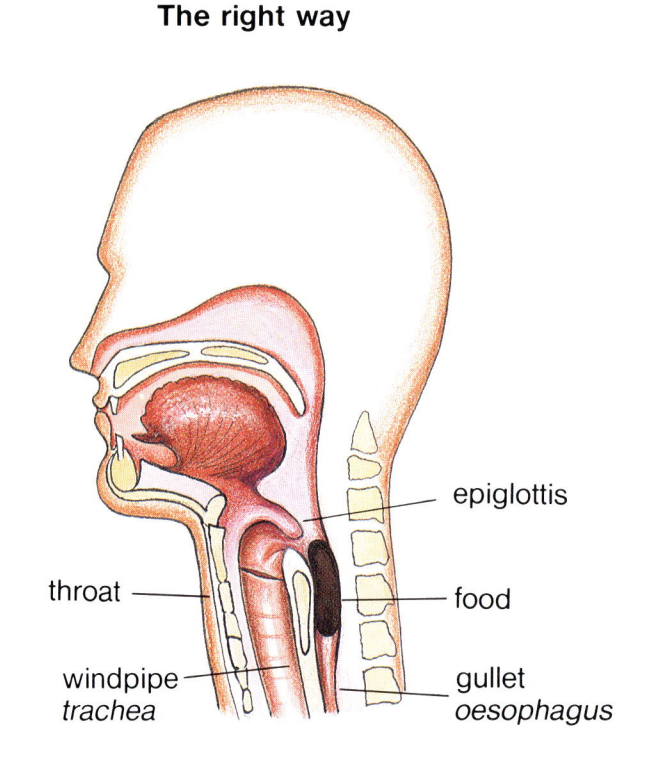

The wrong way

- epiglottis
- food
- throat
- gullet *oesophagus*
- windpipe *trachea*

The right way

- epiglottis
- food
- throat
- gullet *oesophagus*
- windpipe *trachea*

⚠ See for yourself

The chemicals which break down your food into smaller pieces are called **enzymes**. The saliva, or spit, that you make in your mouth contains enzymes. These break down the **starch** in foods such as potatoes and bread, and turn the starch into sugar. The sugar dissolves more easily as it goes down into your stomach. You can see how this enzyme works by keeping a piece of dry bread in your mouth for a few minutes. It will soon taste sweet. You make over a litre of saliva every day.

Did you know?

Your appendix is a thin, worm-like tube at the top of your large intestine. Animals which eat grass, such as rabbits or cows, use the appendix to help them digest their food. But humans have no use for it any more. Some people suffer from appendicitis, when the appendix becomes swollen. They have to have an operation to take it out.

Did you know?

Your small intestine is only 2 to 3 centimetres wide, but it can be as much as 6 metres long.

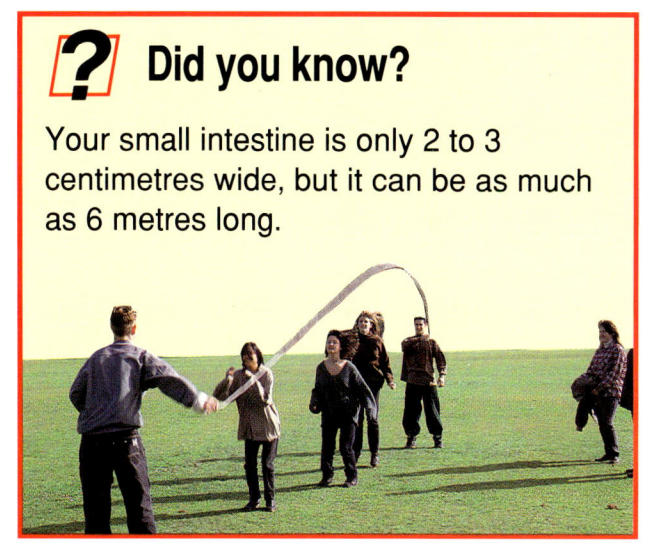

Which foods are good for you?

You need to eat a balanced diet to keep healthy. This means eating foods containing a selection of protein, carbohydrate, fibre, fat, vitamins and minerals. Too many fatty foods or too much sugar (a type of carbohydrate) can make you unhealthy.

This Madeira cake spread with butter tastes very good, but it is full of fats and sugars.

Hamburgers are tasty treats but they are not very nourishing. So we should not eat them too often.

Salad is good for you because it is low in fat and high in vitamins.

Spaghetti contains carbohydrates for energy and protein for the growth and repair of tissue.

What does your brain do?

Without a brain, you would not be able to move, think, learn or remember, or feel anything. Your brain is the control centre of your body. Information about the outside world travels along a huge network of wire-like nerves to your brain.

Nerves run all over your body. They also carry instructions from your brain to your body. The main pathway between your nerves and brain is your spinal cord. This is a long bundle of nerves running through your backbone, or spine.

When the information reaches your brain, your brain sorts it out and decides what action, if any, to take. It then tells your body. Your brain looks a bit like a pinkish-grey lump of blancmange. It is made of up to 10,000 million nerve cells. It is divided up into different parts, each with a different job to do.

Parts of the brain

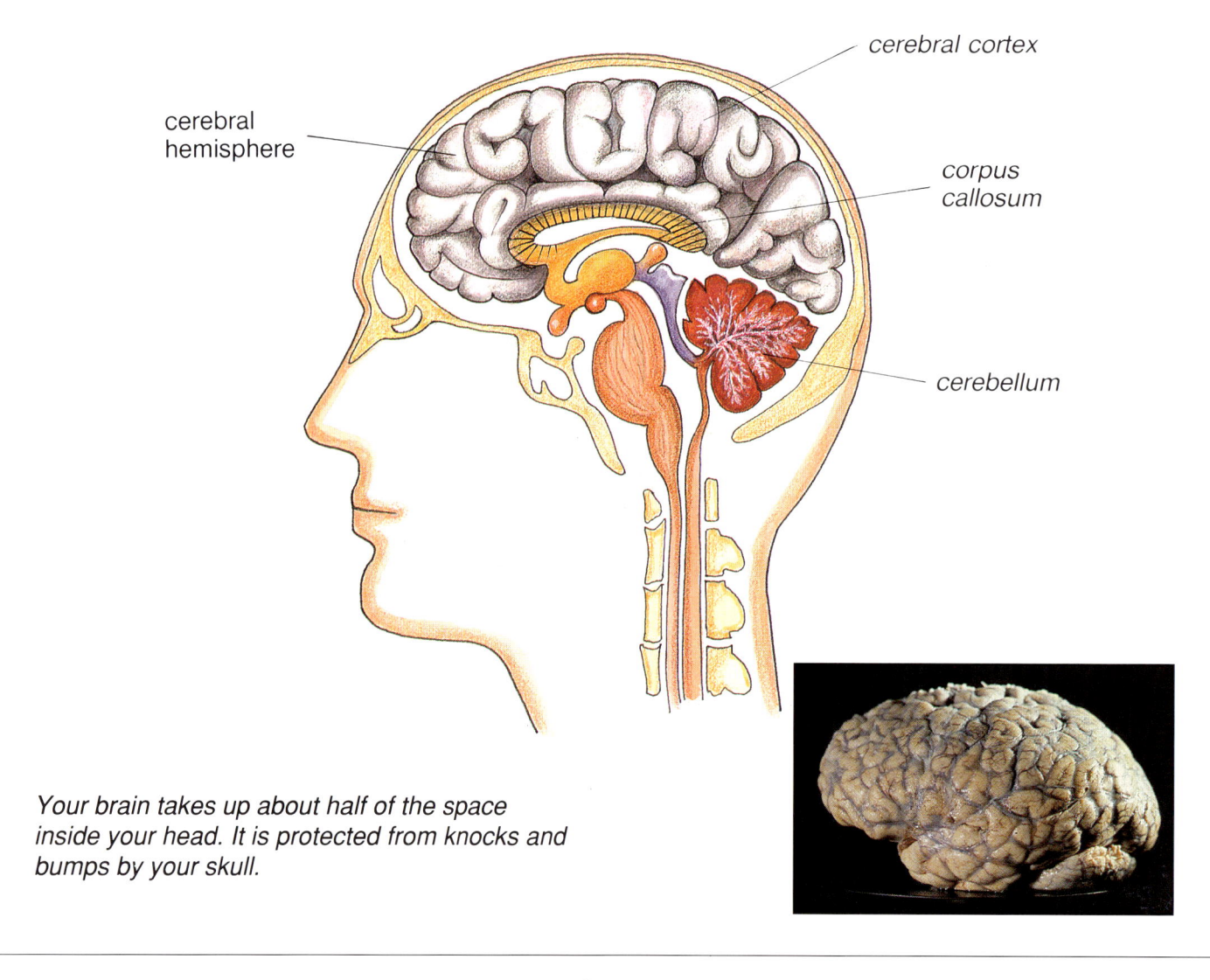

- cerebral hemisphere
- cerebral cortex
- corpus callosum
- cerebellum

Your brain takes up about half of the space inside your head. It is protected from knocks and bumps by your skull.

Why are people left or right-handed?

Which hand do you write with? Your left or your right? Most people write with their right hands. Only about 1 person in 10 is left-handed.

The biggest part of your brain is called the cerebral cortex. It is divided into two halves, called hemispheres. Each hemisphere controls the opposite side of the body. The hand you write with depends on which side of your brain controls language and speech. If the right-hand side is in control, you will be left-handed. If the left-hand side is in control, you will be right-handed. A very small number of people are ambidextrous. This means that they can write with either hand.

? Did you know?

An adult's brain weighs about 1.5 kilograms. People used to think that the more intelligent a person was, the bigger their brain. We now know that this is not true. All adults have brains about the same size.

! See for yourself

Your brain stores some of the information it receives as memories. These may last for just a few minutes or for many years. Can you remember your first day at school, or your last birthday, or your telephone number? Try this test to see how good your memory is.

Lay out eight objects on a table or a tray. Look at them for about 20 seconds. Now look away and see how many objects you can remember. How well have you done? Is it easier if you remember the first letters of each object, and then put the letters together as a made-up word? The letters here could make up the word 'SCUMPAWS'.

SCUMPAWS

How do you see?

Sight is your most important sense. It gives you more information about the outside world than all the other senses - hearing, smell, taste and touch - put together. You see with your eyes - two, jelly-filled balls protected in socket holes in your skull.

Light passes through the front of your eye and an **image** is **projected** on to the back of the eye. You see a clear, sharp picture because the light is **focused** by a **lens**. This lens can change shape to focus light rays from distant objects, or objects which are closer to it.

At the back of your eye is a layer of nerve cells, called the retina. You have two types of nerve cells, called rods and cones. Rods only see in black and white. They can see quite well in dim light. Cones see in colour. But they only see in good light. The light hits the rods and cones, and nerve signals are sent from your eye to your brain. They travel along a large nerve, called the optic nerve. Your brain sorts out the signals and puts together the picture that you see.

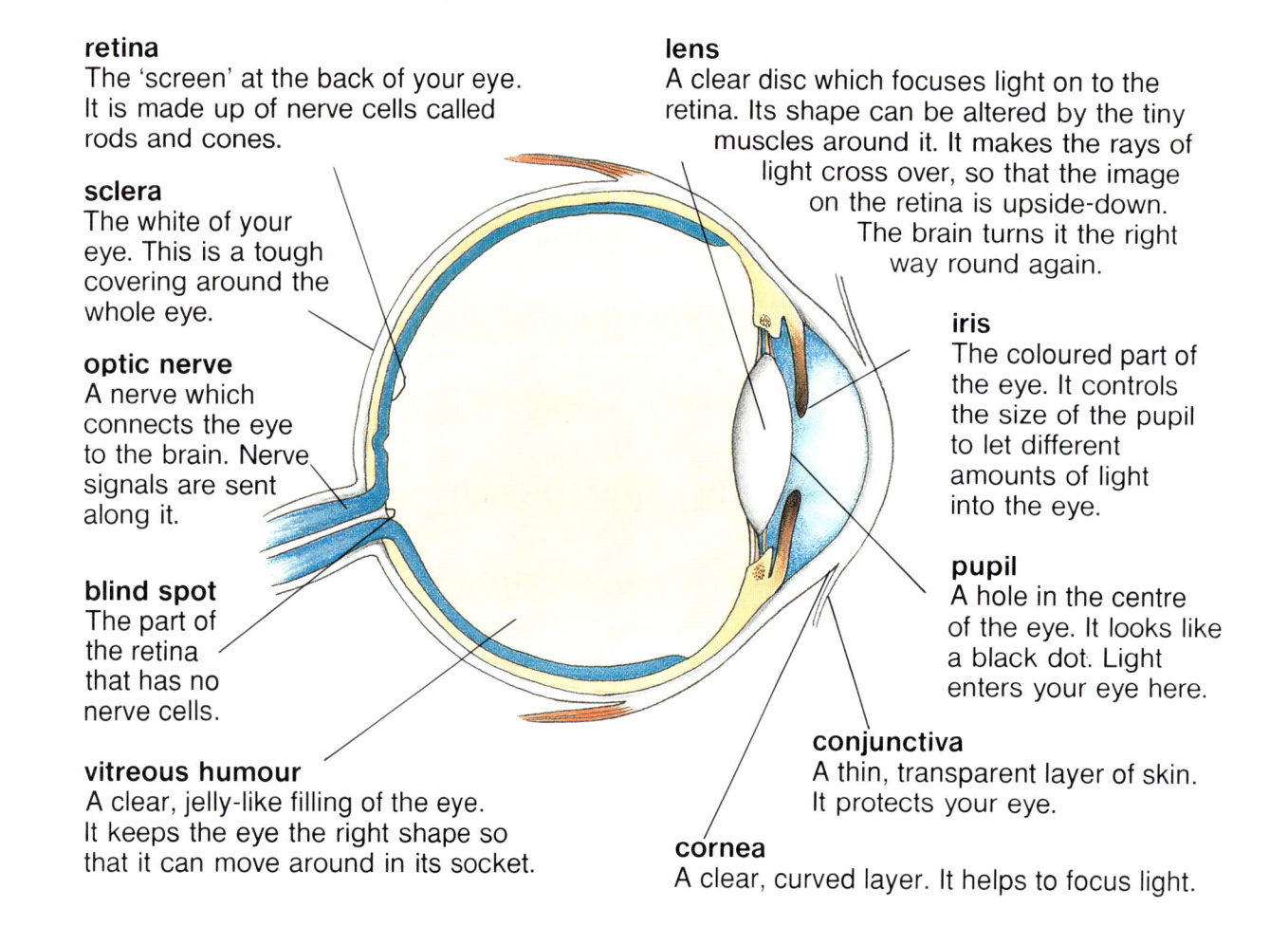

retina
The 'screen' at the back of your eye. It is made up of nerve cells called rods and cones.

sclera
The white of your eye. This is a tough covering around the whole eye.

optic nerve
A nerve which connects the eye to the brain. Nerve signals are sent along it.

blind spot
The part of the retina that has no nerve cells.

vitreous humour
A clear, jelly-like filling of the eye. It keeps the eye the right shape so that it can move around in its socket.

lens
A clear disc which focuses light on to the retina. Its shape can be altered by the tiny muscles around it. It makes the rays of light cross over, so that the image on the retina is upside-down. The brain turns it the right way round again.

iris
The coloured part of the eye. It controls the size of the pupil to let different amounts of light into the eye.

pupil
A hole in the centre of the eye. It looks like a black dot. Light enters your eye here.

conjunctiva
A thin, transparent layer of skin. It protects your eye.

cornea
A clear, curved layer. It helps to focus light.

> **? Did you know?**
>
> You have about 7 million cones in each eye, and about 120 million rods.

Why do people have to wear glasses?

Do you wear glasses? Do you know anyone who wears contact lenses? People have to wear glasses or contact lenses because their eyeballs are a slightly different shape from normal and cannot focus light rays properly. Short-sighted people have longer eyeballs than normal. They can only see things at a short distance. They cannot see distant objects clearly. Long-sighted people can only see things at a long distance. They have difficulty seeing things close to them. Their eyeballs are shorter than normal. Wearing extra, artificial lenses such as glasses, in front of the eyes, helps the eyes to focus properly. The sight, or vision, is therefore improved.

> **! See for yourself**
>
> You use one of your eyes more than the other. This is called your dominant eye. Find out which is your dominant eye by holding a pencil at arm's length and lining it up with an object in the distance. Close each eye in turn, and then open them again. When one of your eyes closes, the pencil seems to jump to the side. Which eye are you closing when this happens? This is your dominant eye.

Why are people's eyes different colours?

What colour are your eyes? Are they brown, blue, green or grey? Does everyone in your family have eyes the same colour? What about your friends? Which eye colour is most common?

The colour of your eyes depends on the amount of the **pigment**, melanin, that there is in them. Melanin is also the substance that colours your skin and hair (see page 42). Brown eyes contain a lot of melanin. Blue eyes have very little. But the amount of melanin, and therefore the colour of your eyes, is inherited, or passed down, from your parents.

For each of your features, such as the colour of your eyes or hair, your height and build, you have two genes. One comes from your mother; the other from your father.

Genes are special sets of instructions found in your cells. You look the way you do because of these genes. Some genes are stronger than others. If you inherit one brown eye gene and one blue eye gene, you will probably have brown eyes because the brown gene is stronger. If you inherit two blue genes, you will have blue eyes. Sometimes, there are exceptions to this.

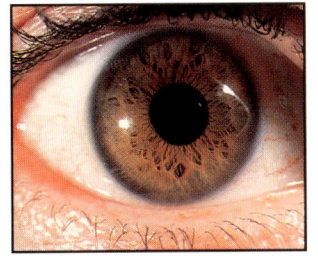

How do you hear sounds?

Sounds are made up of vibrations in the air, called sound waves. Low sounds are caused by slow vibrations and high sounds by fast vibrations. Your earflap makes sure that the vibrations go into your ear, where they travel down the ear canal to the eardrum. This is a thin sheet of skin-like membrane across the end of the canal. The membrane is stretched tight, a bit like a drum skin. When the sound waves hit it, it vibrates too. These vibrations are passed to three tiny bones deep inside your ear. They are called the anvil, hammer and stirrup because of their shapes.

From here, vibrations travel to your cochlea. This is a coiled, snail-like tube, filled with liquid. Special cells turn the vibrations into electrical signals which are sent to your brain along the auditory nerve. This nerve connects the ear to the brain. Your brain sorts the signals into the sounds you hear.

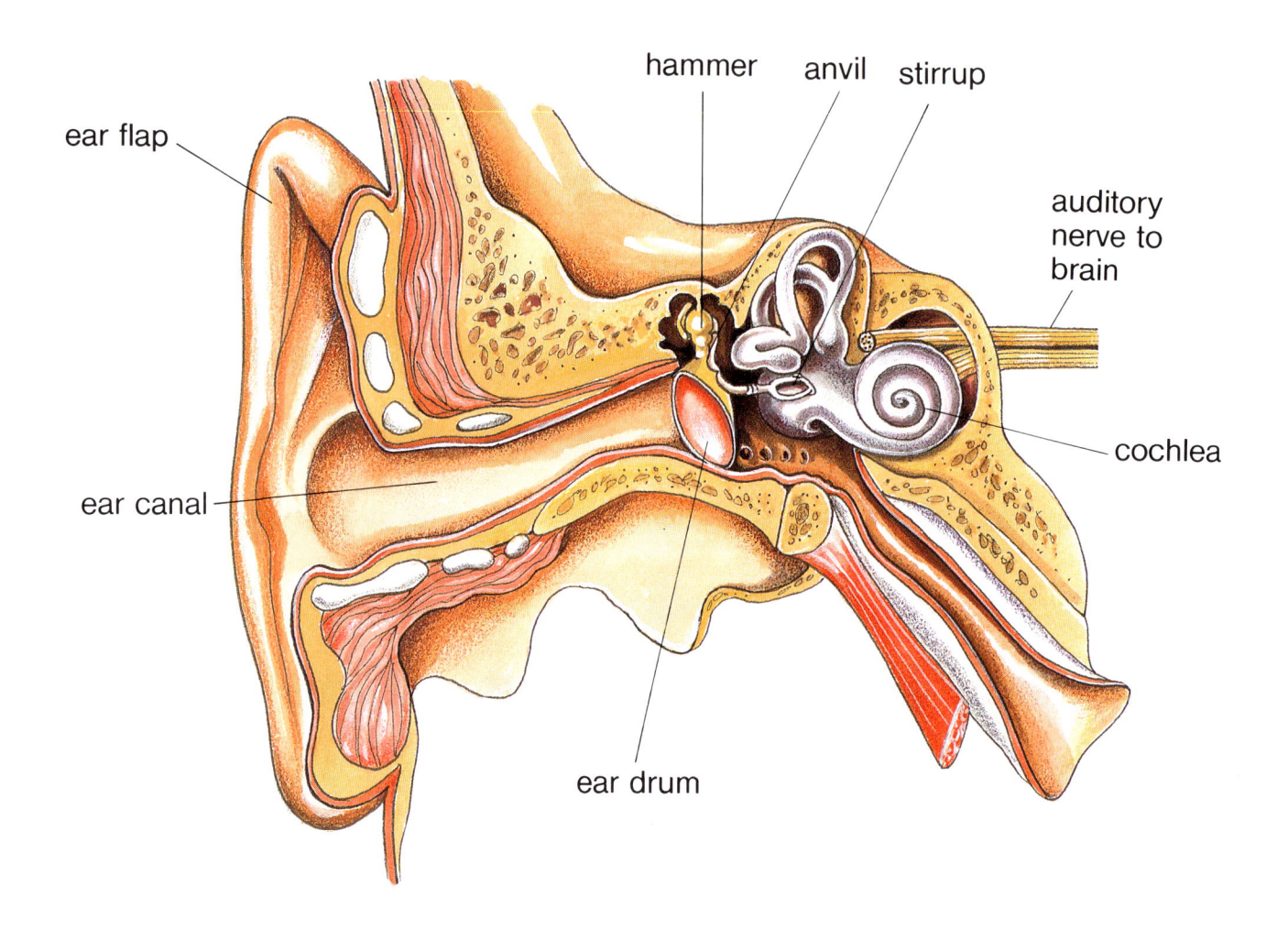

People can hear a wide range of sounds from a quiet whisper to the roar of a jet plane. Children usually have more sensitive ears than adults.

Why do you feel dizzy?

Your ears also contain special parts which help you to balance. These are tubes, called the semi-circular canals, which are filled with fluid. There are three of these tubes in each ear. They are lined with nerve cells. When you move your head, the fluid inside the canals moves and touches the nerve ends. They send signals to your brain to tell it about the change in your head's position.

If you spin round and round, then stop, the fluid in the canals keeps moving. This sends confused messages to your brain. When you stop spinning, your muscles and eyes tell your brain that your body has stopped. The fluid tells it that your body is still spinning. This is why you feel dizzy for a while.

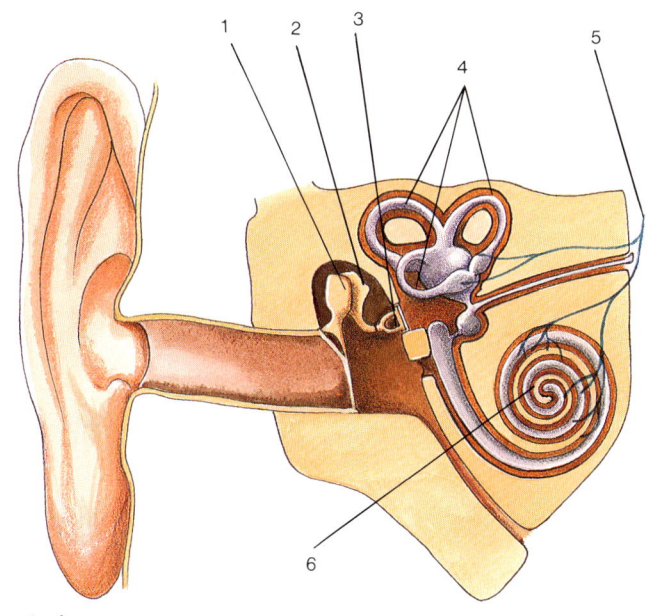

1. hammer
2. anvil
3. stirrup
4. semi-circular canals
5. auditory nerve to brain
6. cochlea

The liquid inside your semi-circular canals is called endolymph.

⚠ See for yourself

You can test your balance for yourself. Choose an object, such as a clock hanging on the wall. Close your eyes, then point at it. Keep pointing and open your eyes. Were you still pointing at the clock? How near were you?

Now spin round twice, then close your eyes and try to point at the clock again. You are probably way off this time because your sense of balance has been confused by the spinning.

You must now be wondering how skaters and ballet dancers can spin round so many times and so fast. Skaters and ballet dancers focus on fixed points as they spin, to stop themselves feeling dizzy. This is called 'spotting'.

How do you smell things?

Smells are made of tiny, invisible chemicals floating in the air. As you breathe in, the smells travel up your nostrils. They are then picked up by a small patch of smell **sensors** in your nasal cavity, the hollow space inside your nose. The sensors have special cells, covered in slimy mucus, which absorb the smells from the air. Then they send signals along your olfactory nerve, which connects the smell sensors to your brain. Your brain sorts the signals and tells you what sort of smell it is, and if it is pleasant or nasty.

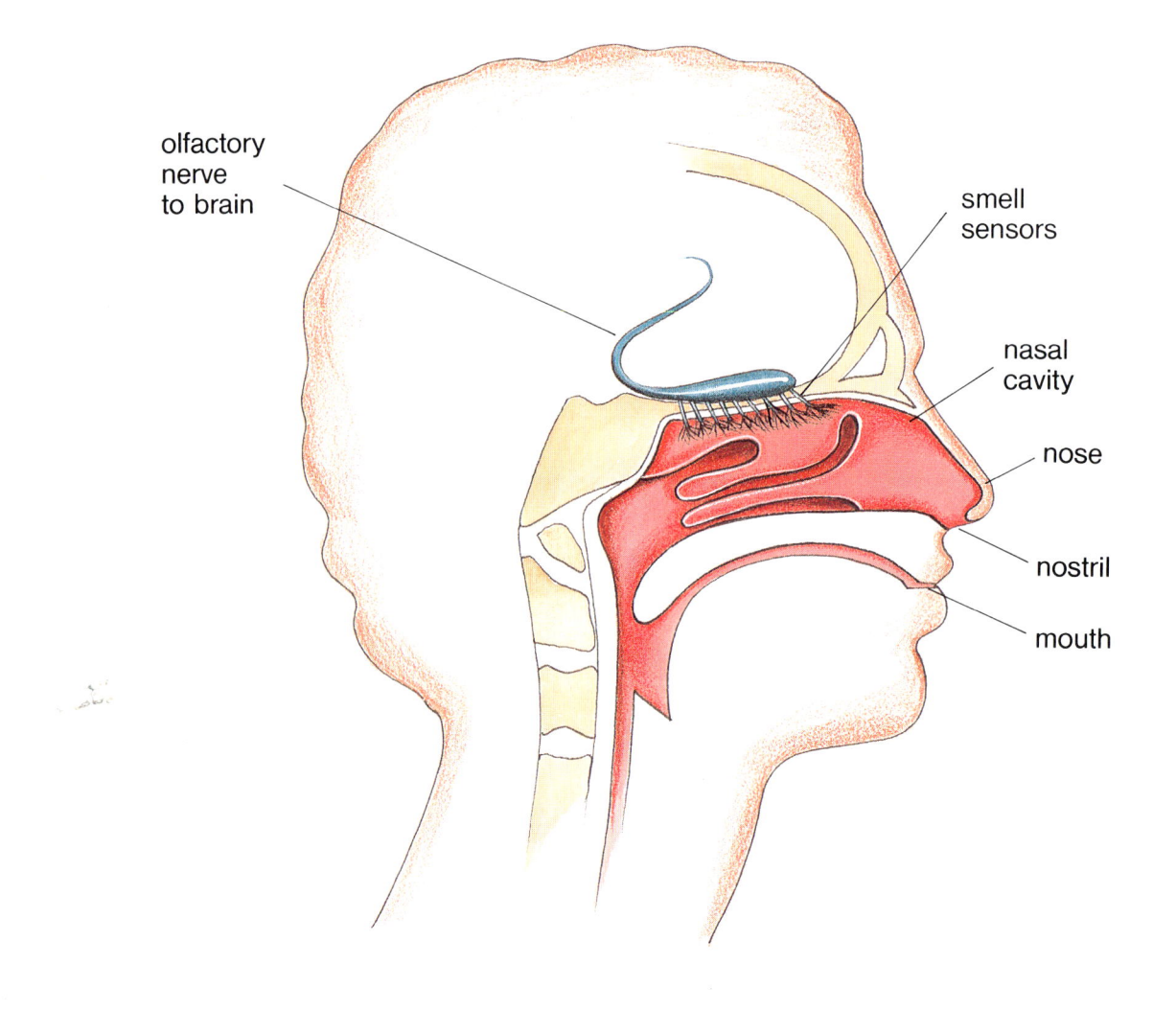

Your smell sensors in your nasal cavity only cover an area about the size of a postage stamp.

❓ Did you know?

Your sense of smell is about 10,000 times stronger than your sense of taste.

Why do people sniff at things?

Sniffing helps you to smell things better. In normal breathing, only a little air, and therefore only a few smell particles, float up into your nasal cavity to be picked up by your smell detectors. A long, hard sniff pushes more air and more smell particles, straight towards your smell detectors to give you a stronger smell.

? Did you know?

Human beings can tell the difference between about 3,000 smells. But this is nothing compared with the sensitivity of a dog's nose. An alsatian dog can smell about 1 million times better than we can.

The top left-hand picture shows a test-tube full of decaying food which is being used in an experiment. It has a nasty smell. Your sense of smell tells you if your food is good or bad. The bad smell of the food in the test-tube warns you that it should not be eaten. The pleasant smell of the meal below makes you want to eat it.

How do you taste things?

What is your favourite taste? Is it something sweet, or something sour? When you eat something, your tongue tastes it. It tells you if your food is hot or cold, if it tastes good or bad, and about its flavour.

Different flavours are detected by tiny taste buds on your tongue. You have over 10,000 taste buds in your mouth. They look like tiny bulges. Most are on your tongue. But there are also some on the inside of your cheeks, on the roof of your mouth and in your throat.

Taste buds can taste four different flavours - sweet, sour, salty and bitter. On different parts of your tongue they can pick up different flavours.

Taste buds pick up flavours which mix with the saliva or spit that you make as you eat. Then nerves carry messages about the tastes to your brain.

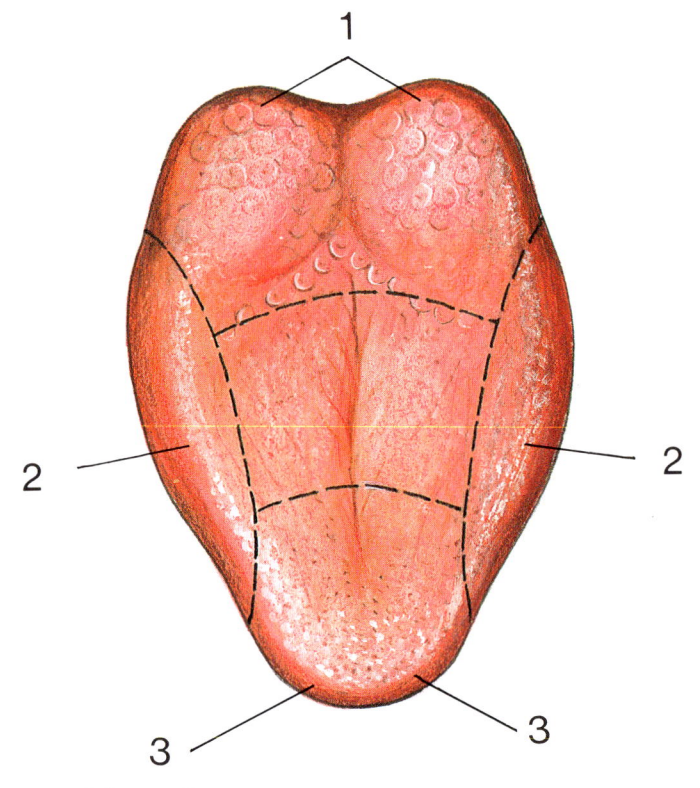

1. bitter flavours
2. sour flavours
3. sweet and salty flavours

Your tongue is a large piece of muscle. It helps you to taste your food and to break it up into pieces small enough for you to swallow.

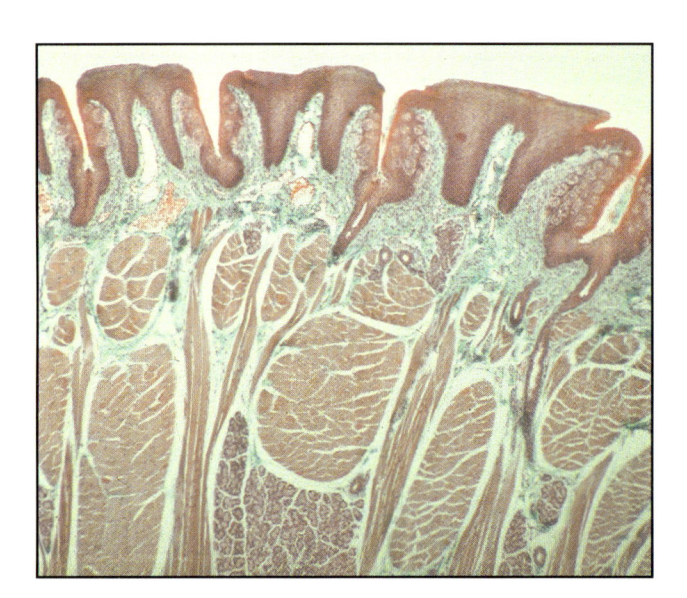

Your taste buds look like tiny bulges on the surface of your tongue.

⚠ See for yourself

Your senses of taste and smell often work together. If you have a cold and cannot smell, you probably will not be able to taste your food very well either. Try this test.

Blindfold a friend. Then hold a piece of onion under their nose. Give them various pieces of food to eat, such as bread, potato or a slice of apple. Can they tell what they are eating? Or does the onion smell confuse them?

How do you feel things?

You touch or feel things with your skin. Your skin touches the things around you. It can feel if something light or heavy is pressing on it. It can feel different textures, such as rough or smooth, and heat and cold and pain.

Your skin is made up of two layers - the epidermis and the dermis. The epidermis is the top layer of hard, dead cells. Below it lies the dermis. This layer contains millions of tiny nerve sensors. Each type is sensitive to a different type of touch and sends signals about it to your brain. Your brain **interprets** the signals and you feel the result. Sensors all over your body send millions of signals every second to your brain.

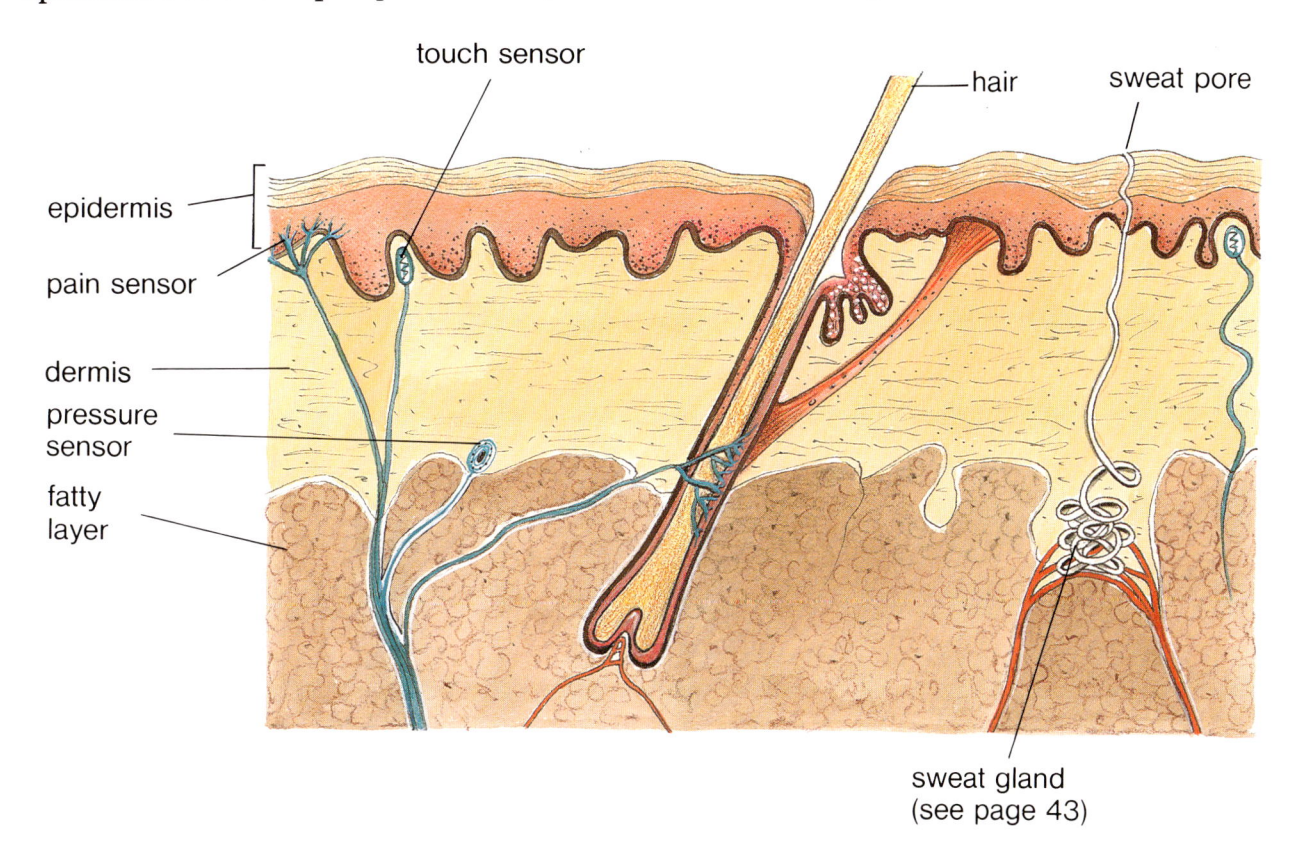

Labels: touch sensor, hair, sweat pore, epidermis, pain sensor, dermis, pressure sensor, fatty layer, sweat gland (see page 43)

⚠ See for yourself

Your skin is more sensitive in some places than others, because there are more sensors in some places. Test this by taping two pencils to a ruler, about 1.5 cm apart. Ask a friend to close their eyes. Then touch them gently with the pencils on their fingertips, arm, neck and so on. How many points can they feel each time? In sensitive places, they should feel the two points. In less sensitive places, they will feel just one point. The most sensitive skin should be on their fingertips, toes and lips.

See for Yourself! Body Science Quiz

1. Does your brain contain the smallest or the largest cells?
2. What is the name of the centre of a cell?
   a) membrane b) cytoplasm c) nucleus
3. Where are your smallest bones?
4. Why does an adult have fewer bones than a baby?
5. How many muscles do you use when you walk?
   a) 5   b) 25   c) 50   d) 100   e) 200   e) 250
6. How many times does your heart beat in a minute?
7. What is the name of the special type of muscle that the heart is made up of?
8. What is the name of the waste gas produced by our cells?
9. Why do you pant when you have been running?
10. What is the name of the flat sheet of muscle under your ribs, which you use for breathing?
11. What type of diet do athletes have to follow to build up their muscles and carbohydrates to give them energy?
12. How long does food take to pass through the body?
    a) 4 hours   b) 24 hours   c) 1 day   d) 3 days
13. Why is salad good for you?
14. Where is your epiglottis?
15. What protects your brain from knocks and bumps?
16. How heavy is an adult's brain?
17. What is the name given to a person who can write with both their left and right hands?
18. Rods and cones are nerve cells in the eye. Which see only black and white? Which see only colour?
19. Where in the body are the hammer, anvil and stirrup?
20. Taste buds can taste four different flavours. What are they?

Answers

Look back to find the answers on these pages.

Question	Page	Question	Page	Question	Page	Question	Page
1	8	6	14	11	20	16	25
2	9	7	15	12	21	17	25
3	10	8	16	13	23	18	26
4	10	9	17	14	22	19	28
5	12	10	19	15	24	20	32

SCIENCE
QUESTIONS & ANSWERS

Animal Science

Anita Ganeri

Acknowledgements

Page 40 - (main picture) K Wothe, Bruce Coleman Limited, (inset) H Schrempp, Frank Lane Picture Agency; page 41 - (left) Peter Parks, Oxford Scientific Films, (right) A Warren, Ardea London Ltd; page 42 - (left) G A Maclean, Oxford Scientific Films, (right) Jane Burton, Bruce Coleman Limited; page 43 -(left)J Shaw, Bruce Coleman Limited, (right) Oxford Scientific Films; page 44 - (pictures 1-4) Kim Taylor, Bruce Coleman Limited, (picture 5) Jeremy Grayson, Bruce Coleman Limited; page 45 - Oxford Scientific Films; page 47 - (main picture) Silvestris, Frank Lane Picture Agency, (inset) Grynienicz, Ecoscene; page 49 Sally Morgan, Ecoscene; page 51 - Jane Burton, Bruce Coleman Limited; page 52 - Oxford Scientific Films; page 54 - (left) Chris Newton, Frank Lane Picture Agency, (right) Silvestris, Frank Lane Picture Agency; page 55 Oxford Scentific Films; page 56 - Michael Leach, Oxford Scientific Films; page 57 - Anthony Bannister, NHPA; page 58 - A MacEwen, Oxford Scienific Films; page 59 - (top) Gordon Langsbury, Bruce Coleman Limited, (bottom) Hans Reinhard, Bruce Coleman Limited: page 60 Mickey Gibson, Oxford Scientific Films; page 61 - (left) David Cayless, Oxford Scientific Films, (right) B Gerard, The Hutchison Library; page 62 - Ian Beames, Ardea London Ltd; page 63 - (left) Christian Zuber, Bruce Coleman Limited, (right) Silvestris, Frank Lane Picture Agency.

Contents

What types of animal are there?	**38**	• Which fish sleeps in a sleeping-bag?	**52**
• Vertebrates	38	• Which fish sleeps the longest?	53
• Invertebrates	39	**What is the difference between frogs and toads?**	**54**
• What are warm-blooded and cold-blooded animals?	39	• Why do frogs have slimy skins?	54
How do insects see?	**40**	• Why do some frogs have brightly-coloured skins?	55
• Why do moths fly towards the light?	41	**How do snakes swallow their food whole?**	**56**
Who likes honey?	**42**	• How do snakes smell?	56
• How do bees make honey?	42	**Why do snakes shed their skins?**	**57**
• What do butterflies eat?	43	**Why do birds have feathers?**	**58**
• Which insects are used as honeypots?	43	• How do birds stay in the air?	59
How do caterpillars turn into butterflies?	**44**	**Why do camels have humps?**	**60**
• How do grasshoppers grow?	45	• How long can camels survive without water?	61
How do spiders spin webs?	**46**	**Why do giraffes have such long necks?**	**62**
• Do spiders use silk in other ways?	47	**Why do elephants have such long trunks?**	**63**
Why are some fish flat?	**48**	**Animal Science Quiz**	**64**
Why don't fish sink?	**49**		
How do fish breathe underwater?	**50**		
• Which fish can live out of water	51		

What types of animal are there?

Scientists think that there could be over ten million types, or species, of animals in the world. But there may be many more, just waiting to be found. Animals range in size from the huge blue whale, the biggest animal that has ever lived, to tiny creatures made of only one **cell**. These animals can be seen only under a microscope.

Animals can be divided into different groups, which makes it easier to study them. The members of each one share certain features or characteristics. Animals can be divided first into two big groups called vertebrates and invertebrates. These are explained below and on the right. You can see also how each of these groups are divided into smaller ones.

Vertebrates

Vertebrates

Vertebrates are animals with bony skeletons inside their bodies. These animals include amphibians, reptiles, fish, birds and mammals. Fish make up over half of all the vertebrates that are known.

Fish Fish live in both fresh water and sea-water. Most have fins and breathe through gills, not lungs (see pages 20-21). They include sharks, seahorses, eels and flat-fish such as plaice.

Amphibians Amphibians can live on both land and water. But they have to return to water to lay their eggs. They include frogs, toads, newts and salamanders.

Reptiles Alligators, crocodiles, snakes, turtles and lizards are all reptiles. They have scaly skin and lay their eggs on land. The dinosaurs which ruled the Earth until about 65 million years ago were reptiles.

Birds Birds are the only animals with feathers. They all have wings and most can fly, though not all. Birds include parrots, peacocks, penguins and ostriches.

Mammals Kangaroos, mice, dolphins and human beings are all mammals. All the members of this group have some hair or fur, and feed their babies on milk.

Emperor penguin.
Rainbow lorikeet.
Grey kangaroo.
Dormouse.
Coral snake.
Loggerhead turtle.
Spotted salamander.
Poison-arrow frog.
Blue shark.
Common seahorse.

Invertebrates

Invertebrates are animals which do not have bones inside their bodies. They include jellyfish, crabs, spiders, earthworms and insects.

Insects There are at least one million species of insects on Earth. Scientists are finding new insects all the time. Insects have six legs and their bodies are divided into three parts — the head, thorax and abdomen. Most have wings. This group includes butterflies, moths, ants, bees and beetles.

Arachnids Arachnids include spiders, scorpions, mites and ticks. They have eight legs and their bodies are divided into two parts.

Crustaceans Crabs, shrimps and barnacles are all crustaceans. They have hard cases protecting their bodies and they mostly live in water. Woodlice are also crustaceans, although they live on land.

Molluscs Molluscs include slugs and snails, clams and cockles, squid and octopuses. They have soft bodies, although most have hard shells to protect them.

Invertebrates

Common blue butterfly.

Honeybee. — head, thorax, abdomen

Seven-spotted ladybird.

Common scorpion.

Funnel web spider.

Common octopus.

Banded snail.

Dublin Bay prawn.

Tortoiseshell limpet.

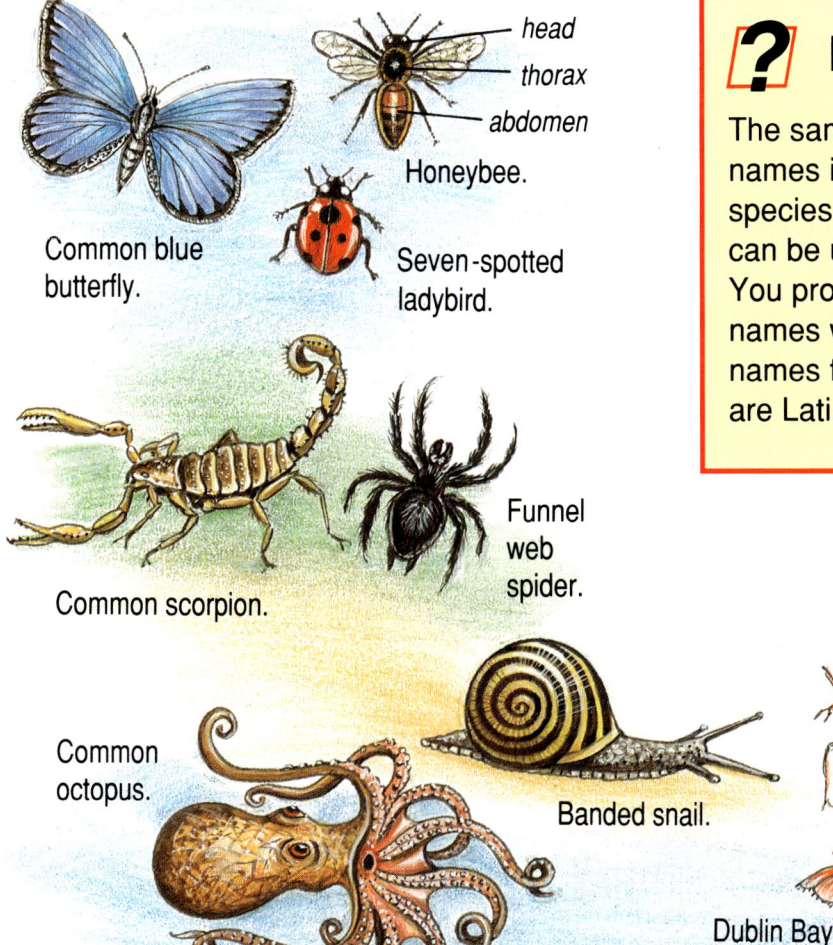

What are warm-blooded and cold-blooded animals?

Birds and mammals are warm-blooded animals. They are called endotherms. Warm-blooded animals keep their body temperature about the same, whatever the weather outside. Their body temperature usually ranges from a warm 36° C to 39° C. This means that they can live active lives even in the coldest places on Earth.

Amphibians, reptiles and fish are cold-blooded. They are called ectotherms. Cold-blooded animals have to rely on the weather to warm them up or cool them down. They are best suited to life in warmer places. In cold weather, they become sluggish and slow.

? Did you know?

The same animal may have different names in different countries. So every species also has a Latin name which can be understood all over the world. You probably know quite a few Latin names without realizing it. Most of the names for dinosaurs, for example, are Latin.

How do insects see?

Most insects have two types of eye. The first type is a set of three simple eyes arranged in a triangle on the top of the insect's head. These eyes are called ocelli. They look like tiny beads. The ocelli are probably used to pick up the differences in the amount of light coming into them.

The other type of eye is called the compound eye. These are the big, bulging eyes that you can see on flies, for example. Each eye is made up of many hundreds of tiny, often six-sided, **lenses**. Each lens has a **nerve** running to the insect's brain. The nerve carries information about the world outside, to the brain which sorts out the information. Compound eyes are very good for judging distances and seeing even the slightest movements. This is why flies are so difficult to swat. They can see you coming!

No one is sure exactly what picture of the world an insect sees. The lenses in its compound eyes cannot **focus**, like our eyes, so the picture is probably blurred and grainy. We also do not know if all insects see in colour or in black and white. But we do know that some insects have excellent eyesight. Dragonflies, for example, can catch mosquitoes in mid-air at night when it is too dark for human eyes to pick them out.

▲ *A Southern hawker dragonfly.*

You can see the compound eyes of this ▶
dragonfly quite clearly.

Did you know?

The giant squid has the biggest eyes of any animal. They measure 40 centimetres across. This is over 16 times wider than your eyes.

A squid's eye.

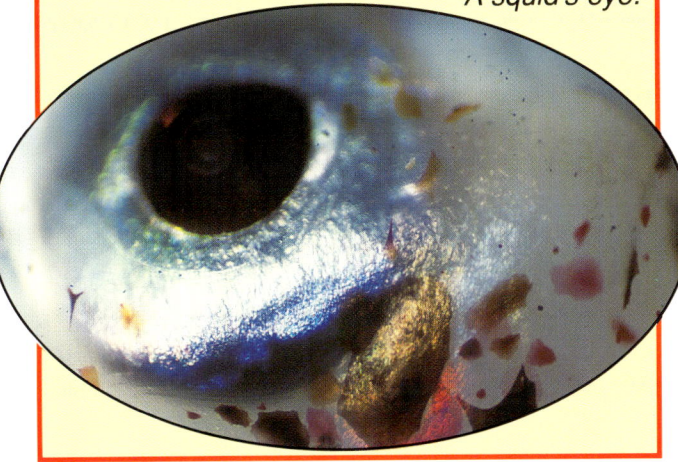

Did you know?

Birds have eyes which look like our own. Birds-of-prey, such as eagles and hawks, have the best eyesight in the animal world. They can see distant objects three times better than you can. This makes them superb hunters.

Why do moths fly towards the light?

Have you ever noticed how moths fly towards a light bulb and then fly round and round it? This is because they mistake the light for the moon. Night-flying moths navigate by keeping the moon at a certain angle to their eyes. If they see a light bulb, they think it is the moon and try to fly with it always on one side. But because the light bulb is much closer than the moon, the moth has to fly round and round in a spiral to keep it to one side.

These moths are flying towards the lamp.

See for yourself

You can see for yourself how moths are attracted to light. In the summer, go outside at night and hang a white or light-coloured bedsheet over a washing-line. Shine a torch through the sheet. You will soon see moths flying towards the sheet and the torch beam. Do not touch them or try to catch them. They are very delicate.

Who likes honey?

How do bees make honey?

Does your garden or nearby park buzz with bees in the summer? The bees are visiting flowers, to feed on the sweet, syrupy **nectar** deep inside them. Honeybees also collect pollen from the flowers. This is a yellow dust made inside the male part of a flower, which sticks to the bees' hairy bodies. You may be allergic, or react badly, to pollen if you suffer from hay fever.

A bumblebee on a ragwort plant.

These honeybees have returned to their hive.

Some of the pollen brushes off if the bees visit the next flower. If the pollen is brushed onto the female part of this flower, it will help to make a seed inside the flower. If the seed finds a good place to grow, it will sprout into a new plant the following year. This process is called pollination.

Honeybees also carry pollen and nectar back to their hives to feed the young bees. Some is also stored as honey for winter food. Bees work very hard making honey. They may have to fly over 100 kilometres to collect enough nectar to make just a tablespoon of it.

Young bees are raised inside six-sided wax cells inside the hive. Honey is stored there as well. The bees make the wax for the cells inside their own bodies. It oozes out through tiny holes in their abdomens and hardens in the air.

? Did you know?

Bees really should not be able to fly at all. Their wings are too small for their bodies. But bees can fly perfectly well. They have to flap their wings about 250 times a second to stay in the air. This makes the buzzing sound that you hear.

? Did you know?

Honeybees are very sociable. They live in **colonies** of as many as 80,000 bees.

What do butterflies eat?

Like bees, butterflies feed on flower nectar. They suck it up through a long tube like a drinking straw. This is called a proboscis. It is coiled up underneath the butterfly's head when it is not in use. Butterflies taste their food with their feet. If they land on something which tastes sweet, they will eat it.

An American painted lady butterfly.

Which insects are used as honeypots?

Honeypot ants live in Australia. They have an amazing way of storing nectar for times when food is hard to find. Some of the ants are fed with so much nectar that their bodies swell from the size of grains of sand to the size of beans. They are too fat to move, so they hang from the ceiling of the ants' underground nest. When the other ants are hungry, the living honeypots **regurgitate** nectar from their stomachs into the mouths of the other ants, for them to eat.

This is how honeypot ants hang in their nest.

⚠ See for yourself

You can tempt bees and butterflies to visit your garden by growing flowers which they particularly like. These include plants such as buddleias, lavender bushes and wall-flowers. Watch the insects feeding on the nectar but do not get too close or frighten them off.

Small tortoiseshell butterfly.

Peacock butterfly.

Bumblebee.

How do caterpillars turn into butterflies?

Caterpillars and butterflies look completely different but they are in fact the same animal at different stages of its growth. To change into a butterfly, a caterpillar has to go through an amazing process, called metamorphosis.

The caterpillar has already been through one change in its growth. It has hatched out of an egg laid by a female butterfly on a plant leaf or stem. The caterpillar then feeds and grows so much that it has to shed its skin and grow a new one several times as it gets too tight. Then the caterpillar spins a silk case, or cocoon, around its body and hangs upside-down from a stem or leaf. It is now called a chrysalis.

The metamorphosis of a red admiral butterfly

1 Caterpillar emerges from an egg.
2 Caterpillar feeds on a nettle.
3 Chrysalis is about to split.
4 Adult butterfly has only just emerged.
5 Adult red admiral has spread its wings.

? Did you know?

Caterpillars spend most of their time eating. The caterpillar of the polyphemus moth has a huge appetite. It munches its way through 86,000 times its own weight in leaves during the first two months of its life.

Inside the chrysalis, the caterpillar's body changes completely. All of its cells are reorganized and its body is rebuilt as a butterfly. A few weeks later, the chrysalis splits open and the butterfly appears. Its wings are soft and crushed but they soon smooth out as blood flows into them.

How do grasshoppers grow?

Some insects, such as grasshoppers, locusts and dragonflies, also go through changes, but not such complicated ones. When young grasshoppers, or nymphs, hatch from their eggs, they already look like very small adults. But they still need to develop their wings, and other parts inside their bodies. As they grow and develop, they shed their skins. This is called moulting. Each time they moult they look more like adult grasshoppers.

This common field grasshopper has just shed its skin.

⚠ See for yourself

Watching a caterpillar change into a butterfly is fascinating. First, collect a small amount of butterfly eggs from a plant in your garden. Summer is the best time to do this. Make sure that you look under the leaves, as this is where a lot of butterfly eggs are laid. Put the eggs on a piece of blotting paper inside a well-sealed box until they hatch. This takes about a week. Meanwhile, find a large cardboard box and punch some air holes in its sides. Do not make the holes too big or the caterpillars will crawl out!

Put a small jar of water inside the box and keep it well stocked with the caterpillars' plant food. This will be the plant that you found the eggs on. Now put the caterpillars on to the plant and wait for them to spin their cocoons. Cover the front of the box with a piece of see-through plastic or cling film. You will then have to wait for the caterpillars to turn into butterflies. Always release the butterflies back into the wild.

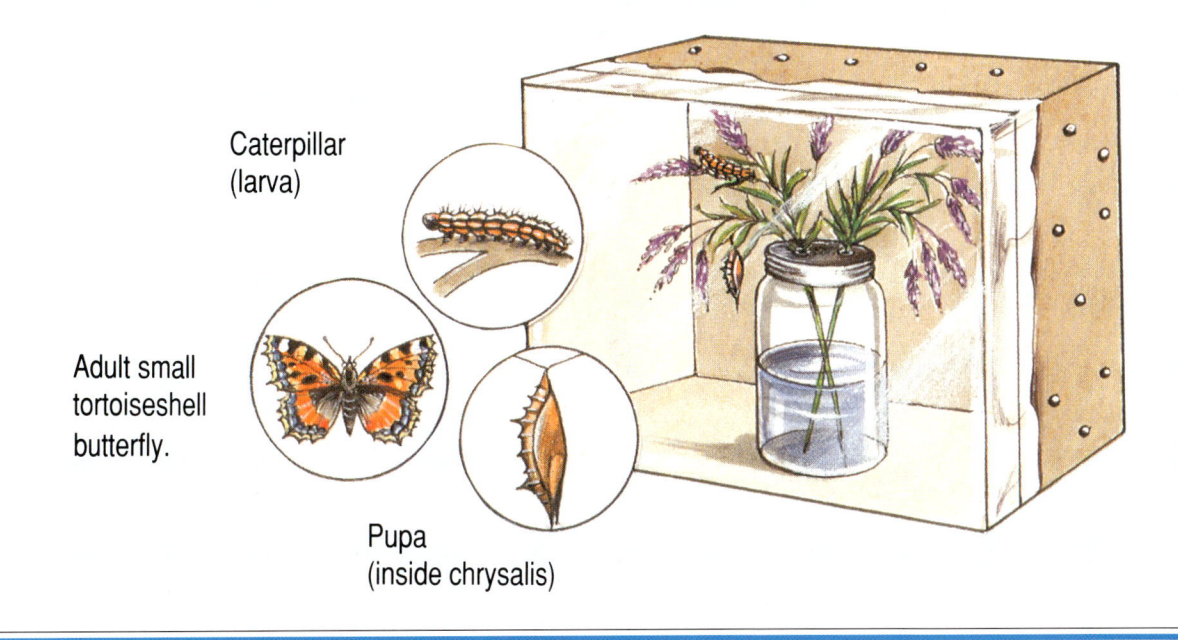

Caterpillar (larva)

Adult small tortoiseshell butterfly.

Pupa (inside chrysalis)

How do spiders spin webs?

Many spiders spin webs to trap insects for food. They weave the webs from silk which they make inside their bodies. Liquid silk is made in **glands** in the spider's abdomen. It is forced out through tiny holes, called spinnerets. In the air, the liquid silk hardens into strands. A spider's silk is made of a special type of **protein** material which does not break up in water. This is why a spider's web does not **dissolve** when it rains.

A strand of the spider's silk is finer than a human hair, but it is stronger than nylon thread and much stretchier. It can be pulled about a third longer than its unstretched length before it snaps.

The biggest spiders' webs are spun by tropical orb weaver spiders. Their webs sometimes measure nearly 2 metres across. They are supported between trees by silk threads up to 6 metres long. In Papua New Guinea, these threads are sometimes used by fishermen as fishing lines.

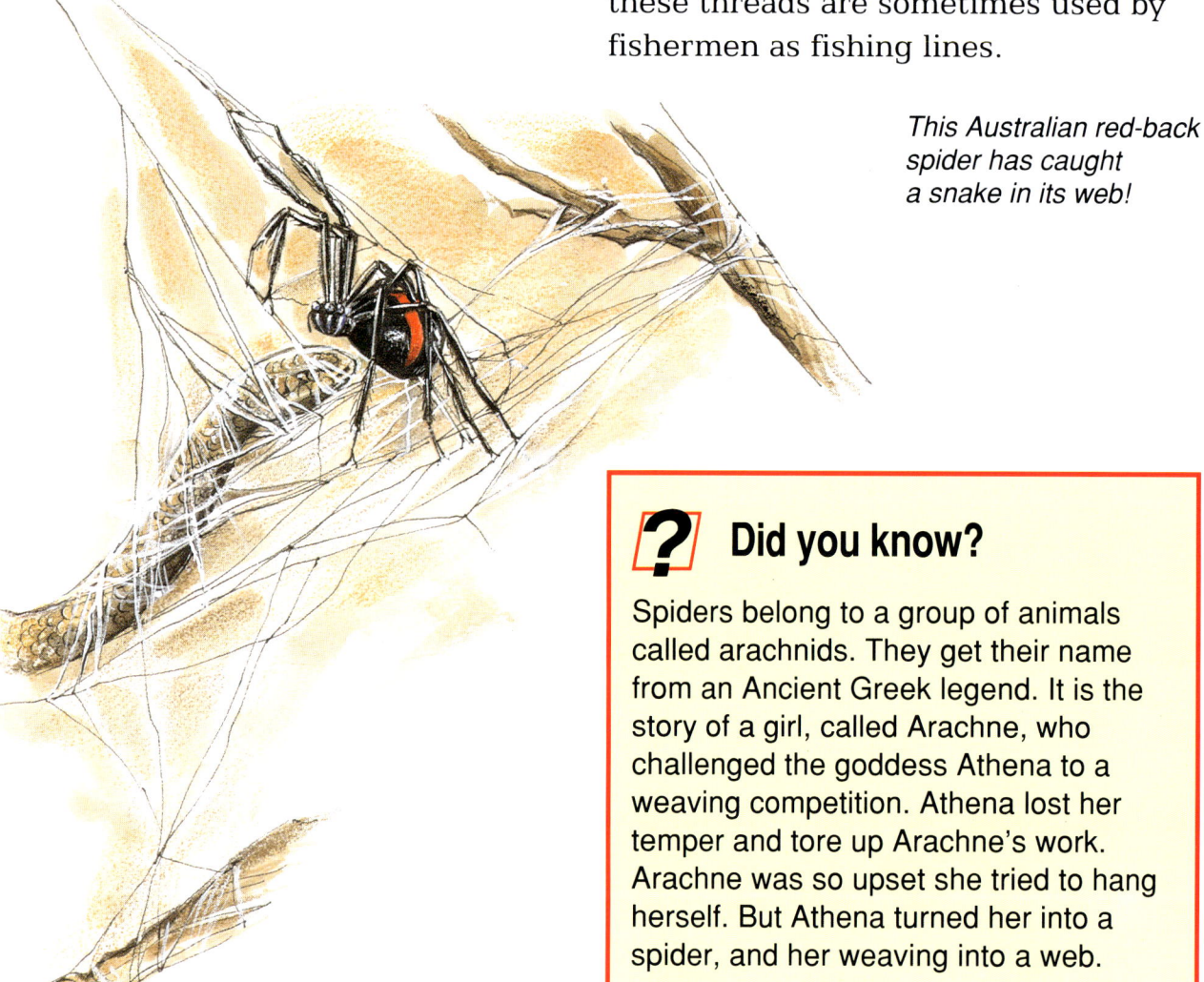

This Australian red-back spider has caught a snake in its web!

❓ Did you know?

Spiders belong to a group of animals called arachnids. They get their name from an Ancient Greek legend. It is the story of a girl, called Arachne, who challenged the goddess Athena to a weaving competition. Athena lost her temper and tore up Arachne's work. Arachne was so upset she tried to hang herself. But Athena turned her into a spider, and her weaving into a web.

Do spiders use silk in other ways?

Not all spiders spin webs, but they all make and use silk in some way. Wolf spiders are hunters. They chase their **prey** on the ground. Female wolf spiders use their silk to spin a sack for their eggs. The sack is attached to the female's abdomen. When she goes out hunting, she drags the bag with her so that her eggs are not left unguarded. In some wolf spider species, the egg sack may be as big as the female herself.

After several weeks, the female bites the sack open and as many as 100 tiny spiderlings crawl out. They climb on to their mother's back and stay there for about a week until they are old enough to fend for themselves.

❓ Did you know?

Before sticking plasters were invented, some people used cobwebs to put on cuts.

◀ *This mother wolf spider is guarding her spiderlings on the nursery web.*

▼ *A mother wolf spider is carrying her spiderlings on her back.*

Why are some fish flat?

Flat-fish, such as plaice or sole, hatch from eggs like other fish. They hatch near the surface of the sea and start life with a normal fish shape. But when they are just a few weeks old, their shape begins to change.

First of all, one eye moves round to the other side of the fish's head so that both eyes are on the same side. Then the fish swims down to lie on the sea-bed. It lies on its blind side with both its eyes staring upwards.

A young plaice changing into an adult

Then gradually, the fish's body flattens out. Instead of a right and a left side, a flat-fish has a top and a bottom side. Flat-fish spend most of their lives lying on the sea-bed. Their shape helps them to hide from enemies and to catch food more easily. Their top sides are often the same colour as the sea-bed so that they can take prey by surprise. Flat-fish can even change colour to match sandy, gravelly or spotted sea-floors. Their undersides are usually white.

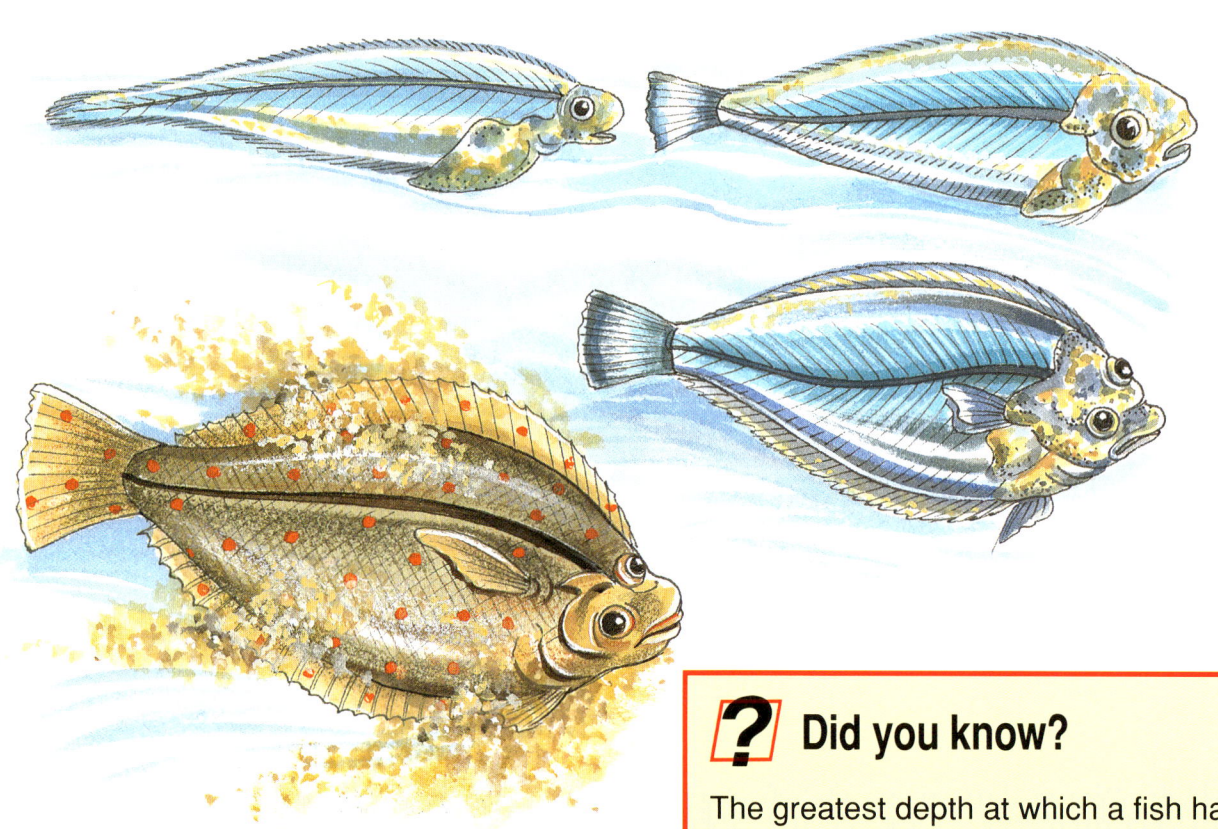

Flat-fish start life looking like ordinary fish, with an eye on each side. As the young fish grows, one eye moves to the other side of its head. Adult flat-fish always lie on one side. They can change their colour to blend in with the surrounding sea-bed.

? Did you know?

The greatest depth at which a fish has actually been seen is 10,917 metres down in the Pacific Ocean. It was a flat-fish, 33 centimetres long, which looked like a sole. At this depth, the water presses down so hard that it would easily crush a person.

Why don't fish sink?

Density is how heavy an object is for its size. Things that are denser than water, sink. Things that are less dense than water, float. Fish do not sink because they can change the density of their bodies.

Most fish have a long, balloon-like pouch inside their bodies. This is called a swim-bladder. It is filled with gas. A fish can change the amount of gas in its swim-bladder so that the fish's body density is the same as the water around it. If there is a lot of gas in the swim-bladder, then the fish is more buoyant, or more able to float than if there is only a little gas in the swim-bladder. Fish do not sink even when they are not moving, because the swim-bladder works all the time.

❓ Did you know?

Sharks do not have swim-bladders to keep them afloat. They have to keep swimming all the time, or they might sink.

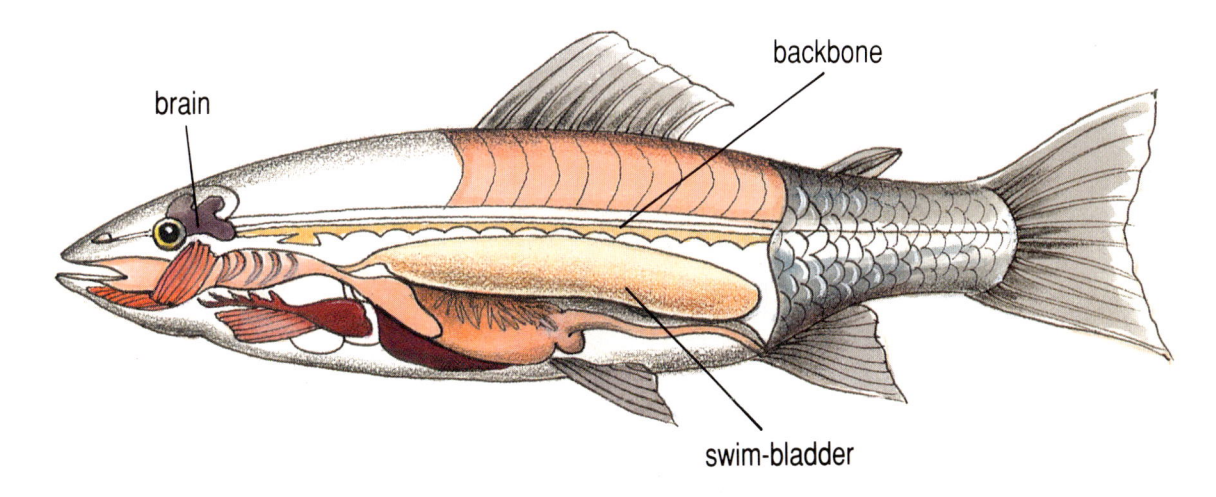

brain — backbone — swim-bladder

❗ See for yourself

Sea-water is denser than fresh water because it contains salt. This makes it easier for things to float in it. Test this for yourself. Half fill a glass with ordinary tap water. Then put a whole, fresh egg into the water. Does it float or sink? Half fill another glass with water, but also add 3 tablespoonfuls of salt. Stir really well so that the salt dissolves. Now add an egg to this water and look at the two glasses. Which egg floats better?

How do fish breathe under water?

Like all other animals, fish need to breathe oxygen to survive. We get our oxygen by breathing air through our lungs. Fish get their oxygen from water. They breathe through gills instead of lungs.

As a fish swims along, it keeps opening and closing its mouth. As it opens its mouth, it closes its gill covers and takes in a large gulp of water. Then it closes its mouth and opens its gill slits. The water is forced out over the gills on either side of the fish's body. Here, oxygen that is dissolved in the water passes into the fish's blood. Waste gases pass through the gills and out into the water. You can see a fish's gills. They are under the slit-like openings just behind its head. They are protected by the gill covers, which look like flaps.

mouth open

gill cover closed

mouth closed

gill cover open; you can see the gills, although they are never as visible as shown here

See for yourself

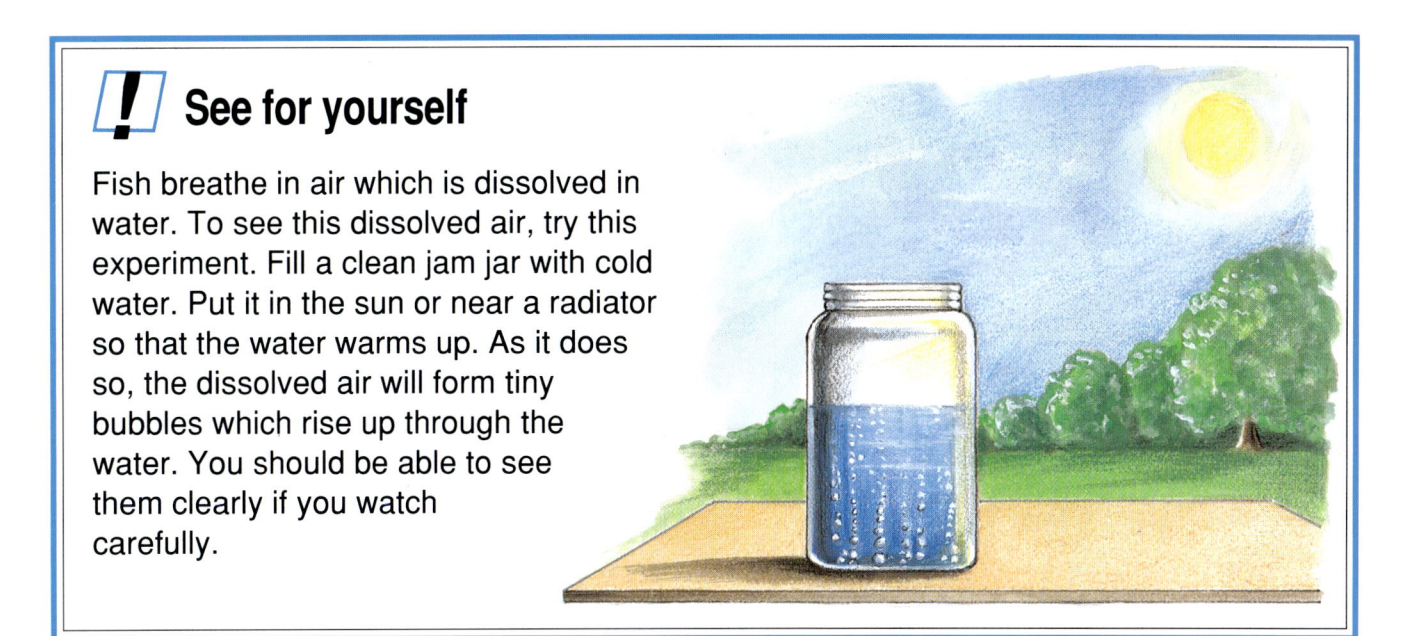

Fish breathe in air which is dissolved in water. To see this dissolved air, try this experiment. Fill a clean jam jar with cold water. Put it in the sun or near a radiator so that the water warms up. As it does so, the dissolved air will form tiny bubbles which rise up through the water. You should be able to see them clearly if you watch carefully.

Which fish can live out of water?

Mud-skippers are happy to be fish out of water. They live in the mangrove swamps which grow at the mouths of some tropical rivers. When the tide goes out, the mud-skippers skip about on the mud looking for their food of worms, insects and shellfish.

These fish breathe by keeping their mouths and gills full of water. They make regular trips to the small pools of water in the mud for fresh mouthfuls. Mud-skippers can also take in oxygen through their skin, like frogs (see pages 24-25). To do this they need to keep their skin moist by rolling in the damp mud.

Did you know?

Fish were the first animals ever to live on land. About 350 million years ago, a group of fish left the water and **adapted** to life in the open air. They gradually developed into the earliest types of amphibians and reptiles.

Mud-skippers stop their eyes from drying out by rolling them back into their sockets.

Where do fish sleep?

Fish cannot close their eyes because they do not have eyelids. But they still need to sleep, just as you do. Some lie on the sea-bed or bury themselves in the sand. Others shelter in cracks in the rocks or sleep among clumps of seaweed. In this way they are protected from hungry night-time hunters.

A dot-dash butterfly fish from the tropics. It is resting among the corals with its eyes wide open.

Which fish sleeps in a sleeping-bag?

Parrot-fish live in tropical coral reefs. They get their name from the hard, beak-like mouths which they use to bite off lumps of coral to eat. At night, parrot-fish have a clever place to sleep. They build a clear bubble of sticky **mucus** around their bodies, like a sleeping-bag. The mucus comes from special glands inside their mouths.

It takes a parrot-fish about half-an-hour to build its sleeping-bag. In the morning, it takes the fish about the same time to break free again. Scientists think that the sleeping-bag helps to stop hunters, such as moray eels, picking up the smell of the parrot-fish. In this way, the fish can sleep safely.

This male parrot-fish has spun its mucus cocoon for the night. This will help to keep the fish safe from predators.

Which fish sleeps the longest?

Lung-fish in Africa usually **hibernate** in the long, hot African summer, when the swamps and streams in which the fish live, often dry up. The fish can then survive until the rains come again. This special type of hibernation is known as aestivation.

As the water level drops, the lung-fish burrow into the soft mud on the water bed. They block the entrance of the burrow with mud. Then they curl up and, like parrot-fish, build a mucus cocoon around themselves. They leave only an opening for their mouths, which point up towards the surface and breathe the air coming through the mud entrance.

Lung-fish usually only have to survive like this for a few months, though some lung-fish have been known to hibernate for up to four years. During this time, they live off their own muscle tissue, which breaks down into **nutrients**. These nutrients keep the heart, lungs and the rest of the body working. As you can tell from their name, lung-fish have lungs for breathing when they are out of water. They also have gills for breathing when they are in water.

The lung-fish is curled up in its burrow during the dry season.

The lung-fish emerges when the rain comes again.

What is the difference between frogs and toads?

Frogs and toads are amphibians, or animals that spend part of their lives in water and part on land. Frogs and toads are very closely related. The main difference between them is their appearance. Frogs have smooth skins and long, powerful legs for jumping. Toads have warts on their skins and shorter, squatter bodies. Frogs always live close to water, but toads can survive in drier places as well.

This common grass frog has got a much smoother skin than the natterjack toad.

Why do frogs have slimy skins?

Frogs have special glands in their skin which make slimy mucus. This helps to keep their skin moist and soft. Like most adult amphibians, adult frogs have lungs for breathing on land. But they also take in oxygen through their skin. If the skin dries out, it cannot take in oxygen. Frogs never stray far from water because of this need to keep their bodies damp. Frogs can also breathe through the moist skin lining their mouths.

Natterjack toads, like the one above, are nocturnal. They also like to live in salty ponds near the sea.

? Did you know?

Most adult frogs grow bigger than tadpoles. But the paradoxical frog does quite the opposite. As a tadpole it grows about 25 centimetres long. But the adult frog is only about a quarter of this length.

Why do some frogs have brightly-coloured skins?

Frogs and other amphibians are tasty food for other hungry animals. Many have **evolved** brightly-coloured skins to protect themselves. The bright colours warn their enemies that these frogs taste terrible. This is because their skin also produces a poison.

Poison-arrow frogs in South America make such a strong poison that a single drop of it could kill a monkey. Hunters in the Amazon rainforest make deadly weapons by dipping their spears into frog poison.

A poison-arrow frog.

⚠ See for yourself

Frogs and toads begin life as eggs laid in the water. These hatch into fish-like tadpoles which breathe through gills. Their bodies gradually change and turn into adult frogs which live on land and breathe through lungs.

To see how eggs hatch into tadpoles, collect just a tablespoonful of frogspawn (frog eggs) from a pond. The best time to do this is in March or April. Take the frogspawn home in a jam jar filled with water. Then transfer it to a fish tank or aquarium. Fill the tank with pond or tap water, and add some mud and rocks from the pond to make it feel more like home. Add some pond plants for food. Then keep a close watch until the tadpoles hatch. You must return them to the pond before their legs develop or they will die. In their own environment they will then be able to grow into frogs.

1 Frogspawn of the common frog.
2 Tadpoles hatch from the spawn.
3 The tadpoles grow and develop.
4 The young frog is now ready to venture on to land.

How do snakes swallow their food whole?

A snake's jawbones are held together by loose, stretchy straps, called ligaments. These allow its jaw to open wide enough for the snake to swallow whole animals as large as deer, pigs and sheep. The snake's ribs also move outwards to make room for the prey inside the snake's body. Snakes have to swallow their food whole because their teeth are not designed for biting and chewing.

Some snakes kill their prey with poison from their fangs before they swallow it. Other snakes, such as pythons and boa constrictors, coil their bodies around their prey and squeeze it to death. Pythons and boas are the largest snakes and can tackle the biggest meals. One python was found to have swallowed a bear. Another had swallowed a leopard. Large meals last a long time. Many snakes only have to eat once a month.

A pit viper.

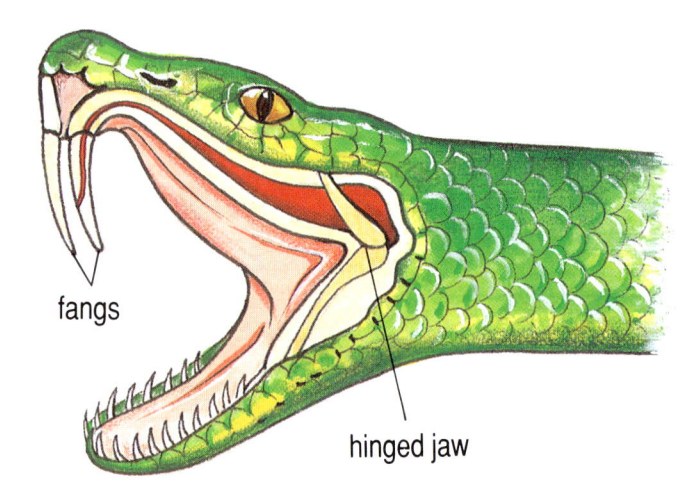

How do snakes smell?

Believe it or not, snakes smell with their tongues. This is why they flick their forked tongues in and out. The tip of the tongue picks up tiny smell particles from the air. Then the tongue flicks back in and puts the smells into special pockets in the roof of the snake's mouth. These are lined with sensitive cells which can tell if the smell is coming from a possible mate or a possible meal.

A cottonmouth snake.

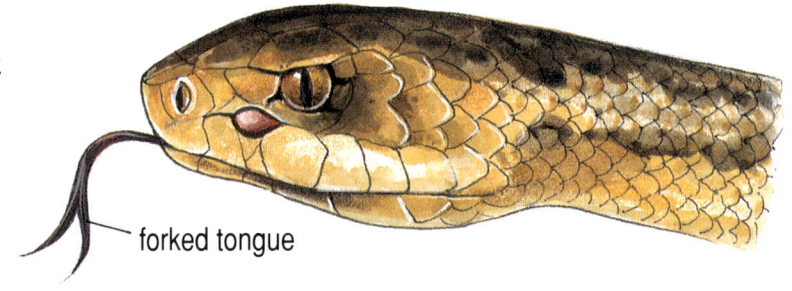

This Indian python is eating a rat.

Why do snakes shed their skins?

Snakes have to shed their scaly skins several times a year. This is because they grow too big for their old skins. Their skins also get worn out as the snakes slither across the ground. When a snake is ready to shed its skin, it rubs against a rough surface to loosen it. Then the snake crawls out of it, already wearing its new, larger skin. The old skin is as thin as paper.

? Did you know?

The reticulated python is the longest snake on Earth. It can reach 10 metres in length. The shortest snake is the thread snake. It is only about 12 centimetres long and as thin as a matchstick.

This Eastern tiger-snake has shed, or sloughed, its old skin which is very pale and fragile. This new skin has clear patterns and bright colours.

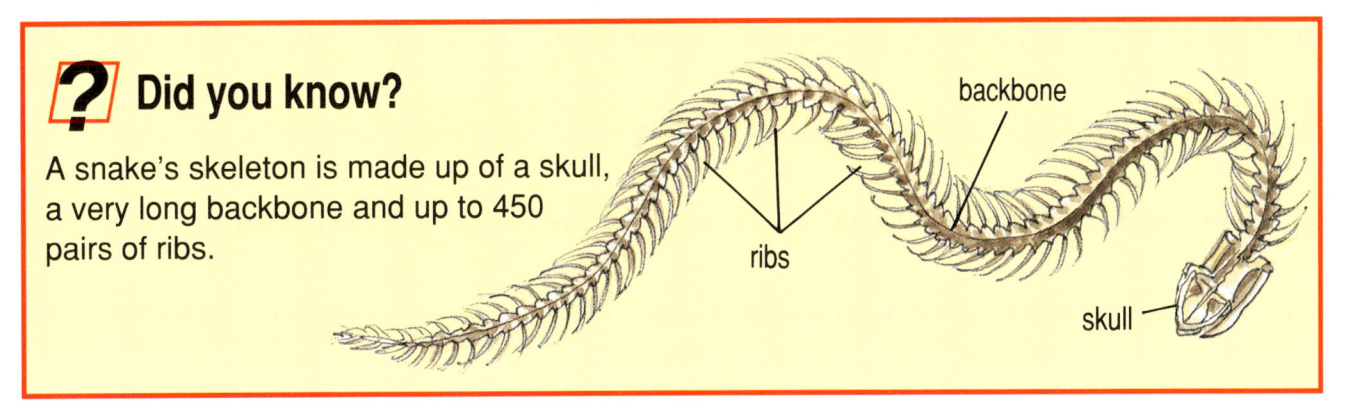

? Did you know?

A snake's skeleton is made up of a skull, a very long backbone and up to 450 pairs of ribs.

Why do birds have feathers?

Birds are the only animals that have feathers. Their whole bodies, except for their beaks and feet, are usually covered in feathers. In fact, feathers make up about a sixth of the bird's total weight.

Feathers are made of the same material as scales, horns, nails and hair. It is called keratin and is very tough and hard-wearing. Each feather is made up of a central shaft with lots of barbs on either side. These fit together like the teeth in a zip.

Birds have different feathers for different jobs. Fluffy down-feathers keep them warm. Contour feathers give birds' bodies their shape. Tail feathers are used for steering and balance in the air, and for balance and braking on the ground. Wing feathers are the biggest of all. They help the bird to fly.

Feathers take a lot of battering. So, once or twice a year, the old feathers fall out and new ones grow. This is called moulting. Most birds moult a few feathers at a time so that they can still fly.

Most water-birds and seabirds have waterproof feathers. They take a great deal of care of them. They preen their feathers to keep them in shape, and use their beaks to coat them with oil which comes from a special gland. This oil keeps the feathers waterproof.

Birds have different shaped wings depending on how they live. For example, each winter, Canada geese fly long distances to warm climates. They have long, wide wings to keep them in the air.

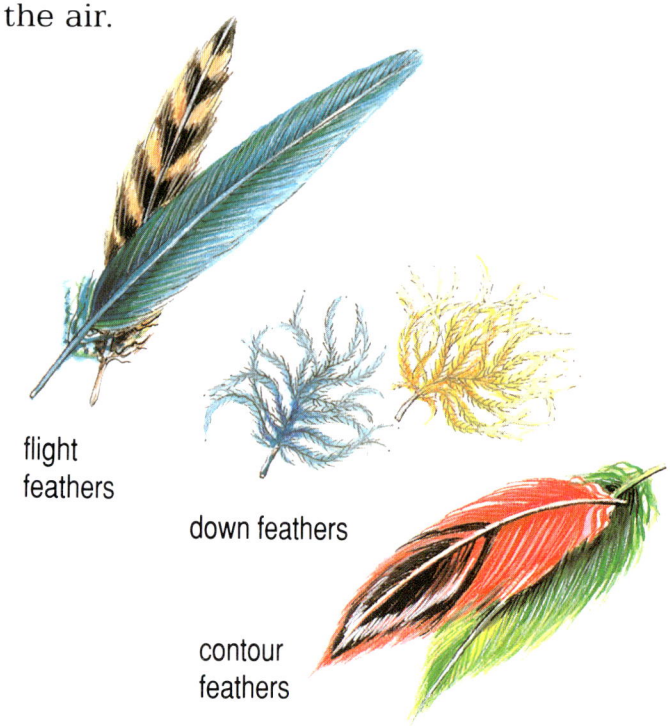

This close-up photograph of a feather shows the interlocking barbs and the even smaller hooks, called barbules.

flight feathers

down feathers

contour feathers

? Did you know?

The Arctic tern flies from the Arctic to the Antarctic and back every year, spending eight months of the year in flight. The return journey is over 40,000 kilometres. This is the longest single journey made by any animal.

The peregrine falcon is the fastest bird. When it dives down on small birds in mid-air, it can reach a speed of 270 kilometres per hour.

An Arctic tern.

? Did you know?

The tiny ruby-throated hummingbird has only about 950 feathers on its body. The swan, though, has over 25,000. This is more than any other bird. About 20,000 of these feathers grow on the swan's neck and head.

A mute swan.

How do birds stay in the air?

Birds can fly faster and further than any other flying creatures. Some fly faster than express trains. Others can fly half-way round the world and back every year. Insects and bats can fly too, but not as well as birds.

Birds are such good fliers because of the shape of their wings. They are curved on top and flat underneath. This is called an aerofoil shape. Aircraft also have this design for their wings.

As the bird flies, air flows over the top of the wing. It flows quite fast so that it does not press down hard on the wing, pulling the bird down. The air underneath the wing presses much harder. It pushes the wing up so that the bird stays in the air.

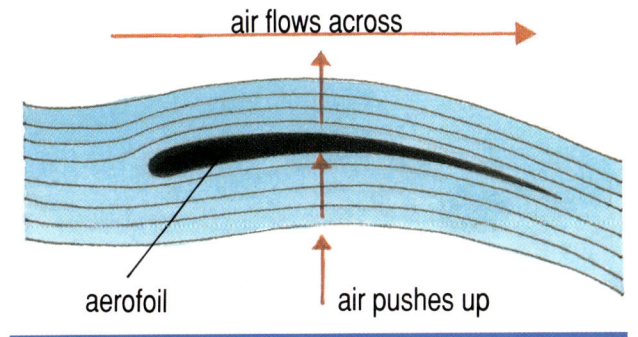

air flows across

aerofoil   air pushes up

! See for yourself

When air presses down softly on things, it makes an area of low pressure. When it presses down hard, it makes an area of high pressure.

To see for yourself how a wing works, you will need a thin strip of tissue paper. Hold the paper to your lips and blow over the top of it. Blow fast and the paper will rise up. This is because there is more air pushing it up than flowing over it.

Why do camels have humps?

Camels can eat the thorniest, driest desert plants which other animals avoid. But they can also survive for long periods without any food at all. This is when the camels' humps become very important to them. The humps contain a store of fat, full of energy, which the camel can use instead of food. A camel's hump can weigh up to 14 kilograms. When all the fat is used up, the hump becomes floppy and skinny. Camels can also change some of the fat supply into liquid.

In many desert areas, camels are used to carry goods and people over the sand. A long line of camels and their riders is known as a caravan.

❓ Did you know?

One-humped camels are called dromedaries, or Arabian camels. Two-humped camels are called Bactrian camels.

How long can camels survive without water?

Camels can go for days and even weeks on end without drinking anything at all. In the open desert, a person would die after just one day without water. But when camels do drink, they can take in over 100 litres of water at a time.

Camels are designed to waste as little water as possible. Their droppings are very dry and their urine is **concentrated**. They do not sweat much, so they lose very little water in that way.

Camels also have other ways of helping them to survive in the desert. They can close their nostrils to keep sand out of their noses. They also have long eyelashes to keep sand out of their eyes. Their webbed, splayed feet act like sand-shoes so that they do not sink into sand. Camels also have only a thin covering of fur on their bellies so that extra heat can escape.

All these features make camels extremely useful desert animals. Desert people use them for transport, and for their milk, meat, leather and wool. In the Sahara, people give camels as wedding presents and have camels taken from them as punishments.

These camels are being given water to drink from a well dug in a dry river bed.

This camel is closing its nostrils to keep out the dust.

❓ Did you know?

About 5,000 years ago there would have been no need for camels in the Sahara. The climate was very different then. Cave paintings in Algeria at this time show a green, jungly landscape with giraffes, lions and hippos.

Why do giraffes have such long necks?

Believe it or not, giraffes have only the same number of bones in their necks as you do. But each of the seven bones is as long as this page. This means that giraffes have necks up to 2 metres long.

Giraffes live in the African scrublands. Their favourite food is leaves from acacia trees. With their long necks, giraffes can reach the very highest leaves. These are well out of reach of other animals, so giraffes do not have to fight for food.

Giraffes also have very long tongues, about as long as your arm from your elbow to your fingertips. They use their tongues to pull the branches down so that they can pick off the leaves with their rubbery lips. Some of their teeth have special grooves to strip the leaves off.

Acacia trees have prickly thorns on their branches. But these do not bother the giraffes. They have bristly hairs on their lips to keep the thorns away from their skin.

Giraffes can gallop at over 48 kilometres per hour on their long legs. But they do have problems bending down to drink. They have to stand with their front legs wide apart to reach the water.

? Did you know?

Giraffes are the tallest animals on Earth. Adult male Maasai giraffes reach over 5 metres in height. The tallest giraffe on record was George, at Chester Zoo in Britain. He was over 6 metres tall.

Why do elephants have such long trunks?

An elephant's trunk is formed from its upper lip and its nose. An adult African elephant's trunk may measure 2.5 metres from the base to the tip. Elephants use their trunks for many different jobs. They use them like drinking-straws to suck up water. An elephant needs to drink over 100 litres of water a day. They use them also as hosepipes to squirt water over their bodies to cool down and clean themselves. A trunk makes a useful snorkel when an elephant is crossing a river.

An elephant also uses its trunk as an extra hand for picking up food and for scratching and touching things. Without its trunk, an elephant would not be able to eat food from the ground. Its neck is too short.

The tip of the trunk is very sensitive. It also has nostrils for smelling. An elephant's trunk is strong enough to pull a tree out by its roots but delicate enough to pick up a peanut.

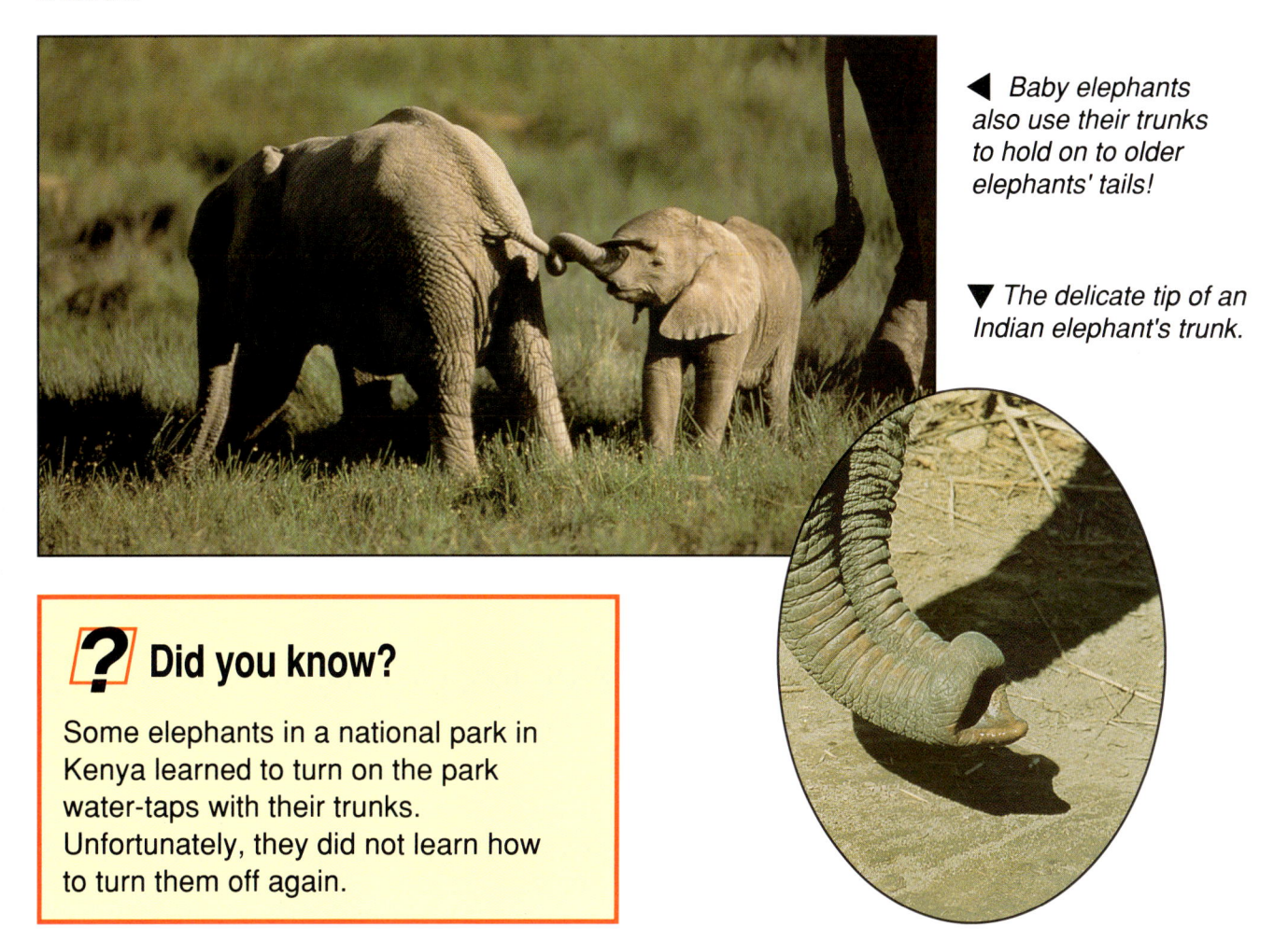

◀ Baby elephants also use their trunks to hold on to older elephants' tails!

▼ The delicate tip of an Indian elephant's trunk.

❓ Did you know?

Some elephants in a national park in Kenya learned to turn on the park water-taps with their trunks. Unfortunately, they did not learn how to turn them off again.

See for Yourself!
Animal Science Quiz

1. What is the name given to animals with no bones in their bodies?
2. Why do moths fly towards light?
3. Which birds have the best eyesight?
4. How many times a second does a bee have to flap its wings to be able to stay in the air?
   a) 200   b) 225   c) 250   d) 275   e) 300
5. How do butterflies taste their food?
6. How do honeypot ants store nectar for when food is hard to find?
7. How much does the caterpillar of the polythemus moth eat in its first two months of life?
8. How do spiders spin their webs?
9. Which fish can change its colour to match the surrounding sea-bed?
10. What does a fish use its 'swim-bladder' for?
11. Which fish can live out of water?
12. How do frogs take in oxygen?
13. What is the name of the longest snake on Earth?
14. What is a snake's skeleton made up of?
15. What material are feathers made of?
16. At what speed can the fastest bird travel?
17. What is stored in a camel's hump?
18. How many kilograms can a camel's hump weigh?
    a) 3   b) 12   c) 14   d) 17   e) 22
19. How fast can a giraffe gallop?
20. How many litres of water does an elephant need to drink in a day?
    a) 100   b) 200   c) 300   d) 400

Answers
Look back to find the answers on these pages.

Question	Page	Question	Page	Question	Page	Question	Page
1	39	6	43	11	51	16	59
2	41	7	44	12	54	17	60
3	41	8	46	13	57	18	60
4	42	9	48	14	57	19	62
5	43	10	49	15	58	20	63

SCIENCE
QUESTIONS & ANSWERS

Plant Science

Anita Ganeri

Acknowledgements

Page 70 - Schaffer, Ecoscene; page 72 - Hans Reinhard, Bruce Coleman Limited; page 73 - (top) Tweedie, Ecoscene, (bottom) Anthony King; page 74 - Sally Morgan, Ecoscene; page 75 - (left) Kloske, Ecoscene, (right) Nicholls, Ecoscene; page 76 - Robert Tyrrell, Oxford Scientific Films; page 77 - (top) Heather Angel, (bottom) Harry Fox, Oxford Scientific Films; page 78 - Jane Burton, Bruce Coleman Limited; page 80 - (top) Sally Morgan, Ecoscene, (bottom) WWF/Timm Rautert, Bruce Coleman Limited; page 81 - (left) Brian Rogers, Heather Angel, (right) Heather Angel; page 82 - (left) Jane Burton, (right) Marie Read, Bruce Coleman Limited; page 83 - (left) MWF Tweedie, NHPA, (right) Sally Morgan, Ecoscene; page 84 - Paul Ormerod, Heather Angel; page 85 - (inset) Peter Stevenson, Planet Earth Pictures, (top) John Anthony, Bruce Coleman Limited, (bottom) Ian Harwood, Ecoscene; page 86 - (left) L Campbell, NHPA, (right) Patrick Clement, Bruce Coleman Limited; page 87 - (left) Tom Leach, Oxford Scientific Films, (top right) Andrew Mounter, Planet Earth Pictures, (bottom right) Andrew Mounter, Planet Earth Pictures; page 88 - (main picture) P J Herring, Heather Angel, (inset) Oxford Scientific Films; page 89 - (top) Heather Angel, (bottom) Doug Allan, Oxford Scientific Films; page 90 -(left) Dave Jacobs, Robert Harding Picture Library, (top right) Ecoscene, (bottom right) Sally Morgan, Ecoscene; page 91 - (top left) M Newman, Frank Lane Picture Agency, (bottom left) Sally Morgan, Ecoscene, (right) Sally Morgan, Ecoscene; page 92 - (main picture) Gryniewicz, Ecoscene, (inset) Heather Angel; page 93 - (left) Breck P Kent, Oxford Scientific Films, (right) Patrick Clements, Bruce Coleman Limited.

Contents

What types of plant are there?	**68**
• Flowering plants	68
• Non-flowering plants	68
• How are plants different from animals?	69
Why are plants green?	**70**
• How do plants make their food?	70
• Why do plants have leaves?	71
How do plants help you to breathe?	**72**
• How do plants breathe?	73
Why do plants have roots?	**74**
Which plants have roots that grow in the air?	**75**
Why do plants have flowers?	**76**
• Why do flowers smell?	76
• What do petals do?	77
• Which flowers look like insects?	77
How do plants make seeds?	**78**
• How do seeds grow into new plants?	78
• Which plants grow the fastest?	80
• Which plants grow the slowest?	81
• Which is the biggest plant?	81
Which plants eat meat?	**82**
• Which plants smell like meat?	83
• Which plants live off other plants?	83
Why do trees have bark?	**84**
• Why does bark make different patterns?	84
• Where does cork come from?	85
How do plants protect themselves?	**86**
• How do plants survive the cold?	87
• Which plant has collapsing leaves?	87
• Which plants glow in the dark?	88
• Which plants look like pebbles?	89
How can desert plants live without water?	**90**
• Why do cacti have spines?	91
• Why do some deserts suddenly burst into flower?	91
What is seaweed?	**92**
• Which plants can forecast the weather?	93
• Which plants can test pollution?	93
Plant Science Quiz	**94**

What types of plant are there?

Scientists who study plants are called botanists. They think that there are over 375,000 different species, or types, of plant in the world. Plants come in all sizes. There are tiny algae made of just one **cell**, which live mainly in water and look like little green blobs, and there are towering trees, taller than houses. Plants range in shape from fern **fronds** and seaweed strands, to orchids that look like bees. These plants develop and grow all over the world, and in very different **environments**, from the coldest, windiest mountain slopes to the steamiest jungles.

To make plants easier to study, botanists have divided them into different groups. These are based on what a plant looks like, whether or not it has flowers, and how the plant grows. You can see how these groups work below.

Flowering plants

This is by far the biggest group of plants. It has about 250,000 species. The plants in this group produce flowers. They include poppies, daisies, grasses, shrubs, and trees such as horse chestnut and cherry trees.

Cherry blossom (prunus pandora).

Non-flowering plants

These are plants which do not produce proper flowers. There are several different groups of them.

Algae are very simple plants, with no proper leaves, roots or flowers. They grow in water or damp places. Some algae are smaller than full stops. You can only see them under a microscope. Seaweeds are the biggest types of algae (see pages 40 and 41).

Mosses and liverworts are simple plants which like to live in damp places. They have no proper roots or flowers. They do not grow from seeds as some plants do, but from **spores**.

Ferns and horsetails also grow from spores, not from seeds. Ferns are tough plants which can grow quite tall because they have strong stems.

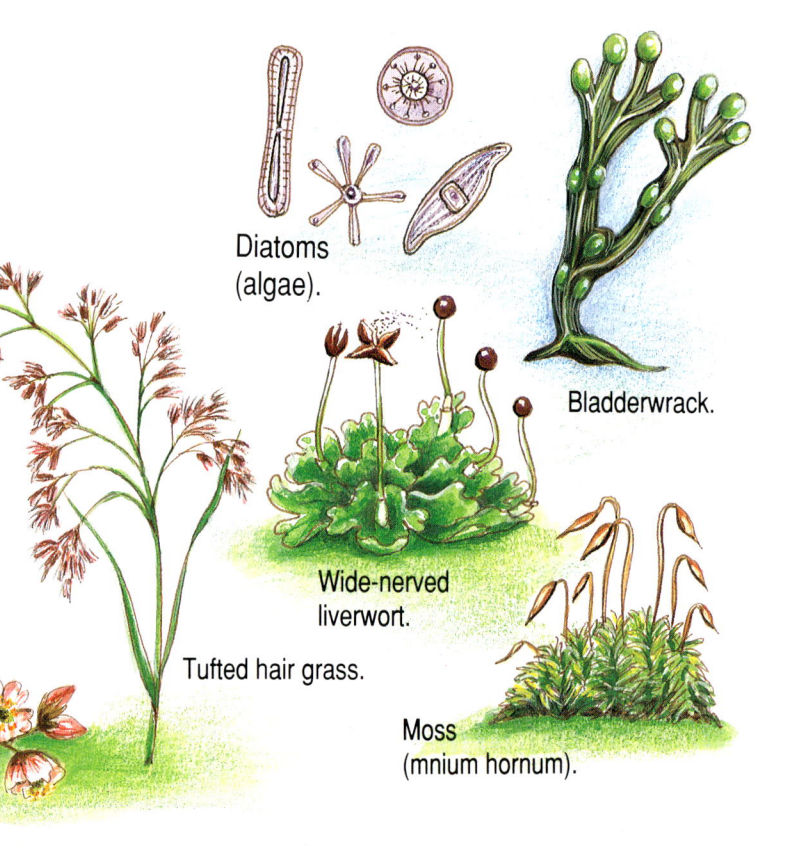

Diatoms (algae).

Bladderwrack.

Wide-nerved liverwort.

Tufted hair grass.

Moss (mnium hornum).

> **? Did you know?**
>
> There is no difference between plants and trees. A tree is simply a type of plant with a thick, woody stem which we call a trunk. Trees are taller than most other plants. There are three groups of trees – broad-leaved trees, conifers and palms (see pages 12 and 13).

Fungi include toadstools, mushrooms and moulds. They are so strange that some botanists do not think that they are plants at all (see pages 42 and 43).

Lichens are mixtures of algae and fungi. In lichens, the algae and the fungi cannot survive without each other's help. There are many different kinds of lichen. Look out for them growing in crusts on walls or rocks. Leafier lichens sometimes grow on the bark of trees, and on walls.

Conifers are trees, such as pine, fir and redwood trees. They have cones instead of flowers and fruit.

How are plants different from animals?

There are many differences between plants and animals. But the most important ones are to do with how they get their food. Animals have to move around and search for their food. This is what you are doing when you go to the supermarket. But plants stay in one place all the time, and most of them can make their own food (see pages 10 and 11). There are some sea animals, such as sponges and corals, which do not move either, but they have to get their food from the water around them as they cannot make it for themselves.

Some animals disguise themselves as plants to avoid being seen and eaten by their enemies. Similarly, it is useful for some plants to look like animals.

Velvet shank fungus.

Lichen.

Common horsetail.

Bracken (fern).

Douglas fir.

Monterey pine.

Why are plants green?

Most plants have green leaves. This is because they contain a special green pigment, or colouring, called chlorophyll. Just under the top surface of the leaves is a layer of special cells, known as palisade cells. Inside each there are tiny disc-shaped containers, called chloroplasts. These are full of chlorophyll.

How do plants make their food?

Plants need plenty of sunlight, water and air to make their own food. During the day, the chlorophyll in the plants' leaves absorbs, or takes in, light from the sun. The plant uses this to turn carbon dioxide from the air, and water from the ground, into a sugary food. Plants give off oxygen as a waste product, although some is used for breathing (see page 15). This process is called photosynthesis. The food can be stored inside the plants and used when it is needed.

Animals and people take advantage of plants' ability to make their own food. They eat many plant species and plant food stores as well (see pages 26 and 45).

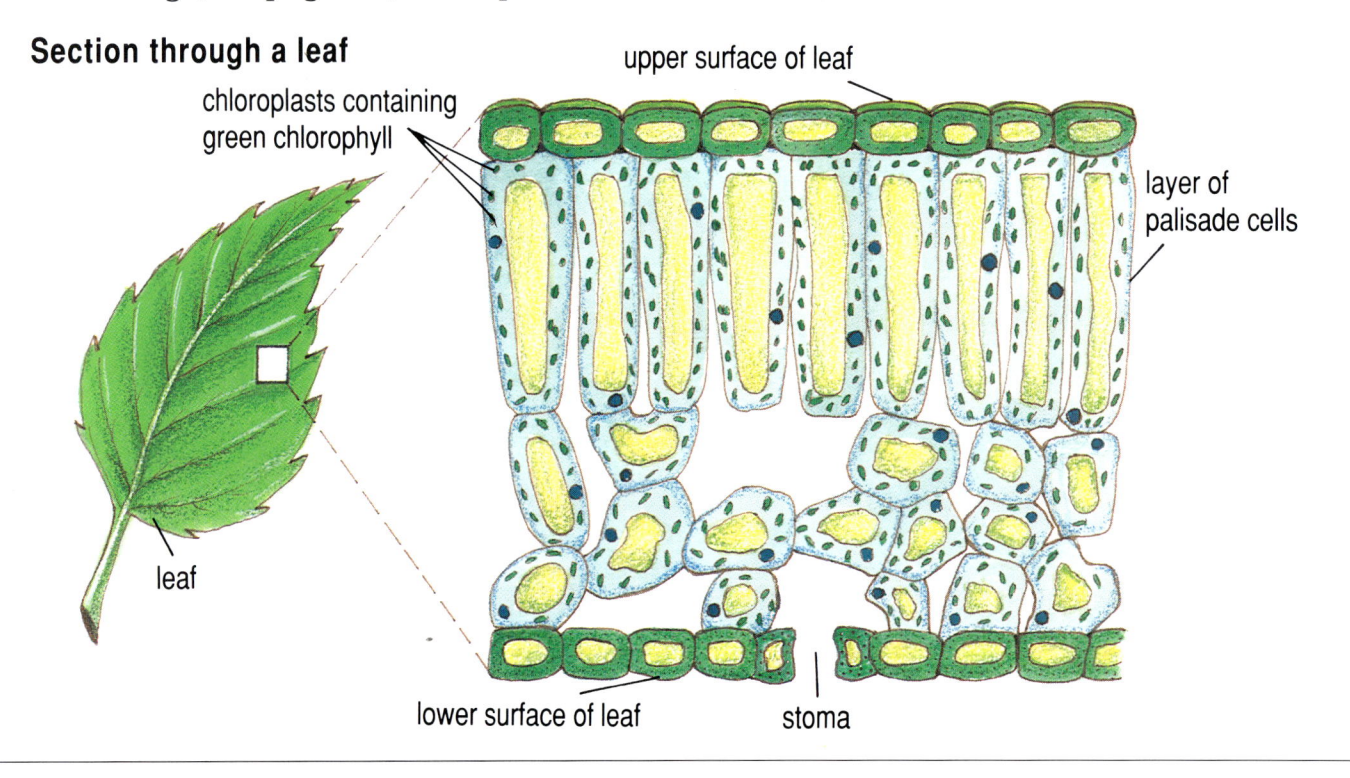

These leaves are opened out to catch as much sunlight as possible.

Section through a leaf

- chloroplasts containing green chlorophyll
- upper surface of leaf
- layer of palisade cells
- leaf
- lower surface of leaf
- stoma

Why do plants have leaves?

Leaves come in a huge variety of sizes and shapes, from pine-needles to palm fronds and from waterlily pads to oak leaves. But they all have the same main purpose – to make food. Leaves are arranged on the plant's stem in a special way, so that each leaf traps as much sunlight as possible. Plants also breathe through their leaves (see page 15) and lose water through them (see page 19).

Banana palm.
Oak.
Scots pine.
Waterlily.

See for yourself

Plants will always try to grow towards the light, because without light a plant cannot photosynthesize. You can prove this with houseplants. Stand a houseplant on a sunny window-ledge and watch it over the next week or so. See how the plant leans towards the sun to get as much light as possible.

Did you know?

The raffia palm has leaves almost 20 metres long – over 30 times longer than one of your arms. An oak tree may have over 250,000 leaves.

See for yourself

If there is a pond near your home, collect some pond-water in a clean jam jar. The water should look quite clear at first. Stand the jar in a sunny place and watch it for a week or two. It should turn green quite quickly as the tiny, **microscopic** algae in the water photosynthesize and multiply.

1. Quite clear pond-water. 2. The algae have turned the water green.

How do plants help you to breathe?

When plants photosynthesize, they give off oxygen as waste. This is the gas which all plants and animals, including people, need to breathe to stay alive. Without plants, there would not be enough oxygen in the air for us to be able to survive.

When plants first appeared on Earth millions of years ago, there were no animals. The air was thick with poisonous gases such as methane and ammonia, but no oxygen. Gradually the plants put enough oxygen into the air for animals to develop and survive.

Water plants are also important. They put oxygen into the water. The oxygen dissolves in the water and is then breathed by fish and other water creatures.

When people and animals breathe, carbon dioxide is produced as waste. This is used by plants to help make their food.

> **? Did you know?**
>
> The first oxygen-making plants on Earth were algae, which lived in the prehistoric seas. Sea algae still produce over 70 per cent of all the oxygen in the air.

Here you can see a pond surrounded by plants. It also has algae and waterlilies growing on its surface.

How do plants breathe?

Plants need to breathe just like animals and people. During the day, as well as giving out oxygen, plants also use oxygen and give out carbon dioxide just as you do when you breathe (see page 10). They are able to make their own food, but like you, they have to break it down into energy by breathing, or respiration. This energy is used for growing and repairing worn-out tissue. At night, when plants cannot photosynthesize, they have to take in oxygen from the air outside. In this way, they can carry on breathing.

Plants do not have lungs like you, or gills like fish. The gases from the air pass through tiny holes underneath their leaves. These holes are called stomata. You can read about what else they do on page 19. Plants that live underwater need to 'breathe' the oxygen which is dissolved in the water.

At dawn and dusk, a plant's photosynthesis and respiration happen at the same speed. They balance each other out, so the plant is making and breaking down its food at the same rate. This means that the plant does not have to take in extra ingredients from the air around it. At most other times, one process happens faster than the other.

Seaweeds breathe through tiny holes on their fronds.

! See for yourself

The oxygen made by plants usually vanishes into the air. You cannot normally see it. But try putting some pondweed or waterweed into a clear, clean bowl of water and standing it in the sun for a while. You should soon see tiny bubbles of oxygen coming from the weed.

The tiny bubbles on this pondweed (Elodea crispa) will eventually rise to the surface of the water.

Why do plants have roots?

A plant needs a firm base in the ground, just like a building, so that it is not blown over by the wind. Its roots are like anchors, holding it down in the soil. But they have another very important job to do. Roots take in water and minerals from the ground, which the plant needs to make its food.

The roots of some plants grow very deep into the soil. But most roots branch out over a wider, more shallow area. This gives them a firmer base and a larger patch of ground for collecting water and minerals.

? Did you know?

The deepest plant roots known belong to a wild fig-tree growing at Echo Caves in South Africa. Its roots measure 120 metres, about as long as 1,000 medium-sized carrots.

Parts of a root system

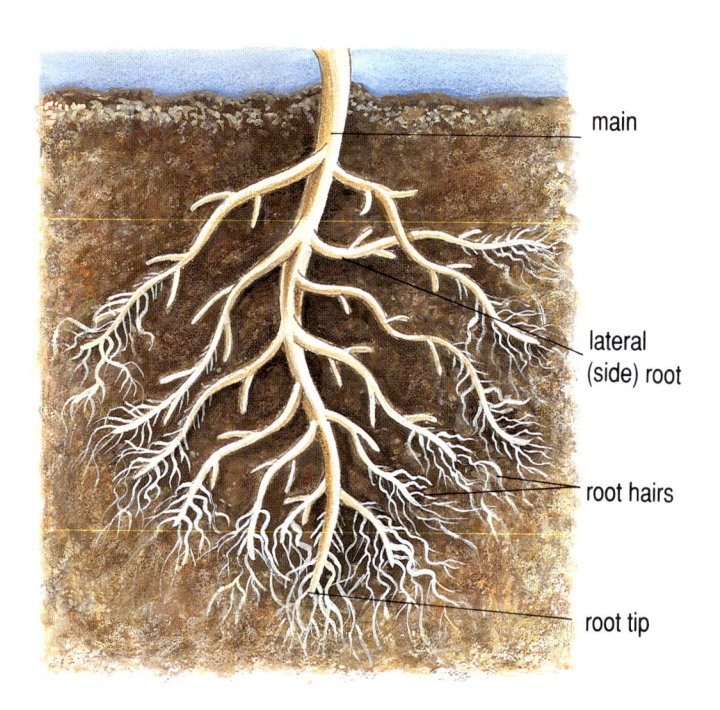

- main
- lateral (side) root
- root hairs
- root tip

The force of gravity makes roots grow deep down into the soil.

Storm-blown beech tree showing base and roots.

Which plants have roots that grow in the air?

Some plants have very odd roots indeed. In the tropical rainforests, there are orchids that live high up on the branches of tall trees. They have roots that dangle in the air. These are called aerial roots. It is very humid and sticky in the rainforest. The air contains a lot of **water vapour**. The orchids' aerial roots take in the water which they need, from the air.

Other rainforest trees have extra roots, called buttress roots, growing out of their trunks. The roots take in extra water and **nutrients** from the rain which runs down the trunks.

Mangrove trees live in the estuaries of some tropical rivers, where the river flows into the sea. As well as normal roots, they use roots growing from their trunks to hold them firmly in the soft mud. These roots are called stilt roots.

These mangrove trees are firmly anchored by their stilt roots.

Some rainforest trees have huge buttress roots growing out of their trunks.

! See for yourself

You can see how plants develop roots by growing your own cuttings. Fill some clean jam jars with about 5 centimetres of lukewarm water. Cut off some lengths of stem from plants such as geraniums or bizzy-lizzies. They should be about 10 centimetres long. Put the cuttings in the water and leave them for a week or so. They should soon grow some roots. Then you can plant them in pots filled with **potting compost**. Water the plants well and leave them to grow.

Why do plants have flowers?

Each plant needs to reproduce, or create new plants, so that its species survives. Many plants have flowers so that seeds can be made inside them. These seeds will eventually grow into new plants.

Flowers contain the plants' male and female parts. They are both needed to make seeds. Some flowers have both male and female parts in the same flower. Others have either one or the other.

The male parts make a fine, powdery dust called pollen. This is what makes you sneeze if you get hay fever. To make a seed, pollen has to travel from the male parts to join with the female parts. This is called pollination. It does not usually happen in the same flower, even if this flower contains both male and female parts. Pollen has to be taken from the male part of one flower to the female part of another. But plants cannot move about, so how does the pollen get there?

Plants have several helpers to transport their pollen. They use the wind, which blows pollen from one flower to another. They also use the services of animals such as bees, butterflies, bats and birds. But first they have to tempt the animals to visit them.

The parts of a flower

This is a section through a poppy flower.

In the tropics, hummingbirds use their long beaks to reach the nectar inside flowers.

Why do flowers smell?

A flower's shape, colour and smell are designed to attract animals to help pollinate it. It also has a sweet syrup deep inside, called nectar, which animals like to eat. The animals visit the flower and get covered in pollen dust as they feed. When they fly off to another flower, some of the pollen

A bumblebee gets covered in pollen as it searches for nectar on this dahlia flower.

brushes off. If it brushes onto the female parts, a seed may grow.

Catkins and other flowers that use the wind to pollinate them are dull and drab. They do not need to tempt animals to visit them. But flowers such as honeysuckle, cherry blossom, pansies and sunflowers use sweet smells and bright petals to attract insects for pollination.

What do petals do?

Plants use brightly-coloured petals to attract insects, as we have seen. Some petals have dark markings on them, called honeyguides. These are thought to guide insects to the flower's store of nectar deep inside the flower. Other petals, such as those on foxglove flowers, are shaped to make sure that insects pollinate them. They have a good landing platform on the outside. Their tight bell shape makes insects, such as bumblebees, force their way inside. The bees cannot avoid getting coated with pollen as they tunnel their way through to the nectar. Petals also help to protect the flower's male and female parts.

Which flowers look like insects?

Some tropical orchids use disguises to attract flies, wasps and bees for pollination. Their flowers look like female insects. They even smell like them, and their petals look like the insects' furry bodies. The disguises are so life-like that male insects visit the flowers and try to mate with them. In the process they get coated with pollen dust, which they carry to the next flower that they visit. The bee orchid, which you can see on the title page, is a good example of a flower that looks like an insect.

The dark honeyguides show up clearly on the pansies' yellow petals.

? Did you know?

The world's biggest flower is the Rafflesia. It grows in the jungles of south-east Asia. Its flower can measure a metre across, which is wider than a car tyre. The smallest flowering plant is a type of duckweed called Wolffia. Over 30 of these plants would fit across the head of a drawing pin.

How do plants make seeds?

When a flower has been pollinated, a male pollen grain joins with the female part of the flower to make a seed. This will eventually grow into a new plant. But first it has to be carried away from its parent plant so that there is not too much competition for space, light, water and nutrients.

A plant needs help to spread its seeds, just as a flower needs help to spread its pollen. Dandelion and sycamore seeds are light enough to be blown away by the wind. They also have special shapes to help them fly.

Prickly burrs contain burdock seeds. They get caught on the coats of dogs and foxes and are carried in this way. Birds enjoy a tasty meal of sweet berries or cherries. Then the seeds inside them pass through the birds and are spread in their droppings.

Other plants, such as laburnum trees, have pods that burst open and shoot the seeds out. If these seeds land in a sunny place with good soil, they will grow into new plants. Laburnum seeds are very poisonous to us, as are many berries.

How do seeds grow into new plants?

Inside a seed there is a food store, and the parts which will grow into a new plant. The young plant lives off this store of food until its leaves are big enough to make their own food. If the seed lands in a good patch of moist soil, its case splits open and the first, small root digs into the soil to anchor it. Then its first shoot appears. Gradually the roots and shoots grow bigger and stronger, and the new plant's leaves grow. This process is called germination.

The dandelion's yellow flower becomes a fluffy seedhead. The slightest breeze will blow the seeds away.

❓ Did you know?

The biggest seeds come from the coco-de-mer palm. This rare plant only grows on the Seychelle Islands in the Indian Ocean. One of its huge seeds may weigh 18 kilograms, as much as 160 apples. Orchids make the smallest seeds. It would take over 560 million orchid seeds to weigh as much as just one apple.

Here you can see how an acorn grows into a young oak tree.

❗ See for yourself

Try growing your own plants from seed. Collect some apple or orange pips. Soak them in water overnight. Find some old yoghurt or margarine pots and punch a few small drainage holes in the bottom. Put a layer of small stones in the bottom and fill the pots with compost. Then plant a few pips in each tub, cover them with a little more compost, and water them well. Cover each pot with a plastic bag, held in place with an elastic band. Keep the pots in a warm place, away from direct sunlight, until the shoots appear. Then take off the plastic bags, move the tubs to a sunnier place and watch your plants grow. When the plants get bigger you will need to replant them in larger pots.

The small stones in the bottom of the pot allow water to drain through, so the soil does not get waterlogged.

Which plants grow the fastest?

Some plants grow very fast indeed. The Pacific giant kelp, the longest type of seaweed, can grow at a rate of 45 centimetres a day. But it stops growing when its strands reach a length of 45 metres. Some types of bamboo grow twice as fast, at 90 centimetres a day.

Bamboo is the favourite food of giant pandas in China. Today, these pandas are very rare because there is not enough food for them. This is partly because of the strange way in which the bamboo grows. It only flowers and produces seeds once every 100 years. Then it dies. In the past, this did not cause any problems. The pandas simply moved to another patch of the forest. But today people have cut down so much of the forest to clear the land, that the pandas have nowhere to go. Many of them starve.

? Did you know?

Albizzia trees like the one below are members of the pea family. They all grow very fast. The fastest growing variety is Albizzia falcata. One of these grew 10.74 metres in just 13 months. If you grew at this rate you would be as tall as a 30-storey building by the time you were ten years old!

Giant pandas feed in the bamboo forests of China.

Which plants grow the slowest?

The slowest-growing tree, the Dioon edule, only grows 0.7 millimetres a year. One of these trees measured just under 10 centimetres, even though it was 150 years old.

The Puya raimondii plant is the slowest plant of all to produce flowers. It grows high up in the mountains in South America. It does not flower until it is between 80 and 150 years old. Then it grows a flower spike, taller than three people. This is covered in as many as 8,000 small white flowers. The plant dies after it has flowered. The Puya raimondii is the biggest type of herb, the strong-smelling group of plants which includes parsley, basil and thyme. They are often used in cooking or for making medicines.

This gigantic flower spike of the Puya raimondii grows in Peru.

Which is the biggest plant?

'General Sherman' is the world's biggest plant and the largest living thing on Earth.

A giant sequoia tree, nicknamed 'General Sherman' after a great American soldier, is the biggest plant in the world. In fact it is the biggest thing that has ever lived on Earth, even larger than the huge blue whale. The tree stands in Sequoia National Park in California, USA. It is over 83 metres tall, taller than 15 giraffes, and measures over 25 metres around its trunk. How much do you measure around your waist? How does this measurement compare with the tree trunk? 'General Sherman' weighs an amazing 2,500 tonnes, more than 400 elephants. It is thought to have enough wood to make 5 billion matchsticks!

Which plants eat meat?

Some plants can make their own food by photosynthesis – but they also eat meat. This is because they often live in boggy places where the soil is not very rich in the minerals which they need. The meat provides them with extra nourishment. These meat-eating plants are called carnivorous plants. They include Venus fly-traps, pitcher plants and bladderworts.

The Venus fly-trap has leaves which are hinged together. They lie wide open, waiting for insects to come and land on their colourful surfaces. Then they snap shut, trapping the insect inside. The plant dissolves the insect's body with special **digestive juices,** and then **absorbs** the liquid. Insects such as dragonflies are the Venus fly-trap's usual victims, but animals as large as frogs have been found inside them. It takes the plant about two weeks to digest a dragonfly.

Pitcher plants have amazing pitcher, or jug-shaped, leaves complete with lids to keep the rain out. Insects are tempted to visit this plant by the stores of sweet nectar under the lids, and around the rim of the pitcher. But the walls of the pitcher are very slippery.

A bluebottle is about to be trapped inside the Venus fly-trap's leaves.

Insects are lying in the bottom of this pitcher plant, about to be digested.

As soon as an insect lands, it loses its footing and slides down into a pool of liquid at the bottom of the pitcher. It cannot get out, and drowns.

Bladderworts live in ponds and lakes. They have tiny pockets, or bladders, on their underwater leaves and stems. Each bladder has a trap-door which it keeps closed until a water-flea or other tiny animal brushes against it. Then it swings open and the creature is sucked inside and digested.

Which plants smell like meat?

Here you can see a Rafflesia arnoldii flower in Sumatra.

Some plants smell like rotting meat to attract flies for pollination (see pages 20 and 22). They include the Rafflesia, which has the biggest and, perhaps, the smelliest flower in the world. Its terrible stink attracts swarms of flies, who think they are in for a tasty meal of meat. Instead, they fly away covered in pollen. Stapelia flowers smell almost as bad. They also look like chunks of rotting meat to fool the flies even more.

Which plants live off other plants?

Plants such as mistletoe and dodders steal food and water from other living plants. These 'thieves' are called parasites. They climb and twist up another plant's roots or stems. As they climb, they send out hundreds of tiny suckers which look a bit like roots. These force their way into the plant's own food and water tubes, and suck out the goodness and moisture.

Mistletoe grows on oak and apple trees. It is only partly a parasite as it can also make its own food. In some countries, people think that mistletoe is magical. It is cut and used for lucky charms.

Mistletoe sometimes grows around tree-trunks.

Why do trees have bark?

The dead, outer covering of a tree-trunk is called bark. It is very tough. The main job of bark is to protect the tree-trunk from attack by animals such as squirrels, deer, birds and insects. Bark also protects the tree from diseases spread by fungi (see pages 42 and 43), and the weather. It stops the tree from drying out, and **insulates** it from very hot or very cold weather.

The bark of this tree has been broken by a green woodpecker to make his nest hole.

Without its bark 'skin', the tree would not be able to grow. The delicate tubes carrying food and water around the tree lie just under the bark. If they are damaged, the tree may die. Tiny holes in the bark, called lenticels, allow the tree to breathe.

Why does bark make different patterns?

Because it is dead, the bark cannot stretch as the tree-trunk grows thicker and fatter. So it cracks, splits and peels, making the different patterns which you can see. Each type of tree has its own special bark pattern. Old oak trees have deep cracks and grooves in their bark. Birch trees have bark which peels off in strips. The strips are paper-thin, but so tough and waterproof that North American Indians once used them to cover their canoes. Pine trees and other conifers tend to have flaky bark. Many young trees have smooth bark that gets more patterned as the trees get older.

Oak.   Silver birch.

Scots pine.

The patterns on different types of bark can be very smooth or quite rough and cracked.

Where does cork come from?

Cork is the bark of the cork-oak tree. The bark is so thick that it can be stripped off without hurting the tree. A new layer of bark soon grows again. Cork can absorb moisture, is slightly elastic and can protect things from heat. This is why we use it to make bottle corks, floor tiles and table mats.

? Did you know?

The bark on a beech tree is only about 1 centimetre thick. But the bark on a redwood tree may be 30 times as thick.

? Did you know?

A tree in Hawaii has bark that is specially designed to protect the tree from the red-hot ashes and cinders which erupt from nearby volcanoes.

Rolls of cork-oak bark have been stripped off a cork-oak tree like the one above.

! See for yourself

You should never peel or strip the bark off a tree. But you can make bark rubbings to keep a record of the different types of bark which you see. Tape a sheet of strong, white paper to a tree trunk. Then rub gently over it with a soft, thick wax crayon until the bark pattern shows through. Write down the name of the tree on each rubbing.

This is how to make a bark rubbing.

How do plants protect themselves?

Plants cannot run away from danger, so they need other ways of protecting themselves from harm. They need defences from animals that attack them for food, and they need protection from the weather. Plants have many clever methods of self-defence, including the use of weapons such as thorns, prickles and poisons.

Holly leaves have double protection. They have shiny, waxy coats to stop them from drying out in the cold wind. They also have prickly leaves to stop animals from eating them. Next time you see a holly bush, look closely at the difference between the upper leaves and those near the bottom. The leaves near the bottom are much more prickly because they are most at risk from animals.

Some plants contain deadly poisons that can put off even the hungriest animals. Many fungi are highly poisonous (see pages 42 and 43). If someone eats a death-cap toadstool it can kill them. Foxglove leaves also contain poisons which can damage the heart. However, they can be used in very tiny amounts to help cure heart diseases.

Above: A holly bush has shiny green leaves and bright red berries.
Right: The Clouded clitocybe fungus growing among the grass can cause stomach pains.

How do plants survive the cold?

Plants growing in cold places such as the slopes of high mountains, or at the Arctic and Antarctic, face two main problems. They need ways of coping with the freezing cold and the biting winds.

The edelweiss plant grows on the slopes of the Alps in Europe. Its flowers and leaves are hairy. This helps it to trap warmth from the sun, and stops it from drying out in the wind. Another Alpine plant, the Alpine snowbell, has an even more unusual way of surviving. It makes and gives out enough heat to melt a tiny area of snow around it, so that it can grow in the frozen ground.

Many mountain plants grow close to the ground, in thick clumps, to keep warm and out of the wind. In some places, trees such as dwarf willows and pines would barely reach your knees.

Beautiful gentians grow in the French Alps.

Which plant has collapsing leaves?

The mimosa plant has an unusual way of stopping insects from eating its leaves. They collapse, all of a sudden, just seconds after an insect lands on them. This helps to shake an insect off, but it also puts off larger animals such as deer. These animals take one look at the wilted, collapsed leaves and set off in search of something more appetising. The mimosa's leaves also collapse when the weather is cold. At night they fold up into a 'sleeping' position. No one is sure why this happens, but it has earned the mimosa the nickname 'sensitive plant'.

A mimosa has open leaves when it is left undisturbed.

The mimosa's leaves collapse when they are touched.

Which plants glow in the dark?

Dinoflagellates are tiny sea plants with just one cell. They are so small that usually they can only be seen under a microscope. But they often form large groups in warm places such as the Indian Ocean. The amazing thing about these plants is that they glow in the dark. Each plant makes a tiny amount of light, and the whole group makes the surface of the water shimmer and sparkle. The light from some very large groups is so good that you could read a book by it.

Some types of jungle fungi also make their own light. They glow green, white or yellow. No one knows for certain why they do this. It may be a means of protection from hungry beetles and other insects. If these insects were lit up, they would be seen too easily by their own enemies.

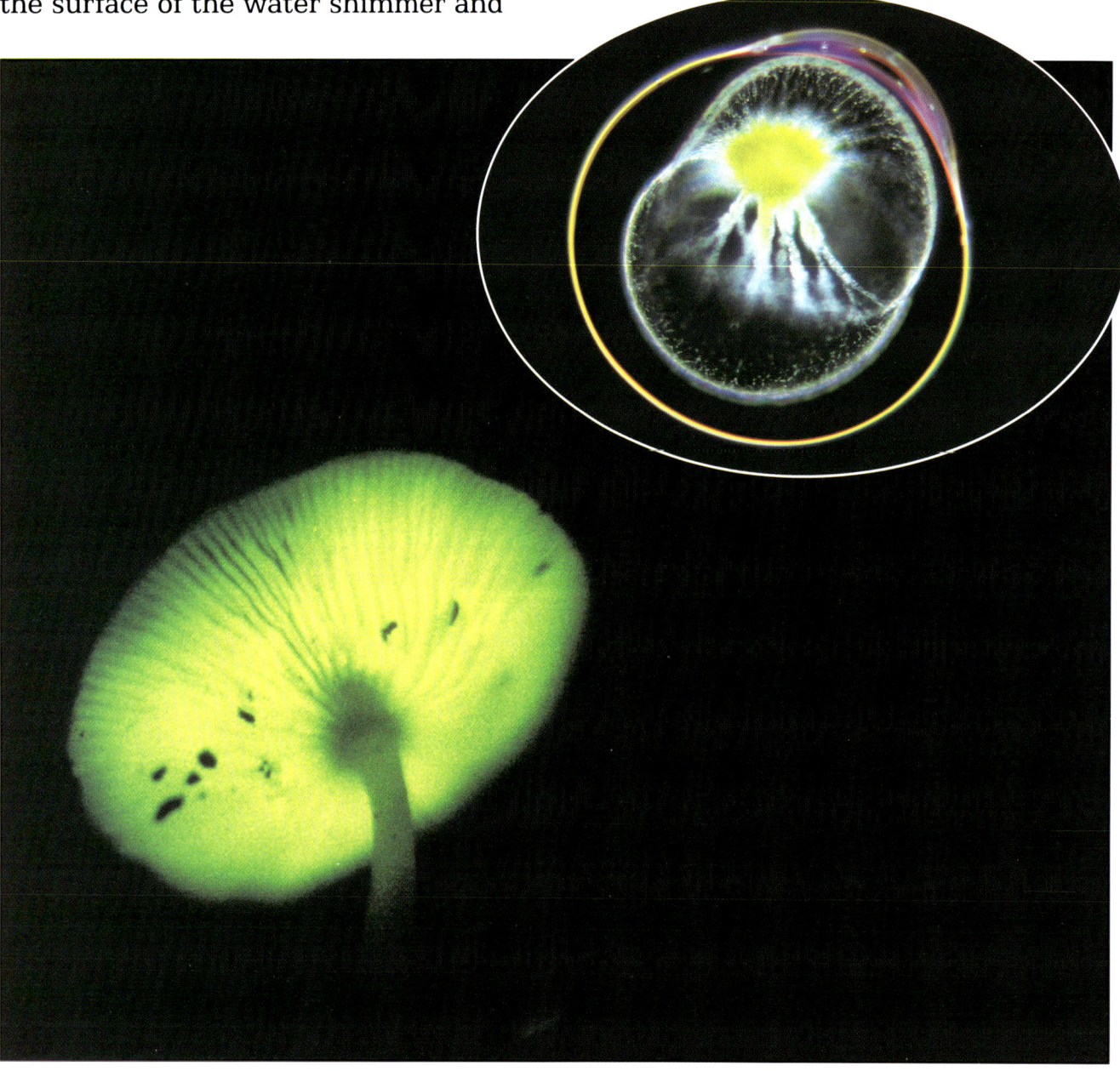

Above: *A fungus glowing on the jungle floor.*
Inset: *You can see the glow given out by this magnified dinoflagellate.*

? Did you know?

Passion-flower vines have very odd leaves. They have strange growths on them, shaped like butterfly eggs. These stop butterflies from laying their real eggs on the leaves. In this way, the false eggs protect the leaves from hungry caterpillars which would have hatched out.

You can see the false eggs underneath this passion-flower leaf.

butterfly egg growths

Which plants look like pebbles?

Some plants use clever disguises to hide themselves from hungry animals. Stone plants live in the deserts of South Africa. They grow on stony ground. Their swollen leaves look so much like pebbles that animals pass them by. The leaves are even coloured mottled brown, grey and white like the real stones around them. This type of disguise is called camouflage. It is only obvious that these 'stones' are plants when their brightly-coloured flowers appear.

Can you tell which are the plants and which are the pebbles?

? Did you know?

Lichens in Antarctica survive by growing very slowly indeed. Their slow growth saves their energy for coping with the harsh weather conditions. These lichens would take about 100 years to reach the size of your thumbnail.

Lichens growing in Antarctica.

How can desert plants live without water?

All plants need some water to live, even if it is only a small amount. In the desert, however, water is very scarce. Plants have to struggle to find enough moisture to survive. Some have very clever ways of doing this.

Cacti grow mainly in the deserts of North America. They store water in their thick stems and use it during the long desert droughts. On a rare rainy day, a large cactus can take in up to a tonne of water. The stems of these plants sometimes have pleats running down them, which allow the stems to stretch as they fill with water.

Cacti belong to a group of plants called succulents. Many succulents also have fleshy leaves that can store water. Others store water in their roots. Succulents have tough, waxy 'skins' to stop water from escaping. Some cacti are covered in fine, white 'wool' which also cuts down water loss and helps to keep the plant cool.

Other desert plants have similar ways of getting enough water to survive. Baobab trees store water in their trunks. These swell up as they fill, and then shrink as the tree uses up the water supply. Creosote bushes have a huge network of shallow roots that stretches over a large area of ground, collecting any drops of moisture, however small.

These three types of cactus are different shapes but they are all thick and fleshy.
Far left: *Saguaro cactus.*
Above: *Prickly pear cactus.*
Left: *Barrel cactus.*

Why do cacti have spines?

Cactus spines are actually leaves. In this prickly form, these leaves can protect the plant against hungry or thirsty animals. They also help to cut down water loss. Large leaves lose a lot of water through their stomata (see page 19). So cacti have developed thin, sharp spines instead of leaves. These lose very little water. Some cactus spines may be up to 15 centimetres long.

Top: Cactus spines lose little water.
Above: Large, open leaves lose a lot of water.

[?] Did you know?

The biggest cacti of all are the giant saguaros which grow in the USA and Mexico. They can stand over 17 metres tall and weigh 10 tonnes, as much as three rhinoceroses. An amazing 9 tonnes of the weight is water stored in the huge stems of these cacti.

Why do some deserts suddenly burst into flower?

In the desert it may be months, or even years, between one fall of rain and the next. So plants have to make the most of any downpour. When it rains, some desert plants such as desert peas, poppies, sand verbenas and sunflowers can grow, flower and make seeds very quickly indeed. This is when the desert suddenly bursts into bloom. Afterwards, the flower seeds lie in the ground until the next rainfall, which may be many months away.

After rain, the desert bursts into bloom.

[!] See for yourself

Try to make your own mini desert and grow some cacti in it. Fill a large, shallow clay flowerpot or box with a mixture of sand and potting compost. Plant a few small cacti and cover the surface with a layer of gravel or small stones. Keep your cacti in a warm, sunny place. They only need watering a little in winter.

What is seaweed?

Seaweed belongs to the group of plants called algae. Many algae are tiny plants that are made of only one cell. They are simple plants with no flowers, proper leaves or stems. Algae can live almost anywhere – on tree-trunks, in ponds and in the sea. Seaweeds are the biggest types of algae. Some can grow over 65 metres long. They grow along rocky shores, or float on the surface of the water, held up by air-filled 'bladders' on their strands. They cannot live deeper down because there is not enough light for photosynthesis (see page 10).

Seaweeds living along the shore often have thick suckers, called holdfasts, at their bases. The holdfasts anchor the plants so that they are not washed away by the tides.

In some countries, such as Japan and Ireland, seaweed is harvested like any other crop. It has many uses as food, as fertilizer for crops, and to make shampoo, toothpaste and even ice-cream.

Above: *Oarweed floats in the sea at low tide.*
Inset: *The bladders on seaweed strands are full of air.*

Which plants can forecast the weather?

Seaweeds are supposed to be able to help you to forecast the weather. If you hang a piece of seaweed by the window, it should dry out if hot weather is on the way, and become softer if wetter weather is coming.

Other plant forecasters include pine cones. A cone contains a pine tree's seeds. In warm, dry weather the cone's scales open up to let the seeds fall out. This is because the seeds will survive better in this type of weather. But the cones remain tightly closed if the weather is bad.

A Virginia pine cone opens all its scales in the warm weather.

? Did you know?

Algae can turn snow red. In 1818, the explorer, John Ross, reported seeing large areas of red snow in the Arctic. Very few people believed his story. But he was telling the truth. Patches of crimson-red snow are caused by huge numbers of tiny, one-celled algae called Protococci.

Which plants can test pollution?

You might have seen orange or green patches of lichen growing on walls or rocks. A lichen is a very odd plant, made up of a mixture of two other plants – an alga and a fungus (see pages 7, 8 and 42). The two plants work as partners. The alga makes food for the fungus by photosynthesis. The fungus provides water for the alga and holds the whole plant firmly down.

Lichens are very sensitive to air pollution. Have a look around the area where you live. How many lichens are growing there? What colour are they? Are they leafy or crusty? If the air is very dirty, no lichens will grow. If the air is very clean, you should find some leafy green lichens. You may only be able to see these lichens in the countryside.

Thick crusts of lichens grow on rocks by the sea.

See for Yourself! Plant Science Quiz

1. All trees can be divided into one of three categories. What are the names of the three groups of trees?
2. What is the pigment called that gives the leaves of a plant their green colour?
3. How do plants breathe?
4. Which plants have roots which grow in the air?
5. What is the name of the fine, powdery dust that is produced by the male part of a flower?
6. Why do some flowers have dark markings, called honeyguides, on their petals?
7. What is the name of the world's largest flower?
8. What is inside a seed?
9. Some types of bamboo are among the fastest growing plants in the world. How many centimetres a day can they grow?
   a) 10   b) 20   c) 40   d) 60   e) 90
10. Which plant eats meat?
11. Where does mistletoe grow?
12. Trees breathe through tiny holes in their bark. What are the holes called?
13. Why does the bark of a tree make different patterns?
14. Which plant has leaves that contain poisons which can damage the heart if eaten?
15. How does the mimosa plant stop insects from eating its leaves?
16. What is the name of the tiny sea plant that glows in the dark?
17. Which plant looks like a pebble?
18. How does the baobab tree, a desert plant, store water?
19. What group of plants does seaweed belong to?
20. How can you forecast the weather using a piece of seaweed?

Answers
Look back to find the answers on these pages.

Question	Page	Question	Page	Question	Page	Question	Page
1	69	6	77	11	83	16	88
2	70	7	77	12	84	17	89
3	73	8	78	13	84	18	90
4	75	9	80	14	86	19	92
5	76	10	82	15	87	20	93

SCIENCE
QUESTIONS & ANSWERS

Earth Science

Anita Ganeri

Acknowledgements

Page 98 - (bottom) Soames Summerhays, Biofotos; page 99 - (top) Sally Bensusen, Science Photo Library, (bottom) Mary Evans Picture Library; page 101 - FLPA; page 102 - Jeff Foott Productions, Bruce Coleman Limited; page 103 - (bottom left) Robert Harding Picture Library, (middle right) John Lythgoe, Planet Earth Pictures; page 105 - (top) SIPA-PRESS, (inset) David E Rowley; page 106 -(right) Dorian Weisel, Planet Earth Pictures; page 107 - (bottom left) Sally Morgan, Ecoscene, (bottom right) A,N,T,, NHPA; page 108 - (bottom left) P A Hinchliffe, Bruce Coleman Limited, (bottom right) John Eastcott, Planet Earth Pictures, (inset) Vincent Serventy, Planet Earth Pictures; page 109 - (top) Ken Lucas, Planet Earth Pictures, (bottom left) Anthony King, (bottom right) Anthony King; page 110 - (middle) John Mead, Science Photo Library, (bottom right) Ken Lucas, Planet Earth Pictures, (inset) Hutchison Library; page 111 - (top) James Holmes, Science Photo Library, (bottom) Alex Bartel, Science Photo Library; page 112 - (bottom) Jim Amos, Science Photo Library, (inset) Ken Lucas, Planet Earth Pictures; page 113 - (top) Ken Vaughn: Planet Earth Pictures, (bottom) Sally Morgan, Ecoscene; page 114 - (bottom) Heather Angel, (inset left) David Woodfall, NHPA, (inset right) David Woodfall, NHPA; page 115 - Paul Trummer, The Image Bank; page 116 - (top) C C Lockwood, Earth Scenes, Oxford Scientific Films, (bottom) John Downer, Planet Earth Pictures; page 119 - (top) Oxford Scientific Films, (inset) Peter Parks, Oxford Scientific Films; page 120 -(bottom) Joe Szkodinski, The Image Bank, (inset) Eyal Bartov, Oxford Scientific Films; page 121 - Ian Griffiths, Robert Harding Picture Library; page 123 - (left) Luiz Claudio Marigo, Bruce Coleman Limited, (middle) Terry Whittaker, FLPA, (right) Luiz Claudio Marigo, Bruce Coleman Limited.

Contents

How old is the Earth?   **98**
- How did the Earth form?   99

What is it like inside the Earth?   **100**
- What are the continents?   100
- How did islands form?   101

How are mountains made?   **102**
- Why are mountain tops often covered in snow?   103

What makes earthquakes happen?   **104**
- Can earthquakes happen under the sea?   105

Why do volcanoes erupt?   **106**
- What are geysers?   107

What are rocks made of?   **108**
- What are gemstones?   109
- Where do metals come from?   110
- What are iron and steel?   111
- What are fossils?   112
- What are fossil fuels?   113

How do rivers flow?   **114**
- What is a delta?   116
- Why do rivers meander?   116
- Why do waterfalls fall?   117

How much of the Earth is covered by sea?   **118**
- What is the difference between an ocean and a sea?   119

What are deserts?   **120**
- Are all deserts sandy?   121
- What are mirages?   121

Why do rainforests grow in the tropics?   **122**
- Why are the rainforests so important?   123

Earth Science Quiz   **124**

How old is the Earth?

Scientists think that the Earth is about 4,600 million years old. The Earth was once a very different place from the planet we know today. It was covered in volcanoes, spitting out hot gases, rocks and **water vapour** into the air. As the Earth's surface cooled, the rocks hardened and formed the ground. The water vapour also cooled, then it **condensed** and fell as rain in violent thunderstorms. Some of the rain dried up on the hot surface. But some filled the first seas, which were almost boiling, and as **acidic** as vinegar. Instead of the oxygen we breathe today, the air was filled with poisonous gases such as carbon monoxide, ammonia, hydrogen sulphide and methane.

Scientists who study rocks are called geologists. In 1984, the oldest rocks so far known on our Earth were discovered by geologists in Canada. These rocks are over 3,960 million years old. The first living things were tiny cells that lived about 3,200 million years ago. The dinosaurs lived from about 200-65 million years ago, but our first ancestors did not appear until about 4 million years ago.

? Did you know?

The Earth is the only planet known to support life. This is because it has the right temperature and because the air is now fit for animals and people to breathe. But there may be life on other planets... what do you think?

The Earth would have looked very much like this 4,600 million years ago, before the first life appeared.

The planet closest to the Sun is Mercury. It is followed by Venus, Earth, Mars, Jupiter, Saturn, Uranus, Neptune and Pluto.

How did the Earth form?

The Earth is just a tiny speck in the Universe. This vast space contains billions of stars, planets and moons. Our part of the Universe is called the Solar System. It is made up of the planets and moons around our Sun. The nine planets are Mercury, Venus, Earth, Mars, Jupiter, Saturn, Uranus, Neptune and Pluto.

Astronomers are scientists who study the stars and planets. Most of them believe that the Universe began about 15,000 million years ago. There is thought to have been an explosion called the Big Bang. This threw clouds of hot gas and dust out into Space.

Astronomers think that the planets formed from these hot clouds, which were pulled together by the force of **gravity**. They also think that the Universe is still getting bigger, from the force of that same Big Bang.

This shows how a 16th century astronomer, Copernicus, saw the Earth and the Universe. He worked out that the Earth spun on its axis and around the Sun.

❓ Did you know?

The Earth measures 40,075 kilometres around the Equator, which is the fattest part of the Earth. It has a surface area of about 510,065,600 square kilometres. It is the third closest planet to the Sun, at a distance of about 150 million kilometres. The Earth's closest neighbour in Space is our Moon. It is about 384,400 kilometres away from the Earth. The diameter of the Earth is about 100 times smaller than the diameter of the Sun.

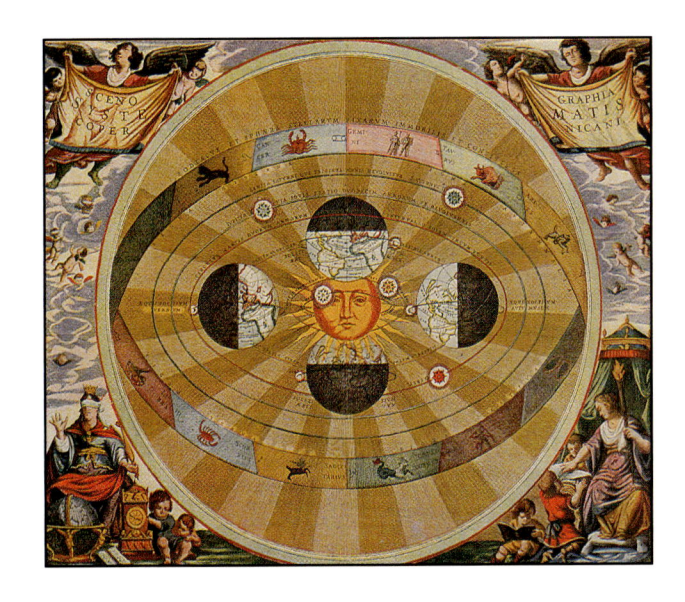

What is it like inside the Earth?

The ground beneath your feet is the outermost layer of the Earth, called the crust. It is made up of hard rock, covered in soil or water. The crust is about 40 kilometres thick on the continents but only about 8 kilometres thick on the sea bed. If you compare the depth of the crust with the overall size of the Earth, it is no thicker than the eggshell on an egg.

The crust floats on the next layer underneath it, which is called the mantle. Here the rocks are so hot that they are almost molten, or liquid. The mantle is about 2,900 kilometres thick.

The third layer is called the outer core of the Earth. It is about 2,200 kilometres thick. This layer is liquid as well, but it is made mostly of iron and nickel, which are metals. The liquid metals cover the Earth's core, which is a ball of solid nickel and iron about 2,500 kilometres wide. The temperature at the centre of the Earth is an amazing 4,500° C, but the pressure on the core is so great that the metals do not melt. Scientists have found out about these layers by studying the shock waves that shoot through the ground after an enormous underground explosion, such as an earthquake (see pages 12 and 13).

What are the continents?

The Earth's crust is not one single slab of rock. It is split into seven enormous chunks, and lots of smaller pieces. These are called plates. The large chunks form the continents – Asia, Africa, Australia, Europe, North America, South America and Antarctica. Which continent do you live on?

The continents have not always been in the same place as they are today. The chunks of crust on which they lie drift on top of the mantle below them. So they are constantly moving. About 250 million years ago, the continents were all joined together. They formed a huge 'super-continent', called Pangaea.

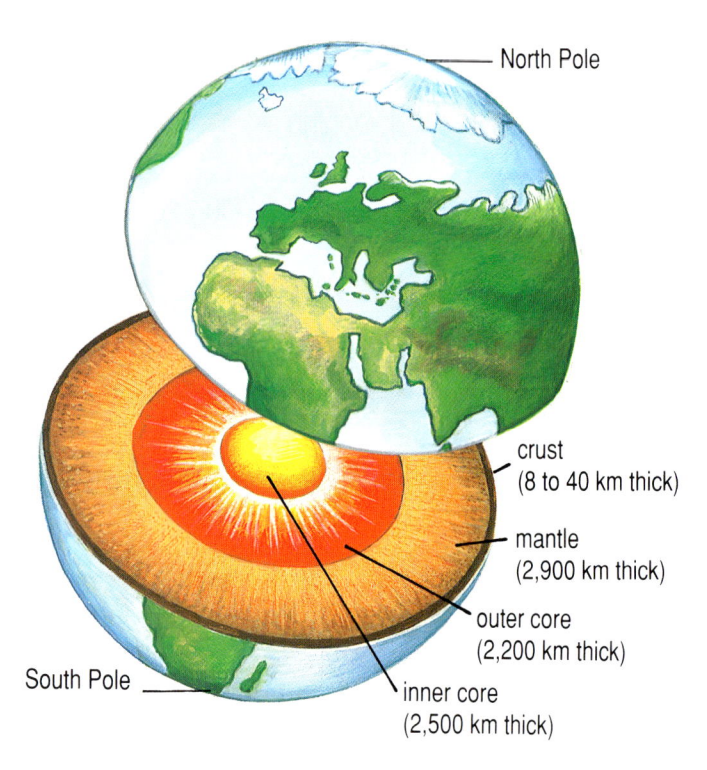

The Earth is made up of layers, a bit like the skins of an onion.

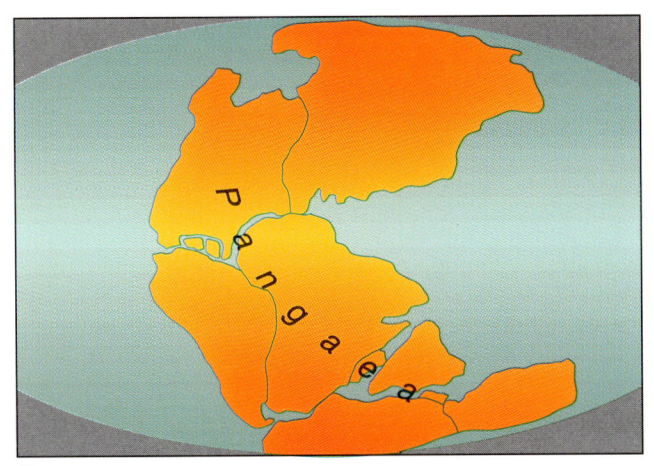

Pangaea.

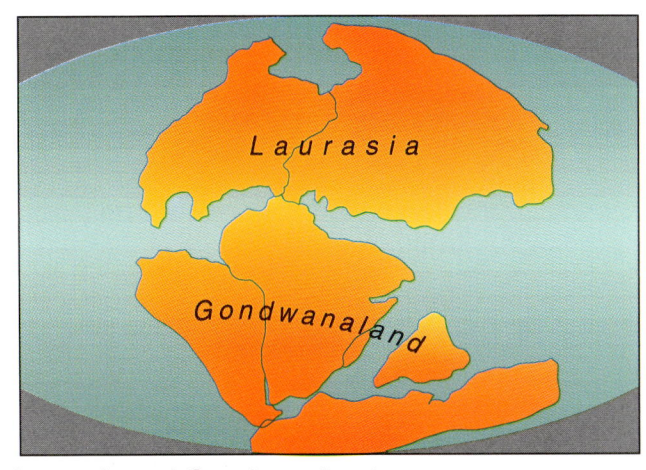

Laurasia and Gondwanaland.

Around it lay a vast ocean, called Panthalassa. About 200 million years ago, Pangaea began to crack up. At first it divided into two large pieces, called Laurasia and Gondwanaland. Then these two pieces began to split again into the continents that we know today, and they drifted into their present positions.

The continents are still drifting. Europe and North America are being pushed about 4 centimetres closer each year.

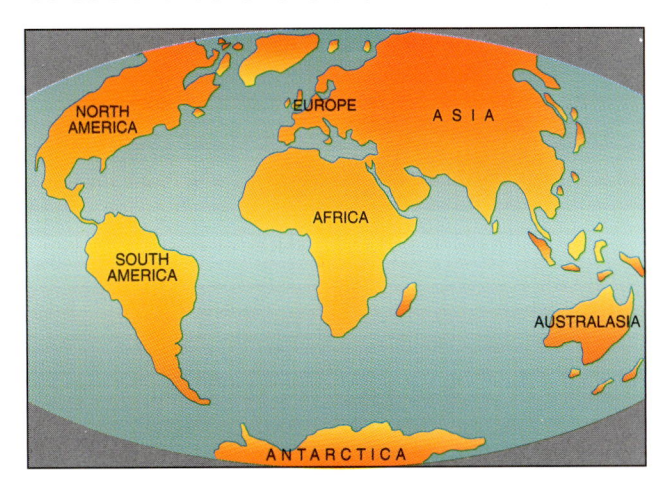

The continents as they are now.

How did islands form?

Islands are areas of land which are completely surrounded by water. Some islands lie on the smaller pieces of the Earth's crust. Others have broken off the continents. Madagascar, for example, was attached to Africa millions of years ago. It now lies about 400 kilometres off the south-east coast of Africa. There are some islands, such as the Hawaiian islands, which are really the tips of underwater volcanoes. Other islands are formed by volcanoes erupting underwater. Surtsey, off the coast of Iceland, erupted from the sea in 1963. The hundreds of tiny islands dotted about the Pacific and Indian Oceans are made from coral (see pages 38 and 39).

These two small islands are part of a long chain of coral islands called the Maldives. They lie in the Indian Ocean.

How are mountains made?

Some mountains are formed by volcanic eruptions (see page 14). But most are the result of movements of the Earth's crust. The rocky plates that make up the crust are always pulling apart or crashing into each other. There are two main types of mountain which are made by the shifting crust.

Fold mountains form when two plates crash into each other and the crust between them folds and crumples like paper. The Himalayas, the world's highest mountains, were formed like this at least 45 million years ago. The plate carrying India crashed into the plate carrying Asia, causing the sea floor between them to buckle up into mountains. Fossil seashells can still be found high up in the Himalayas.

Block mountains have flatter tops than fold mountains, and are formed in a different way. A huge block of rock is pushed up between two cracks in the Earth's crust. The Sierra Nevada range in the USA is a good example of this.

How a block mountain forms.

How a fold mountain forms.

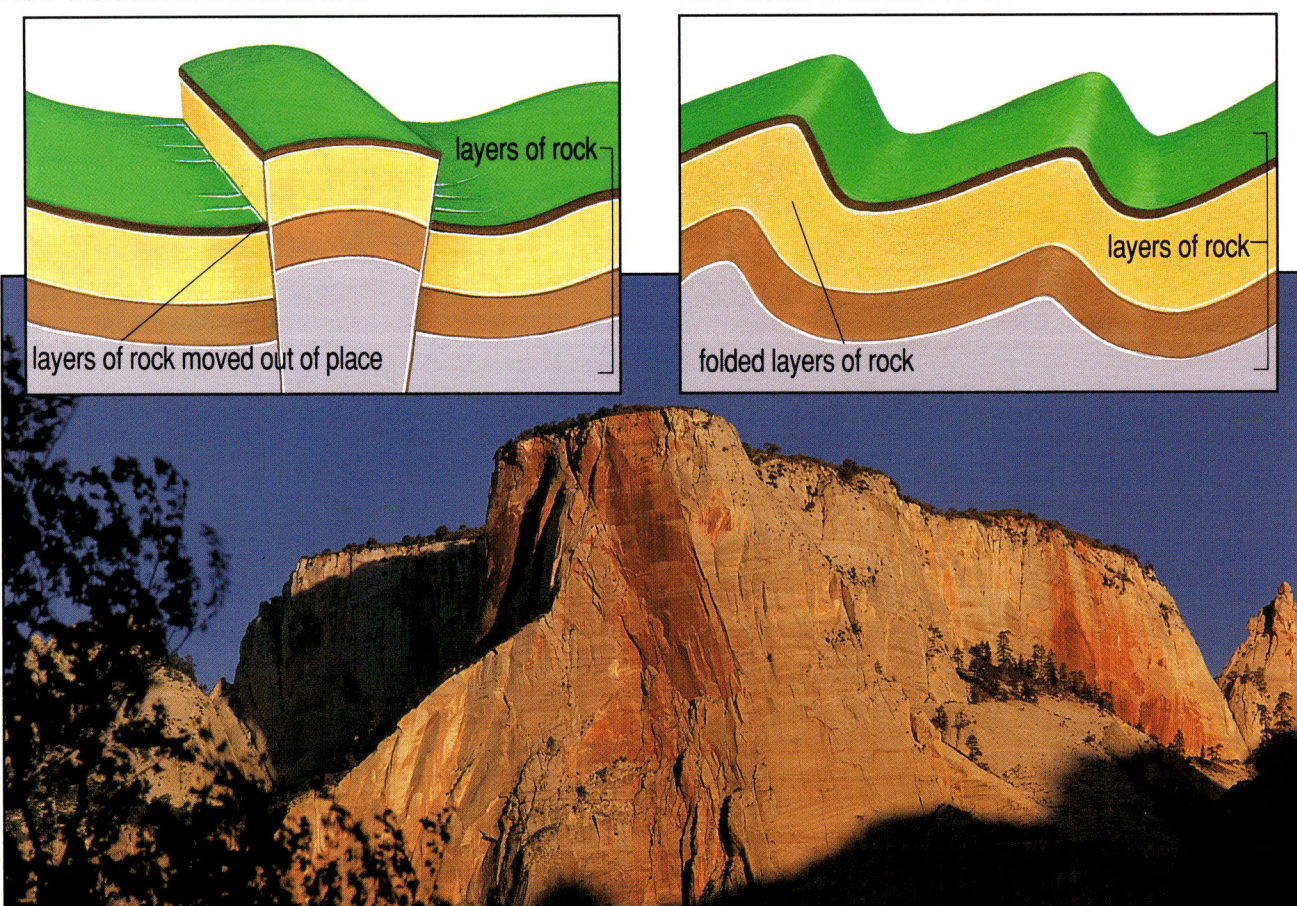

This huge rock in Zion National Park, Utah, USA, is part of the Wayatch Range. It is an example of a block mountain.

102

⚠ See for yourself

You can make your own fold mountains with four strips of plasticine. Arrange them in layers, one on top of the other. These layers are like the Earth's crust. Now hold your palms out flat and press against each of the ends of the plasticine. Your hands are acting as the colliding plates. As they push towards each other, they force the plasticine up into a mountain. You could try making a chain of mountains using longer pieces of plasticine. You may need to ask a friend to help push on one side.

❓ Did you know?

Mount Everest in the Himalayas is the world's highest mountain. It is 8,848 metres high. The first people to climb to the top were Sir Edmund Hillary and Sherpa Tenzing Norgay in 1953.

Mount Everest in Nepal.

Why are mountain tops often covered in snow?

As you climb a mountain, you will notice that it gets colder. The temperature drops by about 1 °C for every 100 metres that you climb. This is why the tops of high mountains are often covered in snow, even though the **climate** may be much milder lower down. Some mountains, such as those in the Himalayas, are so high that the snow on their **summits** never melts. Mountaineers also have to cope with bitter winds and less oxygen than normal, so breathing is very difficult.

This is the Matterhorn in the Swiss Alps. Its pyramid shape was caused by erosion (see below).

❓ Did you know?

Mountains are constantly being worn away by the wind, frost and ice. This process is called erosion. But it happens very slowly indeed. A mountain gets less than 9 centimetres shorter every 1,000 years.

What makes earthquakes happen?

Believe it or not, there are about 500,000 earthquakes every year. Only about 1,000 of these cause any damage, and only about 100,000 can be felt. The rest of the earthquakes make the ground shake so gently that no one notices them. But any **vibration** of the Earth's crust, however small it is, counts as an earthquake.

Earthquakes happen at the edges of the great plates of the Earth's crust. As two plates jostle and strain for position, they suddenly slip and slide. This causes the ground to shake. In the worst earthquakes, great cracks may open up in the ground and swallow up buildings, cars and even people. Most earthquakes last for less than a minute, but an earthquake in Alaska in 1964 lasted for seven minutes. Cracks 90 centimetres wide appeared in the ground.

As the plates move, shock waves shoot through the rocks in the Earth's crust. These are called seismic waves and they can be felt hundreds of kilometres away from the earthquake. Scientists known as seismologists, study these waves to find out more about the restless Earth.

The strength of an earthquake is measured on a special scale, called the Richter Scale. It goes from 1 to 10, and each number up the scale means that the earthquake is 30 times more powerful than the one before it. The worst earthquake so far measured 8.9 on the Richter Scale.

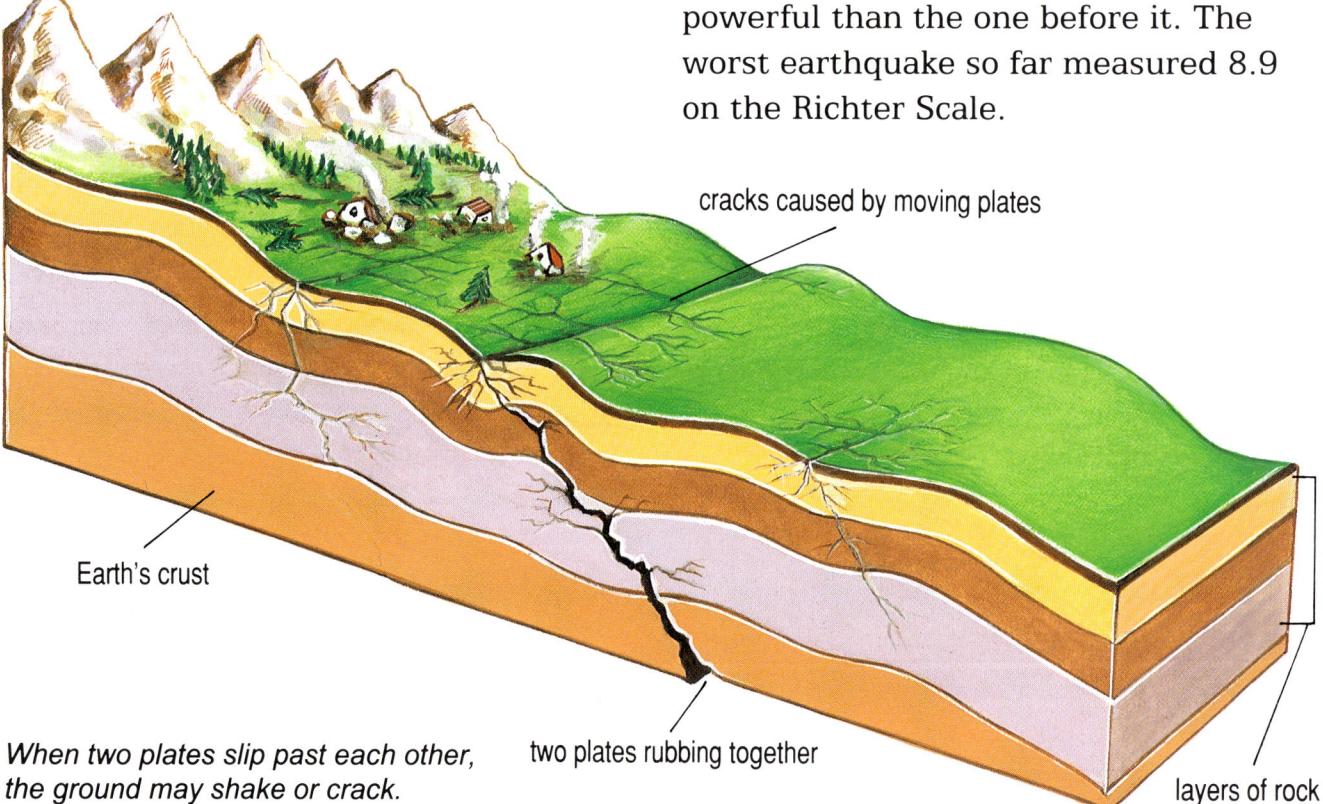

When two plates slip past each other, the ground may shake or crack.

? Did you know?

In September 1985, a terrible earthquake destroyed large areas of Mexico City. Over 2,000 people died. The city's maternity hospital was knocked flat. But amazed rescuers later found 50 new-born babies who had survived under the rubble.

Above: Earthquake damage, California, USA.

Left: Mexico City, 1985.

Can earthquakes happen under the sea?

Many earthquakes happen under the sea and cannot be felt on land. They are known as seaquakes. The deepest happen about 750 kilometres below the surface. Very strong seaquakes can make ships shake violently. Others set off huge mudslides under the sea and can even snap underwater telephone cables.

Underwater earthquakes or volcanoes can also cause enormous waves, called tsunamis. These can speed over the sea and crash on to islands and coasts, drowning houses and people. The highest tsunami so far recorded was 85 metres high, taller than a twenty-storey building.

? Did you know?

About 90 per cent of all earthquakes happen in the area around the Pacific Ocean known as the Ring of Fire.

The Ring of Fire in the Pacific.

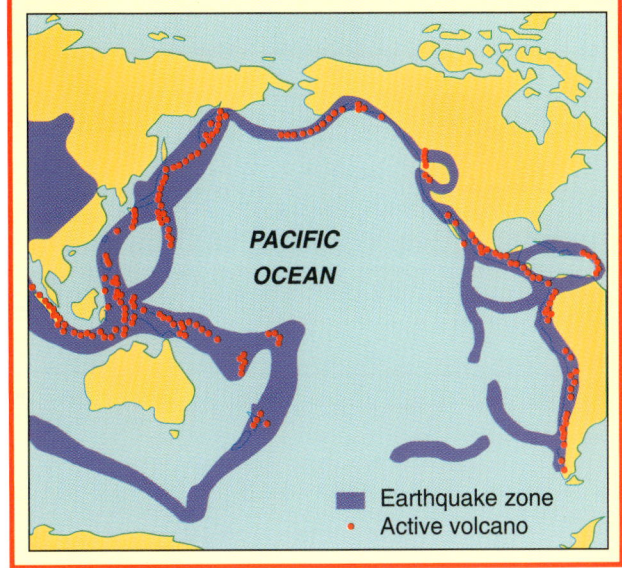

Why do volcanoes erupt?

An erupting volcano is one of the most dramatic sights on Earth. Deep under the Earth's crust lies a layer of red-hot liquid rock, called magma. A volcano erupts when pressure builds up underground and forces the magma up and out through cracks in the Earth's surface. After it has burst through the surface with rocks, dust and gases, the magma is called lava.

Volcanoes are different shapes, depending on how violently they erupt and the type of lava that pours out of them. Thick, sticky lava builds up a cone-shaped mountain as it cools quickly and hardens. Thin, runny lava flows much further before it cools and hardens. It forms low volcanoes, called shield volcanoes.

? Did you know?

Lava can flow at speeds of over 600 kilometres an hour. This is about twice as fast as an express train.

Lava is oozing out of this volcano in Hawaii, and flowing fast down the sides.

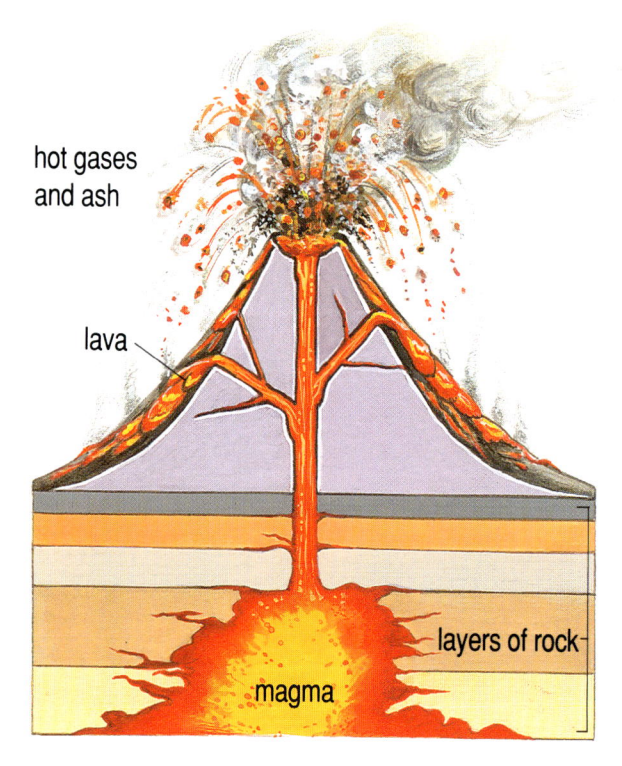

A cone volcano.

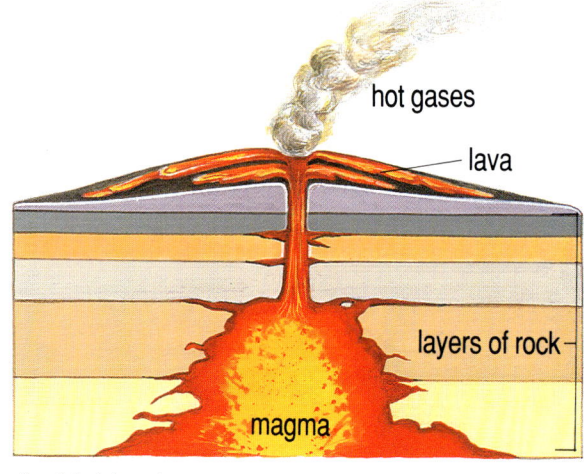

A shield volcano.

🛈 See for yourself

You can make your own working model of a volcano. You may need to ask an adult to help you. First, make a cone-shaped mountain out of sand or soil. Mix a teaspoon of baking soda (bicarbonate of soda) with some warm water in a test tube. Shake the tube so that the soda dissolves. Then add a few drops of washing-up liquid and a few drops of orange food colouring. Mix the ingredients together. This is your lava. Gently push the test tube down into your sand mountain. Now add a few teaspoonfuls of vinegar to the test tube until the mixture starts to bubble and fizz, and pours out down the sides of the volcano.

❓ Did you know?

There are about 10,000 geysers in Yellowstone National Park, USA. One of these is called Steamboat Geyser. It is the tallest active geyser in the world. It shoots up to a height of 115 metres.

What are geysers?

Geysers are fountains of scalding-hot water and steam which shoot out of the ground. They happen in places where there are lots of volcanoes, such as Iceland. The rocks under the ground are red hot. They heat any underground water until it is so hot that it bursts out of cracks in the ground.

The word 'geyser' comes from the Icelandic word, 'geysir', which means gusher. In Reykjavik, the capital of Iceland, hot water from geysers is pumped into people's homes and used in their central heating systems.

This geyser is shooting out hot water in Whakarewarewa, Rotorua, New Zealand.

What are rocks made of?

The ground under your feet is made up of rocks. Most of these formed millions of years ago. They may be covered with soil or grass, or water in the rivers, lakes and seas. The rocks themselves are made up of substances called minerals. These are chemicals which form naturally inside the Earth. They include silicon, iron and carbon.

Rocks may be made of one type of mineral or a mixture of several different types. Hard granite rock, for example, is made of three main minerals: mica, quartz and feldspar. There are over 3,000 different types of mineral, but most rocks are made out of 30 or so of the most common ones. Rocks are divided into three types: igneous, sedimentary and metamorphic. Igneous rocks include those that shoot out of volcanoes, and rocks such as granite and obsidian. They form when magma from inside the Earth cools and hardens.

Sedimentary rocks, such as sandstone and limestone, form in layers. The bottom layers turn to rock as they are squashed by the layers on top of them. Sedimentary rocks often contain **fossils** (see pages 20-21).

Metamorphic rocks form when igneous or sedimentary rocks are pushed back into the Earth and changed underground by great heat and pressure. Marble, for example, is a metamorphic rock made from heated and compressed limestone.

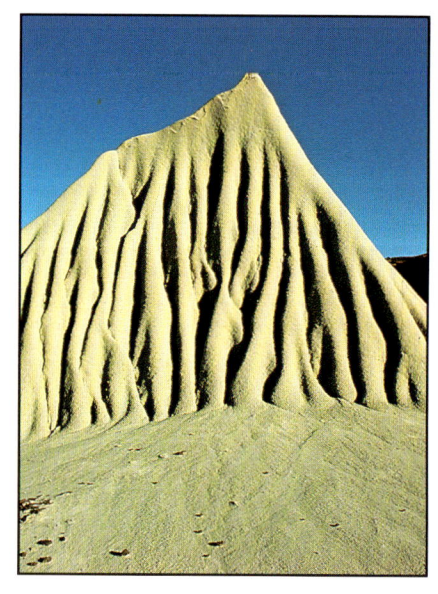

Top: Hard granite rocks on Lundy Island off the coast of England.

Top right: This sandstone formation in Alberta, Canada, has been produced by weathering.

Left: Exposed red and white marble at Marble Bar, Australia.

What are gemstones?

About 100 types of the different minerals are called gemstones. They are very rare and very valuable. They include sapphires, rubies, emeralds and diamonds. Gemstones are mined, or dug, from the ground. Then they are cut, polished and made into beautiful jewellery.

All minerals, including gemstones, are graded according to how hard they are. Diamonds are the hardest minerals on Earth. A diamond can only be cut with another diamond. The softest mineral is talc, which is used to make talcum powder.

This rock contains amethyst, which is a semi-precious stone.

! See for yourself

Minerals often form crystals. These are regular-shaped clusters inside rocks. You can grow your own crystals using alum powder, which you can buy from a chemist. **Dissolve** enough alum in warm water so that no more powder dissolves and you can see a little of it at the bottom of the jam jar. This is called a saturated solution. Then pour a little of this into a saucer. Leave it until the water evaporates and tiny crystals form. Choose the biggest crystal and tie a piece of thread around it. Tie the other end of the thread around a pencil. Half fill a jam jar with more saturated solution of alum. Lay the pencil across the top of the jar so that the crystal hangs down into the mixture. Leave the jar in a warm place and wait for the water to **evaporate.** A larger crystal should form as the alum in the mixture sticks to the first crystal.

1. Small crystals are forming in the saucer.

2. A large crystal has grown inside the jam jar.

Where do metals come from?

Like gemstones, metals are also minerals. They are found in the rocks of the Earth's crust. If a rock contains a lot of a particular type of metal, it is known as an ore. Iron-ore contains iron, copper-ore contains copper and so on. Each type of ore has different amounts of the metal in it. Iron-ore, for example, is about 75 per cent iron. But copper-ore is only about 2 to 3 per cent copper.

Before metals can be used, they have to be mined. Mining can be very hard work. For example, it takes 2 tonnes of rock to produce just 28 grams of gold. Metals are used for making tools, machines and jewellery. Camera films are coated with silver. Fizzy drinks cans can be made out of a very light metal, called aluminium. Copper, and bronze (a mixture of copper and tin), were the first metals used by people, about 3,700 years ago.

An open cast copper mine at Morenci, Arizona, in the USA.

Did you know?

The deepest gold mine in the world is the Western Deep mine in South Africa. It is over 3.7 kilometres deep. At the bottom of the mine, the temperature can reach 55 °C. Special refrigerators are used to keep the miners cool.

Far right: A gold nugget from Venezuela.
Right inset: A gold Ashanti pendant from Ghana.

What are iron and steel?

Iron is a metal that occurs naturally in iron-ore. People mix iron with carbon to make steel. Mixtures such as this are called alloys. When the iron-ore has been dug out of the ground, it is heated in a very hot oven, called a blast-furnace. This melts the iron so that it can be collected more easily. Most of this iron is mixed with carbon to make it into harder steel. There are many different kinds of steel.

Cars are usually made out of steel. Knives, forks and spoons are often made of stainless steel. This means that the steel has been mixed with another metal, called chromium, to stop it going rusty.

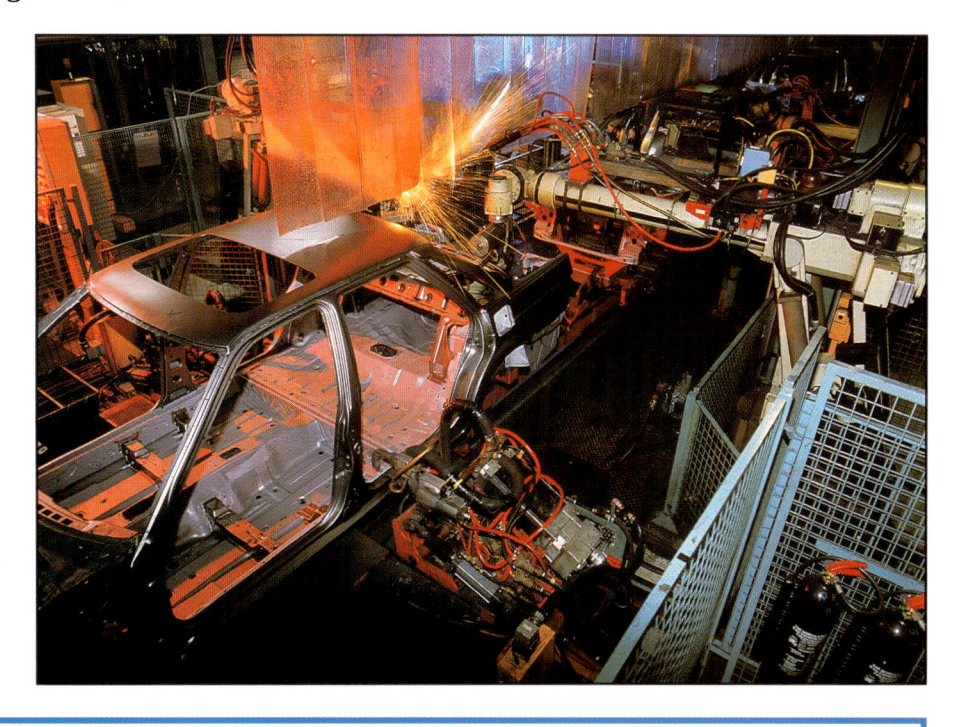

A car body is being welded in a factory. Like most cars nowadays, it is being made by a robot.

⚠ See for yourself

Look around your house and see how many things you can find that are made out of metal. Can you find anything made out of silver, gold, iron, stainless steel, copper, bronze, nickel or aluminium? Make a list of these metals and tick them off as you find them.

Like paper, metal can be recycled, or used again. Metal cans are made from either steel or aluminium. They need to be sorted out into two separate piles before they can be recycled. So if you want to recycle any cans in your house, first test them with a magnet to see if they are steel or aluminium. The steel ones will stick to the magnet; the aluminium ones will not. Now you can take them to be recycled.

Aluminium cans have been squashed together ready for recycling into aluminium sheets.

What are fossils?

Fossils are the hard parts of prehistoric plants or animals, such as dinosaurs, which have turned to stone over millions of years. The most common fossils are of teeth, bones and shells. But dinosaur footprints, eggs and nests have also been found in fossil form. Fossils help scientists to build up a picture of the Earth as it was millions of years ago. In fact, they are the only record we have of the Earth's early history.

The chances of a fossil forming are very small. When a dinosaur died, the soft parts of its body rotted away leaving the hard parts behind. Over many years, they were covered in layers of mud and sand. Gradually the bones were replaced by minerals, and turned to stone. Most fossils are found in sedimentary rocks, such as sandstone and limestone (see page 16). When these rocks are pushed to the surface of the Earth, they are worn away by the wind and weather. This uncovers the fossils.

? Did you know?

The oldest fossils found so far are tiny blob-like cells that lived about 3,200 million years ago. They were discovered in rocks called cherts, in South Africa.

Above: In Dinosaur National Monument Park, USA, a dinosaur's leg bone fossil is being carefully chipped away.
Inset: This fossilized ammonite shell began to form over 194 million years ago in Germany.

What are fossil fuels?

Coal, oil and natural gas are called fossil fuels. This is because they formed from the remains of prehistoric plants and animals. Coal formed from huge trees and plants which grew near swamps 345 to 280 million years ago. When the trees died, they fell into the swamps. Over many years, the weight of material falling on top of them squeezed the water out of the trees and turned them into coal. The remains of the plants can often be seen in lumps of coal.

There are many types of coal. The hardest is anthracite, which gives out a lot of heat when it is burned.

Oil and gas were made from the remains of tiny prehistoric sea animals and plants. Their bodies sank to the sea bed and were buried under layers of sand and mud. Over millions of years, they turned into gas and oil. Oil is found in 'traps' under the Earth's crust.

Oil found under the sea is called offshore oil.

? Did you know?

When a huge fossil bone was found in 1677, people thought it belonged to a giant man. In fact, it belonged to a dinosaur called Megalosaurus. It was the first dinosaur fossil ever discovered. The dinosaurs were not given their name, which means 'terrible lizards', until 1841.

? Did you know?

In 1861, an amazing fossil was found in Solnhofen in Germany. It showed the earliest animal known to have feathers. Scientists called this early bird Archaeopteryx.

The Archaeopteryx had wings and feathers like the birds we know, but it also had claws, teeth and a bony tail.

How do rivers flow?

When rain falls high up on hillsides, some of the water drains away into the ground. The rest runs downhill, as a small streamlet. Gradually it joins up with other streamlets to form a stream. The start of the river's journey to the sea is called the river's source. Other rivers begin life as mountain springs, where underground water bubbles to the surface. The only difference between a river and a stream is that the river is bigger than the streams that flow into it.

A young river is strong and fast flowing. It is pulled downhill by the force of gravity and flows quickly because the mountain-side is steep. As it flows hard and fast, the water wears away the stone on its bed and sides. It carries the worn rocks with it, breaking them down into ever smaller pieces of rock and finally, mud. This wearing-away process is called erosion, and the rocks and mud are known as sediment.

As the river reaches the gentler slopes at the bottom of the mountain, it slows down. The river carries its load of rocks and mud, but it no longer flows strongly enough to erode hard rocks. In its final stage, it meets the sea at the mouth of the river. Here it drops its load of sediment (see page 24).

Above: The mouth of a river.

Far left: A bubbling river source.

Left: An older, slower river.

⚠ See for yourself

When a river drops its load of sediment, it drops the heaviest rocks and pebbles first, followed by lighter particles of mud and silt. You can see how sediments settle with this simple experiment. Collect some samples of different types of soil, gravel, mud and sand. Put three tablespoons of each sample into a large jam jar with a screw top, or a plastic drinks bottle with the top cut off. Now pour one-and-a-half cupfuls of water into the jam jar or bottle. Screw the lid on the jar and give it a good shake, or stir the plastic bottle with a spoon. Leave the mixture until the sediment settles. You may have to leave the mixture to settle for several weeks.

You should then be able to see the different layers quite clearly, with the heaviest grains at the bottom and the lightest on top.

❓ Did you know?

The River Nile in Egypt, below, is the world's longest river. It flows for 6,670 kilometres. The world's shortest river is D River in Oregon, USA. It is only about 37 metres long.

What is a delta?

A river drops its load of sediment when it reaches the sea (see page 22). If the tides and ocean **currents** are strong enough, they sweep the sediment out to sea. When this happens, the river is said to flow into an estuary. But if the river lays down too much sediment at the mouth of the river, or the currents are too weak to carry it out to sea, a delta forms. The sediment builds up on the sea floor, forming islands of new land. The river has to split into smaller branches and flow around the islands to reach the sea. The branches of the river sometimes make patterns which looks like fans or birds' feet.

Why do rivers meander?

As a river slows down on its journey to the sea, it is not strong enough to wear away the hard rock in its path. So the river follows the bands of soft rock, which it is able to cut into. This means that the river sometimes flows in curving, horseshoe-shaped bends, to follow the bands of soft rock. These bends are called meanders.

The water in the Mississippi River delta flows very slowly around marshy islands.

As the river curves, the water flows more slowly along its inner bank, building up this bank with the sediment that it drops. It flows faster along its outer bank, wearing it away. This makes the meander even more curved. Sometimes the curve makes the river flow too slowly, so it cuts a quicker route just before the bend, especially during a flood. This can cut off the curve, making it into a small lake, called an ox-bow lake.

An ox-bow lake which was once a meander on the Mara River, Kenya.

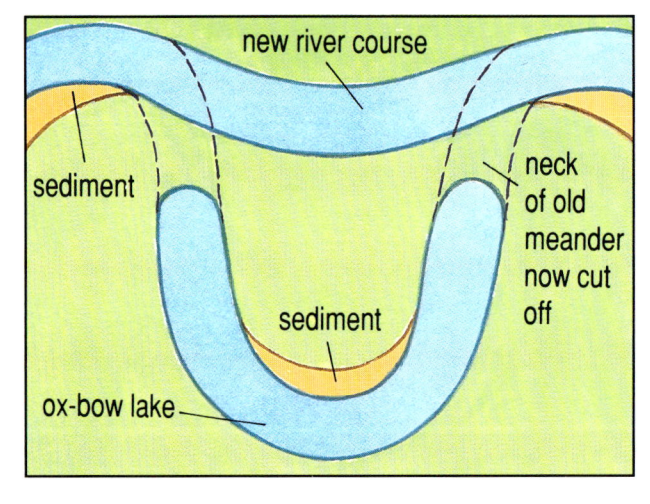

This is how the ox-bow lake on the Mara River was formed.

116

Why do waterfalls fall?

A waterfall forms when a river flows over a band of hard rock on to a band of soft rock. Over thousands of years, the river wears the soft rock away, slowly carving it into a steep cliff. When the cliff is steep enough, the river water flows over the ledge of hard rock, then suddenly drops down. The falling water carries rocks and pebbles with it. At the bottom of the waterfall they wear away a hollow called a plunge pool.

? Did you know?

The highest waterfall in the world is Angel Falls in Venezuela. The water drops 979 metres. The Eiffel Tower in Paris would reach less than a third of the way up the Falls. The Falls were named after an American pilot, Jimmy Angel. He spotted them from his plane in 1933.

? Did you know?

The greatest ever waterfall formed about 6.5 million years ago. The Mediterranean Sea became cut off from the ocean and gradually dried up. When the sea-level rose about a million years later, the water flowed back in over the Straits of Gibraltar in a gigantic waterfall. The Mediterranean took about 100 years to fill up again.

This is how a waterfall forms.

hard rock

soft rock

stones carried by water

plunge pool

How much of the Earth is covered by sea?

If you were an astronaut **orbiting** the Earth in your spaceship, you would be able to see that there is far more water than land on our Earth. In fact, over two-thirds of the Earth is covered in sea-water. Perhaps 'Sea' would be a better name for our planet than Earth! This sea-water lies in the five oceans. They are the Pacific, which is the largest, then the Atlantic, Indian, Southern and the Arctic oceans. The oceans are not separate areas. They link together to form a continuous stretch of water.

The Pacific Ocean covers a third of the Earth. At its widest point, it stretches almost halfway around the world. All seven continents would fit into the Pacific, with room to spare. The Pacific Ocean is about 13 times bigger than the Arctic Ocean, which is the smallest of the five oceans.

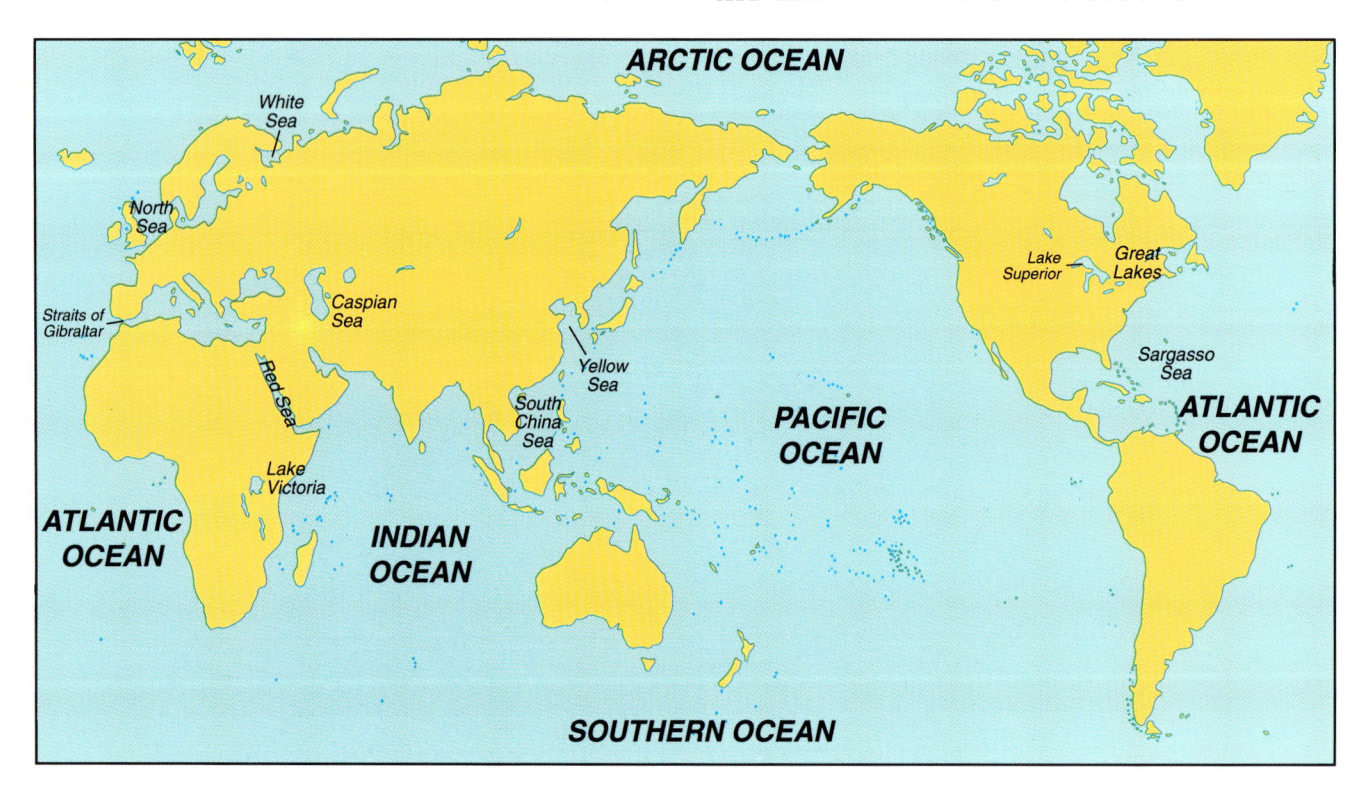

> **? Did you know?**
>
> The Red Sea in the Middle East gets its name from the red colour of its water. This is caused by millions of tiny plants, called algae. The Yellow Sea lies between China and Korea. Yellowish mud and clay that are carried into the sea by rivers give this sea its name. The White Sea off the Arctic Ocean does not have white water. It is called 'white' because it is covered with ice for two-thirds of each year.

The oceans and some of the world's seas and larger lakes (see page 30).

Above: Sargassum seaweed close up.

Left: A mass of Sargassum seaweed floating on the Atlantic Ocean.

What is the difference between an ocean and a sea?

We often use the word 'sea' to mean the oceans or sea-water in general. But oceanographers, or scientists who study the oceans, use the word 'sea' to mean a particular area of water in one of the oceans. Some seas are given names because of a special feature or characteristic. The Sargasso Sea is part of the Atlantic Ocean. It was named after the clumps of Sargassum seaweed which float on its surface. Other seas, such as the Mediterranean Sea, are partly surrounded by land. The name Mediterranean means 'between land'. This sea separates Africa and Europe and is linked to the Atlantic Ocean through the narrow Straits of Gibraltar.

? Did you know?

The South China Sea is the biggest sea. It covers an area of 2,974,600 square kilometres. This is about the same size as the country of Argentina.

? Did you know?

There are mountains and valleys under the sea just as there are on land. In fact, the world's greatest mountain range runs down the middle of the Atlantic Ocean. It is called the Mid-Atlantic Ridge. It is about 65,000 kilometres long. The mountains lie about 2.5 kilometres under the sea. Some of them are 4 kilometres high.

What are deserts?

Deserts are very dry places which get less than 25 centimetres of rain each year. The whole year's rain can fall in just two or three rainstorms. Sometimes years can go by without any rain at all.

During the day, the temperature in the desert may reach a scorching 58 °C. But it can be freezing cold at night. Because of these harsh conditions, only the toughest plants and animals survive in the desert.

Desert plants include cacti, which store water in their stems. There are desert animals, such as gerbils, which shelter in cool underground burrows during the day, and camels, which can go without food or water for days.

Deserts cover about an eighth of the Earth's surface. They are divided into hot and cold deserts. Cold deserts, such as the Gobi Desert, have very warm summers but very cold winters. Hot deserts, such as the Sahara and the Arabia, are hot all year round during the day, and cold at night.

Right: A desert fox emerging from its cool hole in the hot Sinai Desert.
Below: Cacti survive in the harsh deserts of the USA.

Are all deserts sandy?

Only about 15 per cent of all deserts are sandy. Most are covered with gravel, pebbles or bare rock.

In sandy deserts, the wind blows the sand into ridges called dunes. Some are crescent-shaped and are called barchans. The biggest dunes are found in the Sahara. They can be 430 metres high and stretch for 5 kilometres. The dunes move like giant sandy waves as sand is blown up one side of the dune, then trickles over the top and down the other side. They can move up to 50 metres a year, covering desert villages that are in their way.

A barchan dune in the Sahara.

What are mirages?

Mirages trick you into thinking you can see things which really do not exist. We say that they are optical illusions. Thirsty desert travellers often see mirages of tempting pools of water in the distance. But as they get closer, the mirages vanish. Mirages are caused by warm air near the ground, which bends the light coming from the sky and **distorts** its reflection. This makes it look like water.

In summer, you may sometimes see what looks like a layer of water over a hot, tarred road. This is also a mirage, made in the same way.

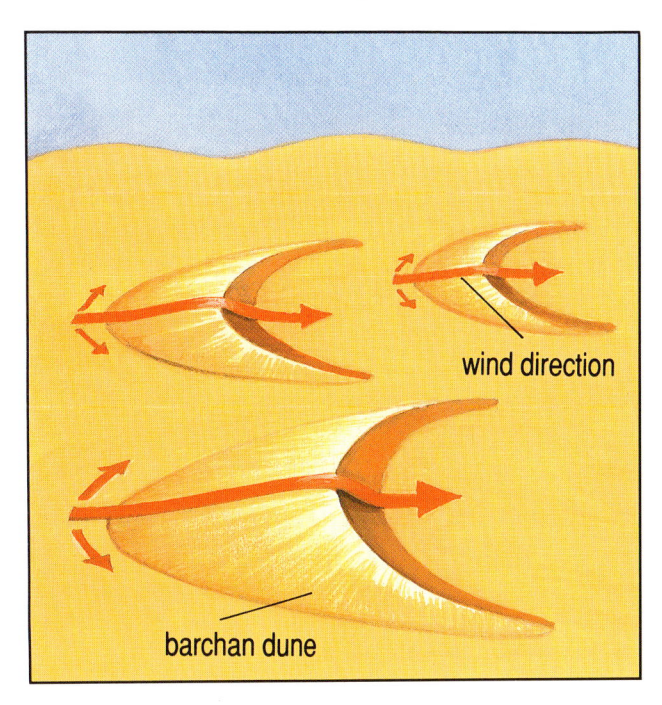

The wind curls round the sides of barchan dunes, making the crescent shapes.

? Did you know?

The Sahara covers about a third of Africa. It is the largest desert in the world. It measures 5,150 kilometres from east to west.

? Did you know?

The Atacama Desert lies along the west side of the Andes Mountains, in Chile. It had no rain at all for 400 years from 1571 until 1971.

Why do rainforests grow in the tropics?

Huge, dense rainforests grow in parts of South America, Africa, South East Asia and Australia. They grow near the tropics, which are on either side of the Equator. Here, it is hot and wet all year round. It rains every day and the air is sticky and humid.

The warm, wet air provides ideal growing conditions for plants. So forests of trees, vines, ferns and shrubs have formed here. The plants grow in three layers. The tallest trees grow in what is called the emergent layer. Some of them are 50 metres tall, and they poke out above the rest of the forest. Below them is the canopy. This is a thick, green layer of treetops which forms a roof over the forest. It can be 10 metres thick. The third layer is called the understorey. It is made up of shorter trees, such as palm trees, and smaller plants, such as vines, ferns and flowers. Very little sunlight reaches the forest floor. Most of it is blocked out by the canopy.

> **? Did you know?**
>
> The world's biggest rainforest grows along the banks of the River Amazon in South America. It is bigger than all the other rainforests put together. This forest alone contains at least a tenth of all the **species** of plants and animals that exist in the world.

Why are the rainforests so important?

Tropical rainforests cover only about 6 per cent of the Earth's surface. Yet over half of all the species of animals and plants in the world are found in them. These species include jaguars, toucans, hummingbirds, tree frogs, orchids, brazil-nut trees, rubber trees... the list goes on and on! Rainforest plants provide us with fruit, nuts, spices and important medicines. For example, about 1,400 types of rainforest plants are known to help fight cancer. The forests are also home to over 1.5 million people, who have lived there for thousands of years. They use the forests' **resources,** without harming the forest.

Below: A Morpho butterfly in the Amazon rainforest.

But the rainforests are being destroyed by other people so fast that there will be none left in about 50 years' time. Trees are cut down for timber, and to make space for farming, ranching and mining. This means that the rainforest people lose their homes, and many animals and plants become **extinct**.

Many of the trees are burnt, which also has a bad effect on the Earth. Burning the trees puts a lot of carbon dioxide gas into the air. This may be making the Earth warmer by stopping heat from escaping into Space. If the Earth becomes even a few degrees warmer, the ice at the North and South Poles could melt and the sea-level might rise. The sea would then drown low-lying places such as New York, London and Sydney.

Above: A Saffron toucanet in the rainforest of south-eastern Brazil.

Left: A Goeldi's monkey in the western Amazon rainforest.

Try to find out how you can help to save the rainforests. We do not have to buy furniture made of tropical hardwoods. There are other woods which come from forests where the trees are always replaced. We can also buy as pets, tropical birds and animals which are born and raised outside the rainforests.

See for Yourself! Earth Science Quiz

Now that you have read this chapter, you could test yourself with these questions.

Questions
1. How old is the Earth?
2. When did our first ancestors appear on Earth?
3. What are the names of the nine planets in our Solar System?
4. How far is the Earth away from the Moon?
5. What is the Earth's crust made of?
6. What are the names of the four layers of the Earth?
7. How tall is the world's highest mountain?
8. Most earthquakes last for less than how many minutes?
    a) 1   b) 2   c) 3   d) 4   e) 5
9. What is the name of the red-hot liquid rock deep under the Earth's crust?
10. How fast can lava flow?
11. What are geysers?
12. What are the three names given to different types of rock?
13. How deep is the deepest gold mine in the world?
14. What are fossils?
15. How much of the Earth is covered in sea-water?
16. What are the names of the five oceans?
17. What makes the Red Sea appear to be red?
18. How many centimetres of rain does a desert normally have each year?
    a) 25   b) 37   c) 48   d) 53   e) 66
19. What are mirages caused by?
20. What are the names of the three layers of plant growth in a rainforest?

Answers
Look back to find the answers on these pages.

Question	Page	Question	Page	Question	Page	Question	Page
1	98	6	100	11	107	16	118
2	98	7	103	12	108	17	118
3	99	8	104	13	110	18	120
4	99	9	106	14	112	19	121
5	100	10	106	15	118	20	122

SCIENCE
QUESTIONS & ANSWERS

Indoor Science

Anita Ganeri

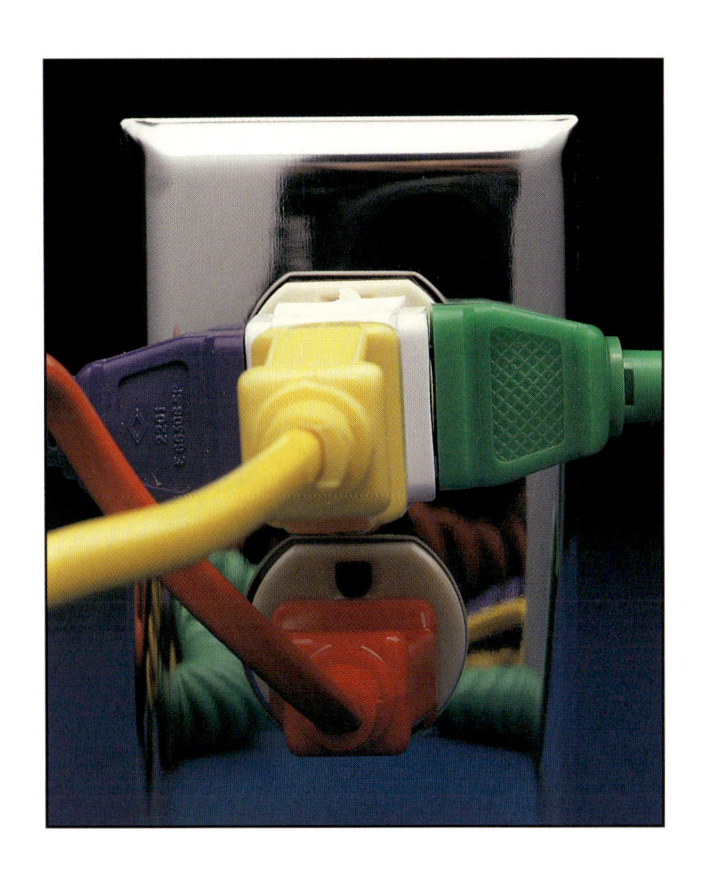

Acknowledgements

page 128 - Garry Gay, The Image Bank; page 129 - (top left) Martyn FChillmaid, Robert Harding Picture Library, (top right) Max Schneider, The Image Bank, (bottom) Oscar Burriel, Science Photo Library; page 130 - Robert Harding Picture Library; Page 131 - (top right) Martin F Chillmaid, Robert Harding Picture Library, (bottom right) Sally Morgan, Ecoscene, (bottom left) Walter Iooss Jr, The Image Bank; page 132 - Sally Morgan, Ecoscene; page 133 - (top) phil Jude, Science Photo Library, (bottom) Robert Harding Picture Library; page 134 - (inset) Arzhur Meyerson, The Image Bank, (main picture) Zefa; page 135 (bottom left) Romilly Lockyer, The Image Bank, (top right) Sally Morgan, Ecoscene, (bottom right) Anthony Cooper, Ecoscene; page 136 -(top left) David Guyon, Science Photo Library, (bottom left) Lorenzo Lees, Ecoscene; page 137 - (bottom left) Sally Morgan, Ecoscene, (top right) Nils Jorgensen, Rex Features; page 138 - (top) Geoff du Feu, Planet Earth Pictures, (bottom left) Last Resort Picture Agency, (bottom right) Zefa; page 139 - (top) Last Resort Picture Agency, (middle) Ever Ready Ltd; page 140 - (left) Garry Gay, The Image Bank, (right) Bill Varie, The Image Bank; page 141 - (left) Sally Morgan, Ecoscene, (middle right) Dr Jeremy Burgess, Science Photo Library, (bottom) Sally Morgan, Ecoscene; page 142 - (left) Norman Tomalin, Bruce Coleman Ltd, (right) Gisela Caspersen, The Image Bank; page 143 - Zefa; page 144 -(top) Adrienne Hart-Davis, Science Photo Libran(l (bottom) Gerhard Gscheidle, The Image Bank; page 145 -(top) Adrienne Hart-Davis, Science Photo Library, (bottom) Sally Morgan, Ecoscene; page 146 - Derik Murray Photography, The Image Bank; page 147 - (left) Sally Morgan, Ecoscene, (right) The Image Bank; page 148 - Sally Morgan, Ecoscene; page 149 - (left) Gray Mortimore, Allsport, (right) Robert Harding Picture Library; page 150 - (top) Colin Molineux, The Image Bank, (bottom) John Kelly, The Image Bank; page 151 - (left) Adam Hart-Davis, Science Photo Library, (right) Last Resort Picture Library; page 152 - (middle) Max Schneider, The Image Bank, (bottom) Zefa; page 153 - (top) Robert Harding Picture Library, (middle) Sally Morgan, Ecoscene, (bottom) Dr Jeremy Burgess, Science Photo Library.

Contents

What is the difference between ice and water? **128**
- Why is syrup difficult to pour? 129

How does water change to ice? **130**
- How do ice cubes cool drinks down? 130
- What makes a fridge keep things cold? 131
- Why does sugar dissolve in a hot drink? 131
- When does water stop dissolving solids? 132
- Why are fizzy drinks fizzy? 133

How does washing-up liquid get plates clean? **134**
- How do towels get you dry? 135

What is electricity? **136**
- Why do your clothes crackle when you undress? 136
- What happens when you plug in an electric kettle? 137
- How does an electric kettle boil water? 138
- What does a battery do? 139

How does a telephone work? **140**

Why can you see yourself in a mirror? **142**
- Why do you look the wrong way round in a mirror? 142
- How can you see yourself in the window at night? 143

How does a pencil make a mark on paper? **144**

How does a magnet pick up pins? **145**

What is the best way of cracking a nut? **146**
- How do scissors cut paper? 147

How do clothes get dry in a spin dryer? **148**

What is fire? **150**
- Why is a flame hot? 151

Why does baking powder make cakes rise? **152**
- How does yeast make bread rise? 152
- Why does food go mouldy? 153

Indoor Science Quiz **154**

What is the difference between ice and water?

Water and ice are two very different substances which you can see in the kitchen. But did you know that although ice and water do not look like each other, they are both different forms of water? Most of the things around you, such as water and metals, can exist in three forms – as solids, liquids or gases. These three forms are called the three states of matter. Ice is the solid form of the liquid, water. The gas form of water is water **vapour**.

All the things around you are made up of tiny particles, called molecules. They are much too small to see. The molecules themselves are made of even tinier particles, called atoms. The different states of matter are caused by the different ways in which molecules in a substance are grouped together.

In a solid substance, the molecules are very close together. They are kept in a fixed shape by very strong **bonds**. In a liquid, the molecules are still quite close together but the bonds between them are not so strong. This is why liquids can flow and change shape. Look at a glass of water – the liquid has taken the shape of its container. In a gas, the bonds are looser still. The molecules move around freely, allowing the gas to spread out.

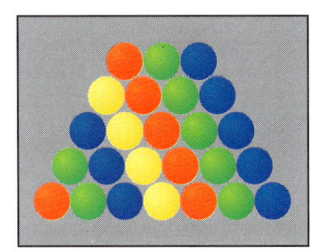

Solid molecules are close together.

Liquid molecules move further apart.

Gas molecules move around freely.

The three states of matter.

Water in its liquid state.

128

? Did you know?

Molecules are very, very small indeed. There are about 50,000 million million molecules in one tiny grain of sand. Each sand molecule is made up of two atoms of oxygen and one atom of silicon. You are made of molecules, too.

? Did you know?

Inside an atom there are even tinier particles called protons, neutrons and electrons. Different types of atoms have different numbers of protons, neutrons and electrons. The rest of the atom is mainly empty space.

? Did you know?

Glass is a liquid, not a solid. But it is extremely viscous, so it does not seem to flow. If you look at a very old window pane, you will see that the glass bulges at the bottom and is thinner at the top. This is because the glass has flowed slowly down over the years.

! See for yourself

If a liquid is warm, it is less viscous and therefore easier to pour. Try this simple experiment to see how this works. Fill two egg cups with two or three tea-spoonfuls of clear honey. Put one egg cup into the fridge and the other in a warm place for a few hours. The warmer honey should be easier to pour than the honey that has been in the cold fridge.

Why is syrup difficult to pour?

All liquids flow but some flow more easily than others. This is why it is easier to pour water or milk than syrup or honey. The thickness and stickiness of a liquid is called its viscosity. The thicker a liquid, the more viscous it is.

Left: Water flows freely because it is not very viscous.

Right: Milk is more viscous than water.

Sticky syrup is very viscous.

How does water change to ice?

When you take ice cubes out of the fridge, you probably do not stop to think how flowing water has changed to solid ice. Things change from one state of matter to another when they are heated or cooled.

If you heat ice (solid water), it turns into liquid water. This process is called melting. If you heat the liquid further, it will turn into water vapour (gas). This is called evaporation. If water vapour is cooled down, it turns back into liquid water. This is called condensation. If liquid is cooled down further, it turns into solid ice. This is called freezing.

Things change from solids, to liquids, to gases when they are heated because the heat makes their molecules move faster and loosens the bonds between them. They change from gases, to liquids, to solids when they are cooled because the molecules slow down and the bonds get firmer as the heat is taken away.

Different substances change from one state of matter to another at different temperatures. Ice melts at 0° C, which is its melting point. It boils and turns into water vapour at 100° C. This is its boiling point. As the water vapour cools below 100° C, it turns back (condenses) into liquid water again. Water turns to ice at 0° C. This is its freezing point.

How do ice cubes cool drinks down?

If you put ice cubes into a drink, they cool it down as they melt. This is because the ice uses heat energy in order to melt. It takes this energy from the drink itself and so the drink becomes cooler. The drink also gets cooler because of the cold water produced as the ice melts.

As the ice warms up, it melts into water.

Ice cubes are cooling these drinks down.

What makes a fridge keep things cold?

There is a system of pipes inside a fridge which carries a special chemical liquid around it. As the liquid passes through the inside of the fridge, it changes to vapour. To do this, it uses energy in the form of heat. The heat is taken from the air around the pipes, which in turn draws it from the food inside the fridge, cooling everything down. The heat is passed out at the back of the fridge. If you put your hand near the back of your fridge, you should feel heat coming from it.

Stocking up the fridge.

? Did you know?

If you put pressure on ice, you raise its freezing point. This means that the outer layer stays liquid for a longer time. This is how ice skates work. As you skate, your weight presses down on the blades and on the ice. This extra pressure stops the ice freezing so that there is a thin film of water under each skate. The water does not grip your skate blades as strongly as ice. So you can skate more easily.

Skaters can move very fast across the ice.

Why does sugar dissolve in a hot drink?

When you put sugar into a hot drink, it disappears quickly and mixes with the liquid. The sugar is dissolved in the liquid. Most solid substances dissolve better in hot liquids than in cold ones. This is because the heat from the hot drink makes the molecules of sugar spread out and move around. The sugar will dissolve even more quickly if you stir the hot drink.

The sugar will dissolve quickly in the coffee, especially if it is stirred.

When you dissolve something in a liquid, you form a solution. So if you dissolve salt in water, you make a salt solution. If a substance is able to dissolve in water, it is called soluble. Salt and sugar are both soluble. If a substance does not dissolve in water, it is called insoluble. Sand is insoluble; so is chalk.

When does water stop dissolving solids?

Start adding some salt to a glass of warm water. There will come a point when no more salt will dissolve in the water. You will see grains of salt sinking to the bottom of the glass because the water cannot hold any more salt. The glass now contains what is called a saturated solution. The hotter the water, the more salt will dissolve in it before the solution becomes saturated. If you leave the solution to cool down, the salt molecules will join up again and you will be able to see the salt crystals once more.

? Did you know?

The sea is a salt solution. Salt is dissolved in the sea water. The saltiest sea water is found in the Red Sea, in the Indian Ocean.

! See for yourself

Try this experiment to see how well different solids dissolve in hot or cold liquids. See how much sugar or salt you can dissolve in warm and then cold water. Add the sugar or salt a teaspoonful at a time. Does it dissolve more quickly in the warm water or the cold water? Does it dissolve more quickly if you stir it? Try other solids such as the ones shown in the picture below.

Try dissolving some of these substances in water: chilli pepper, black pepper, curry powder, flour, sugar, baking powder and coffee granules.

Why are fizzy drinks fizzy?

Gases also dissolve in liquids. Drinks such as lemonade are fizzy because they have carbon dioxide gas dissolved in them. The gas is bubbled into the liquid at the drinks' factory. It is bubbled in under pressure because gases dissolve better at higher pressure. When you take the top off a fizzy drinks' bottle, there is a hiss and fizz as the pressure **decreases** and some of the gas comes out of the liquid.

The gas molecules are spread out throughout the liquid. When they collect together, they form bubbles. If you put a drinking straw into some fizzy lemonade, you will be able to see the bubbles forming on the outside of the straw.

! DON'T see for yourself

Never shake a can or bottle of fizzy drink before you open it. The gas will collect at the top of the container and explode out, which could be dangerous.

Right: Drinks are given their fizz in this bottling factory.

Below: You can see the bubbles in this fizzy drink rising. Some are collecting on the slice of lemon.

How does washing-up liquid get plates clean?

Washing-up liquid works by removing the sticky grease and oil from dirty plates and cutlery, pots and pans. If you hold a greasy plate under a tap, the water will just run off it, leaving the droplets of grease behind. If you add some washing-up liquid to the water, it will take the grease with it. This is because washing-up liquid contains a special substance, called a detergent.

Detergents contain special chemicals. The molecules of these chemicals float around the water in groups. When they come across a globule of grease, they attach themselves to it and lift it off the plate. They surround the grease so that it is trapped and cannot get back on to the plate again. The molecules have long 'tails' which hate water. They bury into the grease and pull it away so that they, too, can get out of the water. Grease is removed faster in hot water. Why do you think this is so? Turn back to page 9 if you cannot guess.

Left: Bubbles of washing-up liquid.

Below: A lot of washing-up liquid has been used to get these glasses and plates clean.

> ## ⚠ See for yourself
>
> Oil and grease do not normally mix in water. If you pour a small amount of cooking oil into a glass of water, you will see that the oil and water will not mix together, even if you give them a good stir. Now add a few drops of washing-up liquid. The detergent should make the oil dissolve in the water.

How do towels get you dry?

When you get out of the bath or shower, you use a towel to dry yourself. But do you know how the towel dries your skin? It is because of a process called capillary action. A towel is made up of lots of fluffy **fibres**. When it comes into contact with water, the water is pulled into the tiny spaces between the fibres. It is sucked into the towel, and away from your skin.

Towelling has a lot of fluffy fibres in it.

> ## ⚠ See for yourself
>
> To see how capillary action works, you will need two clear plastic rulers and a saucer filled with coloured water. You can colour the water with food dye. Hold the rulers close together and stand them in the saucer. You should soon see the water rising slowly between them.

Capillary action also works in plant stems. Here, the flowers have turned blue because blue dye has been sucked up the stems.

What is electricity?

Electricity is a type of energy. We use it to power lots of the things in our homes, such as televisions, electric kettles, computers, hi-fis and lights. Have a look around your house – you might be surprised at how many things need electricity to make them work.

Most offices have a lot of electrical equipment, such as computers and fax machines.

How many electrical gadgets can you see in this kitchen? What are they used for?

Electricity is made by tiny particles, called electrons. These are found inside atoms (see page 7). The electrons carry an electric charge. There are two main types of electricity: static electricity and current electricity.

Why do your clothes crackle when you undress?

Do your clothes ever make a crackling sound when you take them off? Do they sparkle in the dark? Or does your hair crackle when you comb it? This crackling is caused by tiny sparks of electricity, called static electricity. When some types of material rub together, electrons move from one surface to another. The electrons are knocked off the atoms of one surface and then stick on to the atoms of the other. If one surface has many more electrons than the other, some of the electrons jump back on to the other surface again, to balance things out. This is what makes the sparks of electricity.

? Did you know?

Static electricity gets its name because it flashes in one place. It does not flow from place to place, like current electricity (see page 17). Lightning is caused by giant sparks of the same type of static electricity that comes off your clothes.

? Did you know?

Photocopiers use static electricity to make them work. A large drum inside the photocopier attracts ink to it by static electricity. The ink is then transferred to a piece of paper so that it exactly copies the original picture or writing.

The piece of paper will be placed face down on to a sheet of glass on the photocopier.

! See for yourself

Rub a blown-up balloon on your clothes, and place the rubbed side against a wall. The balloon should stick to the wall. This is because electrons jump from your clothes to the balloon, leaving it charged with static electricity. Then, when you hold the balloon against the wall, electrons jump between the two, making them stick together. This works best with man-made materials such as polyester.

This balloon is held on to the wall by static electricity.

What happens when you plug in an electric kettle?

When you plug in and switch on an electric **appliance**, such as a kettle or a radio, electricity flows into it through wires in the wall socket and in the plug. Your kettle can now work. This type of flowing electricity is called current electricity. An electric current can only flow around an unbroken wire, called a circuit. If the circuit is broken, the electricity will not flow.

It is amazing to think that the electricity you use for your kettle is

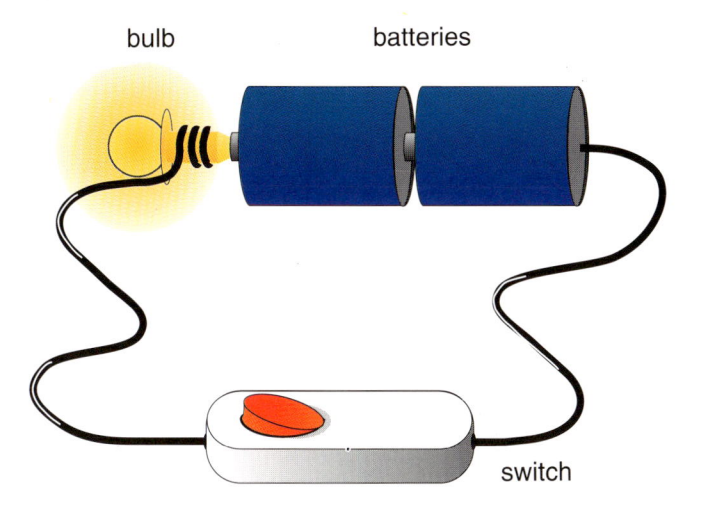

When the switch is turned on, the circuit is complete and the electricity can flow.

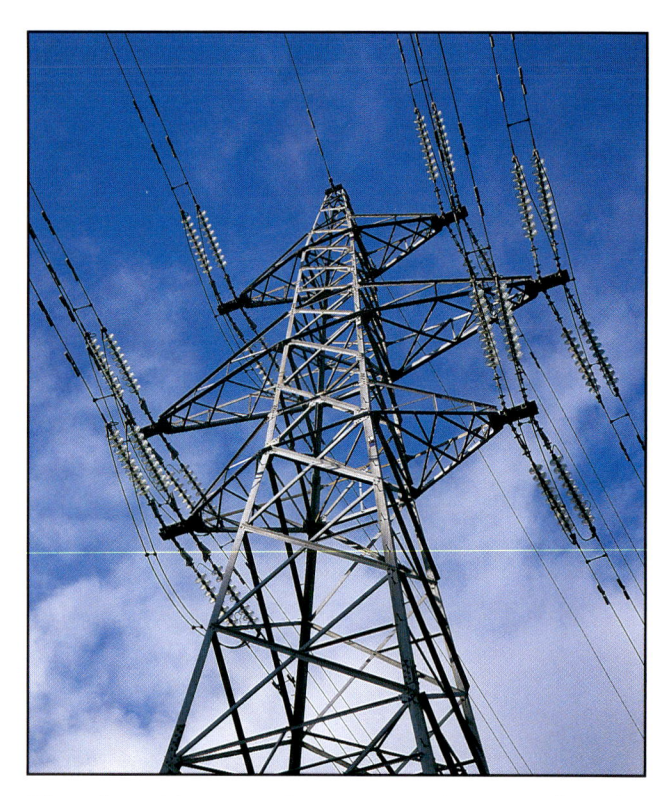

well. When you put the plug in and switch on the socket, you complete the circuit and the electricity can flow. When you switch the socket off, you break the circuit again.

> **? Did you know?**
>
> An electric current is measured in units, called amperes, or amps. The amount of electricity that an appliance such as a kettle uses up in a set time is measured in watts.

Electric cables are often strung along overhead pylons before they go underground.

made in a power station which may be far away from where you live. It travels to your home along wires that are threaded through cables. First, these cables are carried by tall pylons. Then they run underground into your house. Wires carry the electricity into the wall socket. There are wires in the plug as

How does an electric kettle boil water?

When you plug an electric kettle in and switch it on, you complete a circuit. Electricity flows into the kettle where there is a special heater element. This gets hotter and hotter, heating the water inside the kettle until it boils. Most kettles also have a safety device called a circuit breaker. It makes the kettle switch off when the water reaches boiling point.

This is a small petrol-powered generator which can make electricity for the home.

For safety, water must cover the heater element inside the kettle before it is switched on.

⚠️ DON'T see for yourself

Electricity is very useful, but it can also be extremely dangerous. An electric shock can kill. Never play around with plugs or electrical appliances and never use a hairdryer or a kettle if you have got wet hands. Electricity flows through water very easily.

This sign on some electrical appliances warns of the danger of electricity.

What does a battery do?

Torches need electricity to make them work. But you do have to plug them in. They contain their own small stores of electricity in the form of batteries. A battery contains special chemicals. When you switch the torch on and complete the circuit inside it, these chemicals are converted into electrical energy. The battery acts like a pump and pushes the electricity around the circuit to make the light bulb work.

Torches can carry different types of battery.

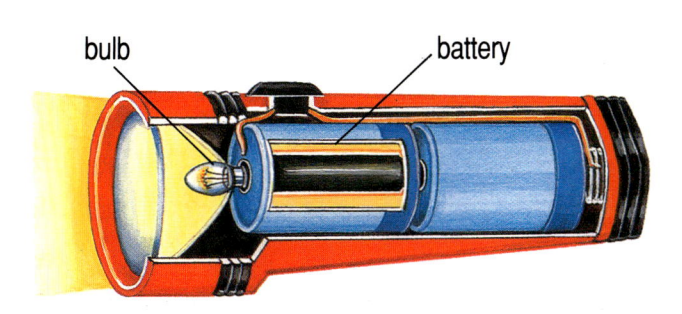

The batteries inside the torch are stores of electricity.

❓ Did you know?

The electricity made by a battery flows one way around a circuit. But the mains electricity, which comes through sockets, changes direction all the time.

How does a telephone work?

Sound is a form of energy. Sounds are made when something **vibrates** and causes the air around it to vibrate as well. The vibrations travel through the air as sound waves, making the sounds that you hear. When you speak, air rushes past your vocal cords in your throat. As your vocal cords vibrate, they make the air around them vibrate as well, so that your voice can be heard. Sound waves travel through the air like ripples through water. Your ears pick up the vibrations caused by the sound waves.

When you want to talk to someone on the telephone, you speak into a mouthpiece. Inside is a microphone, which contains a special device that vibrates as the sound waves hit it. It then turns the sound waves into electrical energy. The electrical signals travel along wires to the telephone exchange. Then they travel along another wire to the person you are calling. In the telephone earpiece, there is a loudspeaker. It contains a device which vibrates as the electrical signals hit it, making the air around it vibrate and produce sound. So the electrical signals are changed back into sound waves, which the person holding the receiver hears as words.

Telephones come in many shapes and sizes.

Thousands of wires inside a telephone exchange.

⚠ See for yourself

To see how sound is caused by vibrating air, try this experiment. You will need a jam jar, a piece of balloon, some shiny foil paper and a torch. Stretch the balloon across the top of the jar and if necessary hold it in place with an elastic band. Stick the foil on top of the balloon. Shine the torch at the foil and speak at it. The reflected beam should make a pattern as you speak.

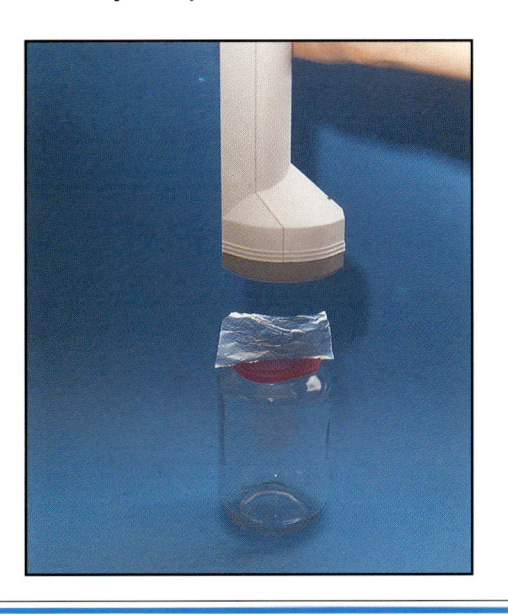

❓ Did you know?

The telephone was invented by Alexander Graham Bell in 1876. Today, there are about 425 million telephones in the world. In the USA, a staggering 422,000 million telephone calls are made each year.

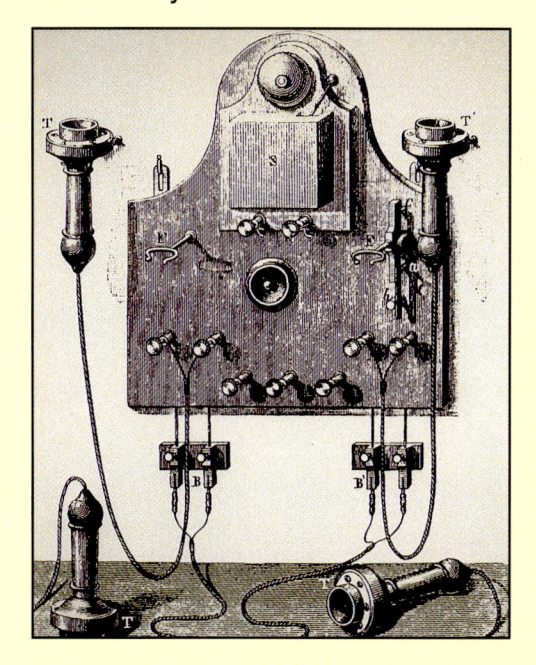

The telephone system developed by Alexander Graham Bell.

⚠ See for yourself

You can make your own simple telephone with two yoghurt pots and a long piece of string. Make a small hole in the base of each pot, poke the ends of the string through and tie a knot so that the string cannot pull through the hole. Keep the string fairly **taut**. You can then speak into one pot, while a friend listens through the other. Your voice will make the air in the pot vibrate, which in turn will make the bottom of the pot vibrate. This will keep pulling and releasing the string, which will make the bottom of the pot at the other end vibrate, causing the air inside the pot to vibrate and produce sound.

Vibrating air produces sound inside the pot.

Why can you see yourself in a mirror?

Light travels in straight lines called light rays. We see things because light rays from the Sun or from electric lights bounce off objects and into our eyes. This is known as reflection. Light behaves a bit like a ball. If it hits something straight on, it bounces straight back off it. If it hits something at an angle, it bounces off at the same angle.

Light rays bounce off a smooth surface better than off a rough surface. A mirror has a very smooth surface which reflects light so well that light bounces straight back off it. Mirrors can be made of glass with a special silver coating on the back, or they can be made of polished metal. When you look at yourself in a mirror, light bounces off you and on to the mirror. It then bounces straight back into your eyes. This is how you see your reflection.

Why do you look the wrong way round in a mirror?

Light is bounced straight off a mirror, in exactly the same way as it hit it, because a mirror has such a smooth surface. This is how you see an exact reflection of yourself. The reflected rays make the parts of your body appear in exactly the same positions as they really are. So your head appears at the top, your feet at the bottom, your left hand on the left and your right hand on the right. But the **image** looks reversed because you are facing it.

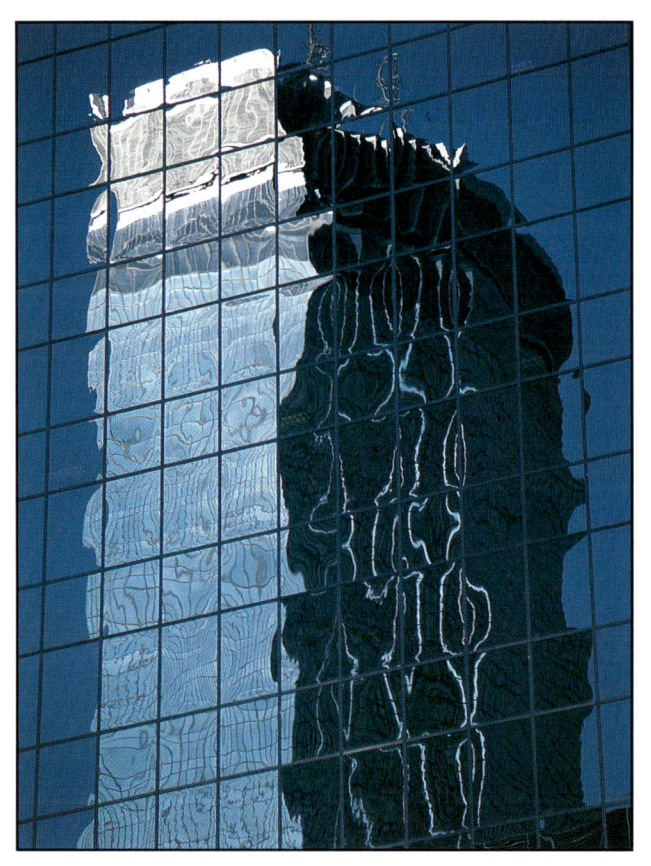

A reflection of a building in the mirrored windows of a tower block.

This woman's right arm is reflected as her left arm in the mirror.

❓ Did you know?

Light is the fastest thing known in the Universe. It travels at a speed of 300,000 kilometres a second.

❗ See for yourself

If you look at some writing in the mirror, it looks the wrong way round. Look at this piece of mirror writing. Can you read what it says? Now look at it in a mirror. You will be able to see it the right way round. Which letters and numbers look the same in a mirror as they do when they are written?

qOTƧ

❓ Did you know?

Ambulances use mirror writing so that car drivers can see the word 'AMBULANCE' the right way round when they look in their driving mirrors. In an emergency, they can then allow the ambulance to drive quickly past them.

ƎƆNAJUBMA

How can you see yourself in the window at night?

During the day, people passing outside your window can look in and see you through the glass. This is because most of the light that hits you, bounces off you and goes out of the window into their eyes. But some of the light that hits you is reflected back into the room by the window.

During the day, you cannot see this reflected light because it is swamped by the large amounts of light coming from outside. At night, though, there is not any light coming from outside. So you can see the light reflected from the window. The glass acts like a mirror, allowing you to see a reflection of yourself.

The darker parts of the glass in this café window act like a mirror.

How does a pencil make a mark on paper?

Have you ever wondered how the writing stays on a piece of paper when you write with a pencil? Inside a pencil, there is a thin stick of a black substance, called graphite. We also call it pencil 'lead', although it has nothing to do with the metal called lead.

Graphite is made up of layers of tiny particles. As you write, you drag the pencil across the paper. A force called friction pulls the layers of graphite off the pencil and on to the paper. So the writing you see is actually a thin layer of graphite.

Friction is a force which makes two surfaces grip each other as they rub together. The rougher the surface, the more friction there is. If you try writing on a very shiny surface, you will find that it does not work as well because there is less friction.

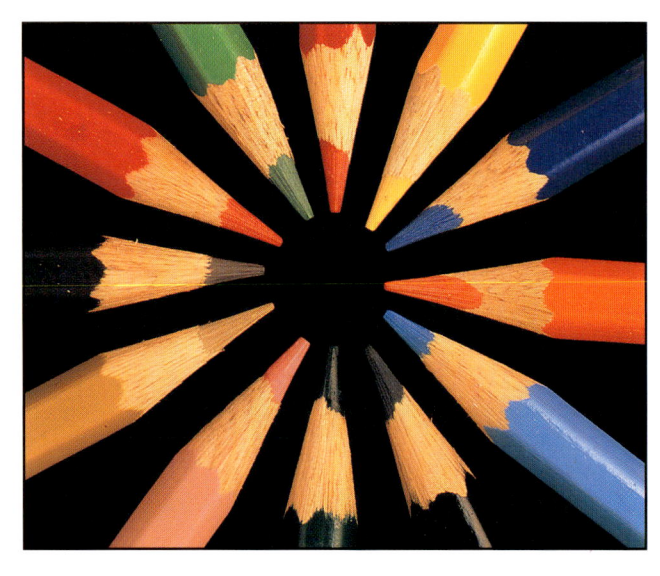

Coloured pencils are made from graphite and clay. 'Lead' pencils also have clay in them.

? Did you know?

Graphite is a form of **carbon**. Diamond is also a form of carbon. Graphite is quite soft but diamond is the hardest natural substance known.

Diamond can only be cut with diamond.

? Did you know?

Some 'lead' pencils are softer and darker than others. This is because they contain more graphite than the harder pencils, which have more clay. Letters and numbers on the side of a pencil show how soft and dark it is. H means that the pencil is hard and pale; B is soft and dark; HB is hard but dark.

? Did you know?

If you rub your hands together, the friction between them makes them feel warmer.

How does a magnet pick up pins?

If you spill some pins or needles on the floor, the best thing to use to pick them up is a magnet. The magnet pulls the pins towards it and makes them easier to collect.

A magnet produces an invisible force called a magnetic force. This attracts certain things towards it. It attracts iron or steel objects, such as pins, but not objects made of most other metals, paper, plastic, or rubber. The magnetic force works in an area around the magnet. This area is called the magnetic field. It is strongest at the far ends, or the north and south poles of the magnet. More pins will stick to the poles than to the rest of the magnet. There is a magnet in your fridge door which helps it to stick shut.

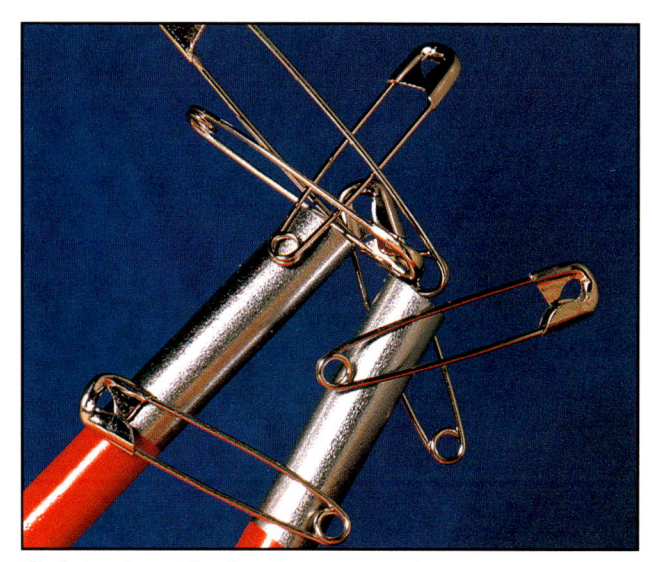

Safety pins clinging to a magnet.

? Did you know?

The Earth itself is a giant magnet. Its magnetic field reaches about 80,000 kilometres out into Space.

! See for yourself

Magnets have been used in compasses for thousands of years, because a magnet will always point to the north if it can swing freely. You can make a simple compass with a needle and some thread. Stroke the needle with a magnet 20 times, always stroking in the same direction. This will make the needle magnetic as well. Tie the thread around the middle of the needle and let it hang so that it is well balanced. The needle will swing and point to the north.

You can make a simple compass with a needle, some thread and a magnet.

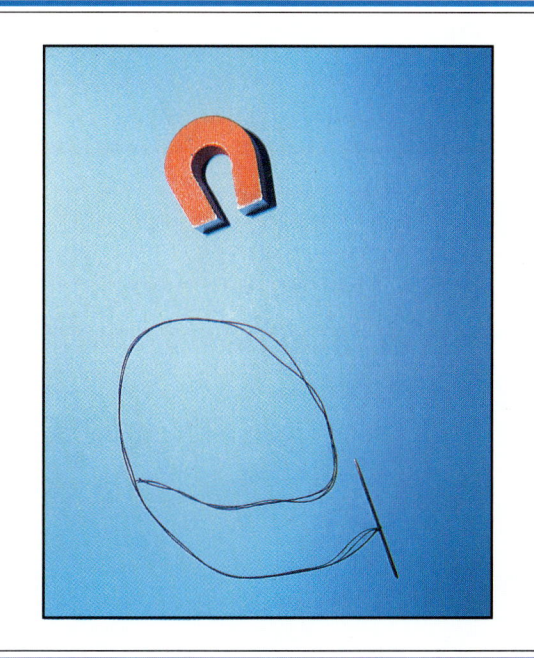

What is the best way of cracking a nut?

We use lots of different machines and tools around our homes. Many of them make life easier for us. Some, such as washing machines and television sets, are very complicated. They use electricity to make them work. But other machines, such as nutcrackers, are much simpler. They use a person's own muscle power to make them work. But it is their design which makes cracking nuts easy.

Nutcrackers are examples of levers, which are some of the simplest types of machine. Some levers are used to move things. The simplest type is a long rod, which is propped up on a set point, called a fulcrum. The lever is used to move a heavy object, called a load. In order to do this, you have to push or pull the lever. This is called the effort. In a lever, the load is closer to the fulcrum than the effort is. You have to move the effort a long way to move the load a short way.

Hard nut shells can be cracked with little effort when nutcrackers are used.

Nutcrackers do not move loads, but they do make it much easier for you to break open nuts with hard shells. The nutcrackers are hinged at one end. This is the fulcrum. The nut is the load and the force you apply on the handles is the effort.

A simple lever

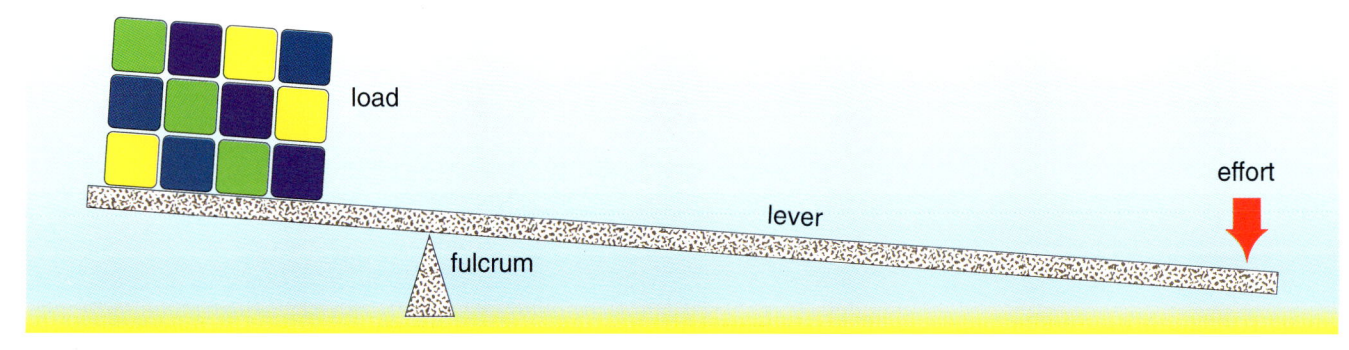

A small amount of effort can move a heavy load.

▎ See for yourself

It is easier to move things with a longer lever. Try to **prise** the lid off a tin with a coin. Then try with the handle of a spoon. Which lever works best?

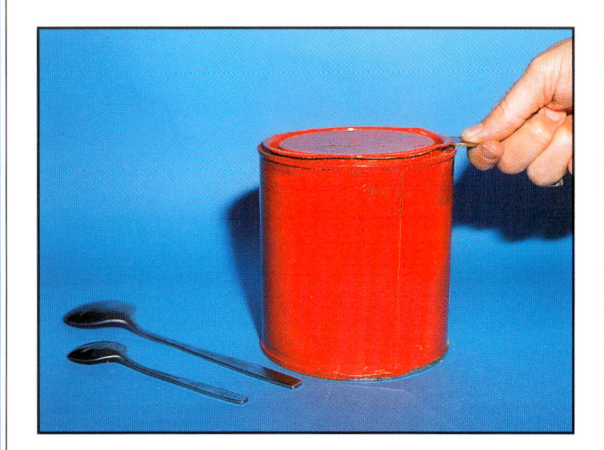

Which of these three levers will help best to open the tin?

❓ Did you know?

There are lots of levers both indoors and outdoors. Many garden tools such as shears, wheelbarrows, forks and spades are levers.

A gardener using a fork as a lever to lift soil.

How do scissors cut paper?

Scissors are a type of lever. If you use the scissors to cut through paper, then the paper is the load. The fulcrum is where the two blades of the scissors are joined. You apply the effort at the handles. When you squeeze both of the handles towards each other, this pushes the blades together and they cut the paper. The closer to the fulcrum you put the paper, the easier it is to cut.

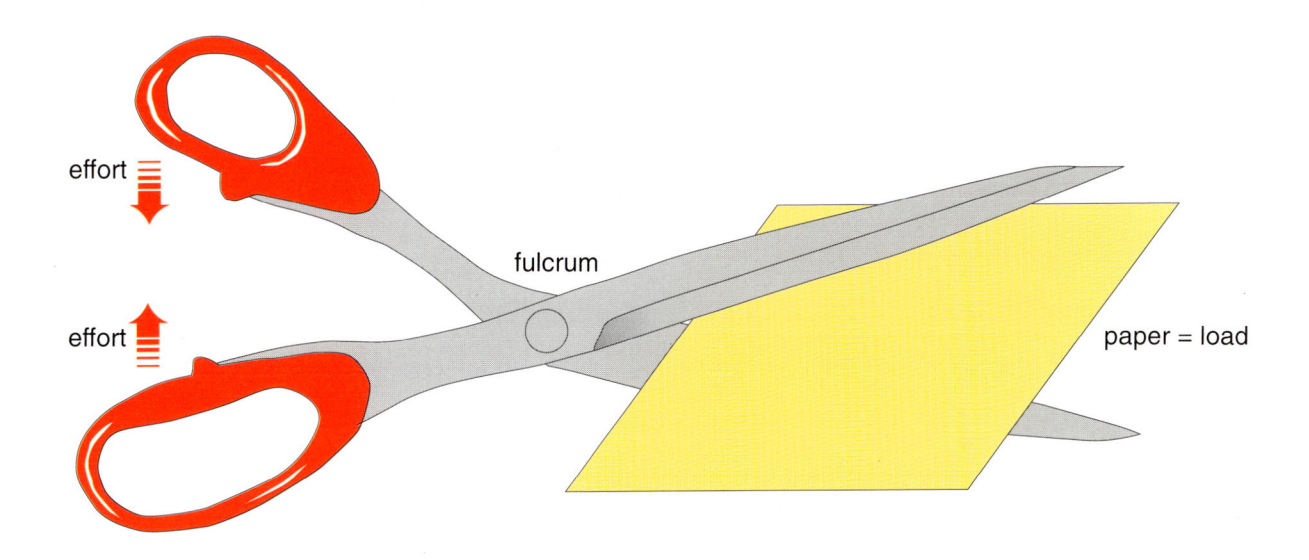

To cut the paper, effort is applied to both handles.

How do clothes get dry in a spin dryer?

Things only move because there is a force pushing or pulling them along. They cannot move by themselves. You have already seen how some forces work, such as friction (see page 26), magnetism (see page 27) and gravity (see page 28). Forces can also change the speed at which something is moving. When things speed up, they are said to accelerate. When they slow down, they are said to decelerate.

If an object is pushed or pulled by a force, it starts moving in a straight line. But it can only change direction or go faster or slower if a different force acts on it. Things that move in a circle, such as wheels or spinning tops, are constantly changing direction in order to spin. They are also pulled by another force, called the centripetal force. This pulls the object towards the centre of the circle so that it keeps going round and round.

If you swing a bucketful of water round fast enough, the water will stay in the bucket. This is because of centripetal force. It keeps the water going round in a circle. If you do not swing the bucket fast enough, the water will spill out.

Centripetal force is used in spin dryers to force water out of wet clothes. The dryer spins wet clothes round very fast in a drum to get them dry. As the drum keeps spinning, the clothes inside it keep spinning too. The water is forced from them as they get flattened against the drum. It then flows out through hundreds of small holes in the drum's walls, and flows outside through a drainage pipe.

Dry clothes have stuck to the sides of the drum with the force of the spin.

❓ Did you know?

If you swing something round in a circle, then let go, the object will always fly off in a straight line. Discus throwers and hammer throwers turn round to gather speed, but when they let go, the discus or hammer move in a straight line.

A hammer thrower spins round several times, getting faster and faster, before letting go of the hammer.

❓ Did you know?

A roller coaster ride at a fair works by centripetal force. As the cars go round very fast in circles, centripetal force acts on them and presses the passengers back into their seats, so they never fall out.

The passengers are forced right back into their seats as they whirl round on the roller coaster.

❗ See for yourself

There are several ways of seeing how centripetal force works. You could try spinning a bucketful of water round and round – but do this outside in the summer, and be prepared to get wet! Another experiment is to tie a cork to a piece of string and whirl it round you. Can you feel the force keeping the cork going round in a circle? Now let go. The cork will fly off in a straight line. Be careful when you do this – make sure you have plenty of room and that no one is close enough to get hit when the cork flies off.

What is fire?

When you see a candle flame or the flame on a gas cooker, you are watching a **chemical reaction**. Fire is very important in our lives. People cook with it, keep warm by it and use it to produce energy and power. But what is fire and why do things burn?

Fire is the light and heat which are given off when something burns. Things burst into flames when they reach a high enough temperature, called their ignition temperature. They burn because they **react** with oxygen in the air. Once something is alight, it makes so much heat of its own that it continues to burn.

A burning gas flame.

A fire needs three things to keep it burning – fuel, heat and oxygen. If one

The flames of this house fire will be put out with jets of water. This takes the heat away.

of these things is taken away, the fire will go out. So, spraying fires with water takes the heat away and puts the fire out. Some fire extinguishers use foam to put fires out. The foam is sprayed on to the fire, smothering it and cutting off its oxygen supply. Foam is always used to smother and put out fires involving oil or petrol. Small foam extinguishers can be kept in the kitchen in case of fire.

All chemical reactions produce new materials. Burning produces ash and soot. It can also produce dangerous fumes. The scientific name for burning is combustion.

Why is a flame hot?

When a candle burns, it produces heat energy which makes it feel hot. It also produces light energy, which is why we can see the flame and why a candle lights up a room.

When the wick of a candle is lit, the heat melts the wax around it.

? Did you know?

Matches are often used for lighting fires. They work by friction (see page 26). When you strike a match on the side of a matchbox, the friction between the match and the box produces heat. This heat makes special chemicals in the matchhead burst into flames. The chemicals react with oxygen in the air and keep burning until you blow out the fire. Never play around with matches – they can be very dangerous.

? Did you know?

Rust is a chemical reaction as well. Things made of iron go rusty if they get wet or are left outside for a long time. The iron reacts with oxygen in the air, making a new brown material called rust. Many knives and forks are made of steel, which contains iron. But they do not go rusty because they also contain another metal called chromium, which protects them. This type of steel is called stainless steel.

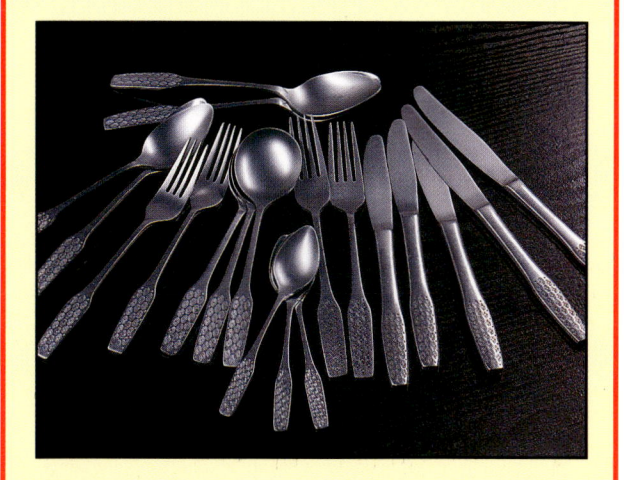

These knives, forks and spoons will not rust because they are made of stainless steel.

Why does baking powder make cakes rise?

When you bake a cake, you often add some baking powder to make the cake rise. Baking powder is made of a chemical called sodium hydrogencarbonate. It is also known as sodium bicarbonate or bicarbonate of soda. When it is heated it gives off carbon dioxide gas. When you mix the ingredients of a cake and put them in the oven, you are in fact bringing about a chemical reaction. The heat releases bubbles of carbon dioxide from the baking powder, making your cake light and fluffy.

How does yeast make bread rise?

You can easily buy packets of dried yeast from a shop. But did you know that yeast is actually a type of fungus, belonging to the same group as mushrooms, toadstools and moulds? It is used in bread-making because, like baking powder, it gives off carbon dioxide. This makes the bread rise. Yeast contains certain chemicals, called enzymes. When bread is made, these enzymes react with sugar to break it down into carbon dioxide and other products.

Right: Cakes rise well when baking powder is used.

Below: These loaves have risen and are ready to be baked.

⚠️ See for yourself

The best way of seeing how yeast works is to bake your own loaf of bread. You will need to ask an adult to help you.

1 Mix 2 teaspoonfuls of dried yeast with 1 teaspoonful of sugar in a mugful of warm water. Leave the mixture to stand for a few minutes until it becomes frothy. The froth is made up of bubbles of carbon dioxide.

2 Now mix 250 grams of strong bread flour with 2 teaspoonfuls of salt and a teaspoonful of butter.

3 Add the yeast mixture and mix the whole thing together with your hands to form a dough. Knead it thoroughly, constantly pulling the dough apart with the palms of your hands and then folding it back again into a lump. This spreads the yeast evenly through the mixture.

4 Then cover the dough with a teacloth and leave it in a warm place for an hour. As the yeast continues to react, it will make the dough rise.

5 Knead the dough again, then place it in a greased loaf tin and let it rise once more.

6 Bake the dough in a hot oven (220 °C) for about 20 minutes or until the loaf sounds hollow when you tap it. Leave it to cool, then eat it!

Kneading soft bread dough.

The frothy yeast will be poured into the flour.

Why does food go mouldy?

Another type of fungus, called a mould, makes food go bad. It sometimes grows on old, stale bread or overripe fruit. Mould is made of tiny threads called hyphae. These spread all over the food, sucking the goodness out of it. They appear as a fluffy green or white covering. Some types of mould are used to treat many illnesses. Moulds are also put into some cheeses, such as blue cheeses, to make them tastier.

See for Yourself! Indoor Science Quiz

Now that you have read this chapter, you could test yourself with these questions.

Questions
1. What three forms are known as the three states of matter?
2. How many molecules are in one grain of sand?
3. What are the particles of an atom called?
4. Why do most solid substances dissolve better in hot liquids than they do in cold ones?
5. What are the tiny particles that make electricity called?
6. What are the two main types of electricity?
7. What type of electricity is used when you turn on a kettle?
8. How does electricity travel from a power station into your home?
9. What is an electrical current measured in?
10. Does the electricity made by a battery flow one way or does it change direction?
11. Are light rays better at bouncing off of a smooth or a rough surface?
12. How fast does light travel?
13. What is the thin stick of black substance inside a pencil called?
14. What is friction?
15. What types of objects will a magnet attract?
16. Where on a magnet is the magnetic field the strongest?
17. What three things does a fire need to be able to keep burning?
18. What is the scientific name for burning?
19. What is the name of the chemicals found in yeast?
20. What is the name of the tiny threads that spread over food and appear as a fluffy green or white covering?

Answers
Look back to find the answers on these pages.

Question	Page	Question	Page	Question	Page	Question	Page
1	128	6	136	11	142	16	145
2	129	7	137	12	143	17	150
3	129	8	138	13	144	18	150
4	130	9	138	14	144	19	152
5	136	10	139	15	145	20	153

SCIENCE
QUESTIONS & ANSWERS

Outdoor Science

Anita Ganeri

Acknowledgements

Page 159 - (top left) Frank Lane Picture Agency, (bottom right) Robert Harding Picture Library; page 160 - (top) Robert Carr, Bruce Coleman Limited, (bottom) Tony Craddock, Science Photo Library; page 161 - (top left) John Cancalosi, Bruce Coleman Limited, (bottom left) Mark Boulton, Bruce Coleman Limited, (right) William Smithey Jr, Planet Earth Pictures; page 162 - (left) Anthony King, (right) Sally Morgan, Ecoscene; page 163 - (top left) N, A, Callow, Robert Harding Picture Library, (bottom left) Anthony King; page 165 - (top) Anna Zuckerman, Bruce Coleman Limited, (bottom) Anthony King; page 167 - Zefa; page 168 - Andra Pradesh, The Hutchison Library; page 169 - (left) Colin Molyneux, The Image Bank, (right) Norman Tomalin, Bruce Coleman Limited; page 170 Alvis Upitis, The Image Bank; page 171 - (left) David Parker, Science Photo Library, (right) C, Newton, Frank Lane Picture Agency; page 172 - Zefa; page 173 - (left) Robert Harding Picture Library, (right) John Wells, Science Photo Library; page 174 - Robert Harding Picture Library; page 175 - Eric and David Hoskins, Frank Lane Picture Agency; page 176 - Jules Cowan, Bruce Coleman Limited; page 177 - Sally Morgan, Ecoscene; page 178 - (top) K, E, Deckart, Zefa, (bottom) Sally Morgan, Ecoscene: page 179 - (top left) Christer Fredriksson, Bruce Coleman Limited, (bottom right) Robert Harding Picture Library; page 180 - (left) John Sanford, Science Photo Library; page 181 - (left) Ronald Royer, Science Photo Library, (right) M, Newman, Frank Lane Picture Agency; page 182 - Anthony King: page 183 - (top left) NASA, Bruce Coleman Limited, (bottom right) NASA, Science Photo Library,

Contents

Why do we need the Sun?	**158**
• How hot is the Sun?	**158**
• How does the Sun's heat reach us?	**159**
How can we use the Sun's energy?	**160**
• How do we collect the Sun's energy?	**161**
How do shadows form?	**162**
• Why is some shadow pale?	**162**
• Why do some shadows change length?	**163**
Why is night dark?	**164**
Why do we have summer and winter?	**166**
• What is a leap year?	**167**
Why do puddles dry up in the Sun?	**168**
• Why do we hang washing out to dry?	**169**
• Why can we see our breath on a cold day?	**169**
What makes it rain?	**170**
• What are rainbows?	**171**
• Why is the sky blue?	**171**
• Why is Space black?	**171**
What is air made of?	**172**
• What is the atmosphere?	**172**
• What is the ozone layer?	**173**
What is lightning?	**174**
• Why does thunder boom?	**175**
Why do leaves fall downwards?	**176**
• Why do plant roots grow downwards?	**177**
• Why does rain fall faster than snow?	**178**
• How do parachutes work?	**179**
How far away are the stars?	**180**
• How many stars are there in Space?	**181**
• Why do stars shine at night?	**181**
Why does the Moon seem to change shape?	**182**
• What is the dark side of the Moon?	**183**
• What are the dark patches on the Moon?	**183**
Outdoor Science Quiz	**184**

Why do we need the Sun?

The Sun is just one of millions of stars in our **galaxy**, the Milky Way. It is just under 150 million kilometres away from the Earth – a very long way indeed. But even at this distance, the Sun is vitally important to all of us. Without the Sun's heat and light, nothing could live or grow on Earth. The Earth would be too cold for anything to survive. There would be no light for plants to make their own food, so there would be nothing for us to eat.

How hot is the Sun?

The Sun is incredibly hot. Its surface temperature is 6,000 °C. At the Sun's core, or centre, the temperature reaches an amazing 16 million °C. This is where the Sun's heat and light is made. Like other stars, the Sun is made up mainly of hydrogen gas. It is so hot in the centre of the Sun that atoms (tiny particles) of hydrogen bump into each other and form another gas, called helium. As

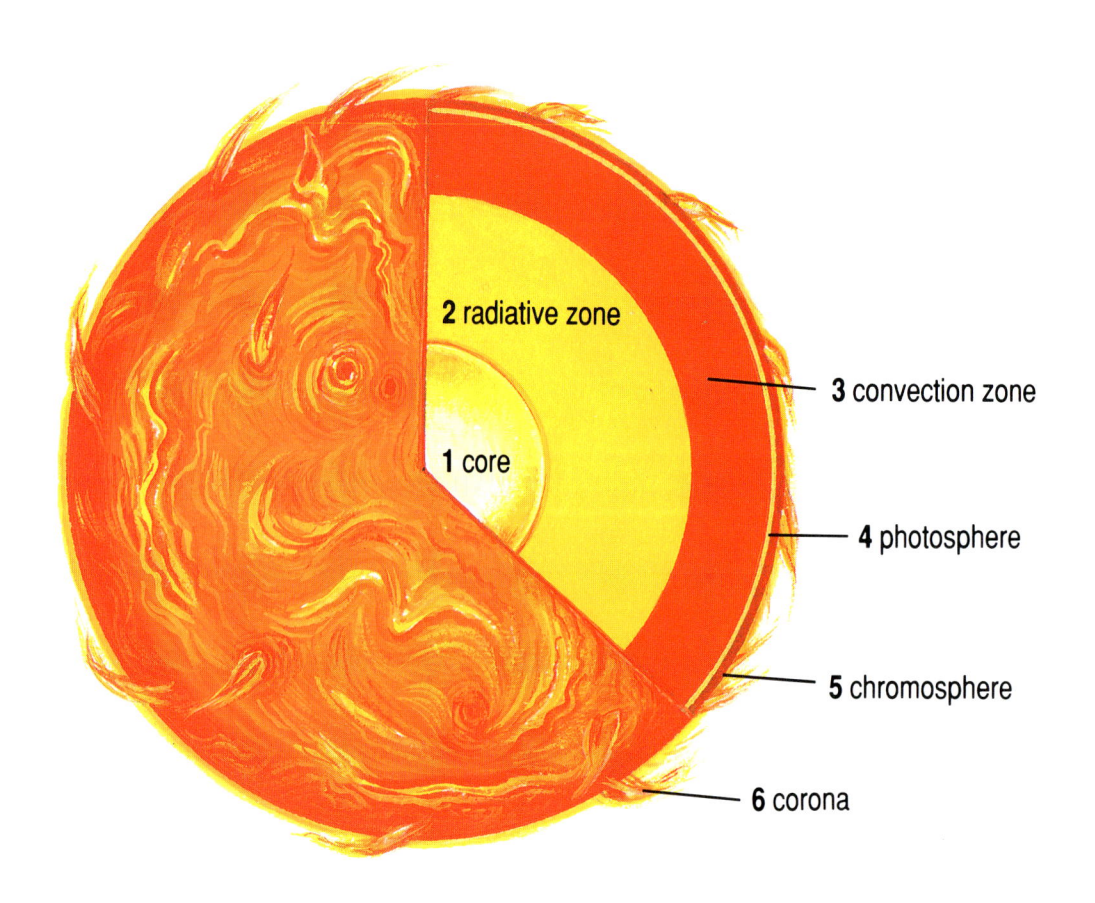

1 core
2 radiative zone
3 convection zone
4 photosphere
5 chromosphere
6 corona

1 energy made here
2 radiation of energy from core
3 energy carried away from core
4 visible layer of Sun
5 rosy ring of gases around Sun
6 outermost envelope of gases

The different layers and areas of the Sun.

this happens, huge amounts of heat and light energy are given off. The Sun burns up about 700 million tonnes of hydrogen every second during these **reactions**. Luckily for us, the Sun has enough hydrogen left to keep shining for at least another 5,000 million years.

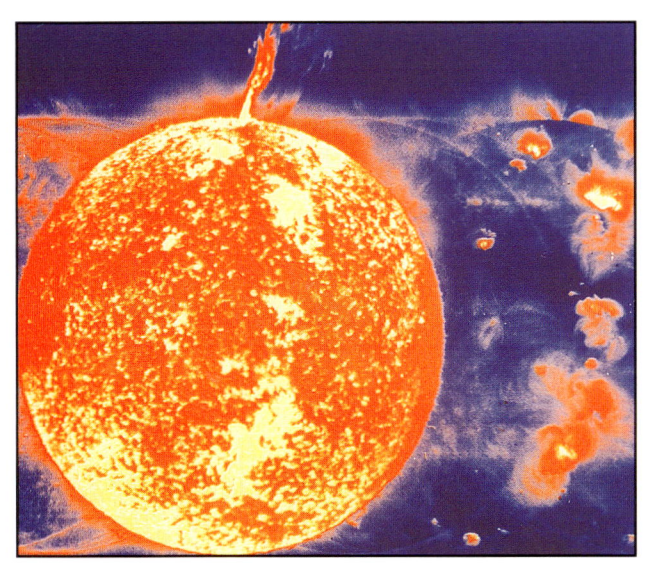

The Sun is mainly made up of hydrogen.

Deserts are baked dry by the Sun.

> **! Don't see for yourself**
>
> NEVER look directly at the Sun, or through binoculars, a telescope or even sunglasses. It will damage your eyes and could even make you go blind.

How does the Sun's heat reach us?

The Sun's heat travels through Space and takes about 8.5 minutes to reach the Earth. Heat travels in several different ways – by convection, conduction and radiation, depending on what it has to travel through.

Heat from the Sun travels to Earth by radiation. This means that it travels in invisible rays, just like the rays of heat coming from a fire. This is the only way that heat can travel through Space. Convection is how heat travels through liquids or gases, such as the sea and the air. Conduction is the way heat travels through solids. Space has no air. It is also empty so heat cannot travel by either of these methods.

Less than a millionth of the heat that leaves the Sun reaches the Earth. Some heat is lost on its way through Space and some will be **reflected** back into Space. The rest is **absorbed** by the Earth's **atmosphere**. There is no atmosphere around the Moon, so it feels much hotter there.

> **? Did you know?**
>
> A piece of the Sun's surface about the size of your thumbnail shines as brightly as at least 200,000 candles.

> **? Did you know?**
>
> The Sun is about 1.4 million kilometres wide. It is big enough to swallow up 1.3 million Earths.

How can we use the Sun's energy?

Each day, the Earth receives enormous amounts of energy from the Sun. This reaches us in the form of heat and light. We need this heat and light in order to survive (see pages 6 and 9). But scientists are now looking at other ways of using all this energy.

Everything we do or use needs energy to make it work. We get our energy from food. Cars get energy from petrol. Televisions, fridges, kettles and computers get their energy from the electricity supplied to them.

Most of this electricity comes from oil, gas and coal, which are burnt in huge power stations. But stocks of these fuels are running out. They also produce gases such as sulphur dioxide, which pollutes the air and causes problems such as acid rain. If we could turn some of the Sun's energy into electricity, we would have a power supply which is not only cleaner but which would never run out. So, how do we go about it?

The white haze hanging over the town is polluted air.

❓ Did you know?

Scientists have worked out that the amount of solar energy reaching the Earth each year is 15,000 times the amount of energy people on Earth use each year.

The Odeillo solar power station in the Pyrenees mountains, France.

How do we collect the Sun's energy?

The Sun's energy is called solar energy. There are two ways of using it. In many hot countries, such as Greece and Israel, people have water-filled panels on the roofs of their houses. During the day, the Sun heats up the water and it is piped around the house. It can be used for baths, showers and washing the dishes.

Another way of collecting the Sun's energy is with solar cells. They turn solar energy straight into electricity. Most solar cells are made of a substance called silicon. They used to be very expensive but you can now buy them quite easily. You might already have some if you own a solar-powered calculator or watch. These have solar cells inside them.

Right: A close-up of some solar cells.

Below: This solar panel in Kenya supplies hot water for washing.

? Did you know?

Cars of the future may use the Sun's energy instead of petrol to make them go. People have already begun experimenting with solar-powered cars. In 1982, a solar-powered car, called *The Quiet Achiever*, travelled right across Australia. Solar cells on the car's body collected the Sun's energy and turned it into electricity.

A type of space-age solar car.

? Did you know?

There are plans to build solar power-stations in Space, where the Sun shines all the time. Most Space satellites are already solar-powered.

? Did you know?

The Ancient Greeks knew about solar heating over 2,500 years ago. They built houses with extra-thick walls. These absorbed lots of heat during the day and released it again at night to keep the houses warm.

How do shadows form?

Light travels in rays which go in straight lines. The light rays cannot bend to go round objects. They can only pass straight through objects which are transparent, like glass. Objects that only allow a little light to pass through are called translucent. Most objects are opaque. This means that light cannot pass through them at all. When light shines on an opaque object, a shadow forms on the other side of the object where light cannot reach. Your body is opaque too. When the sunlight shines on you, you cast a shadow.

Why is some shadow pale?

The darkest shadow forms when light shines straight on to an object from a single point. The type of shadow formed behind the object is called umbra. If light hits the object at an angle, or from more than one point, a paler shadow forms a rim around the dark umbra. This lighter shadow is known as penumbra.

! See for yourself

To see how shadows form, make your own shadow pictures. Shine a torch at a wall. Put your hand out near the wall, so that the torch beam shines on your hand. Make a rabbit shadow or a bird.

A bird shadow has formed.

! See for yourself

To make umbra and penumbra, hold your hand underneath a torch beam. You should see very dark shadow, or umbra, in the middle. Around the edge there should be a lighter area of shadow, the penumbra.

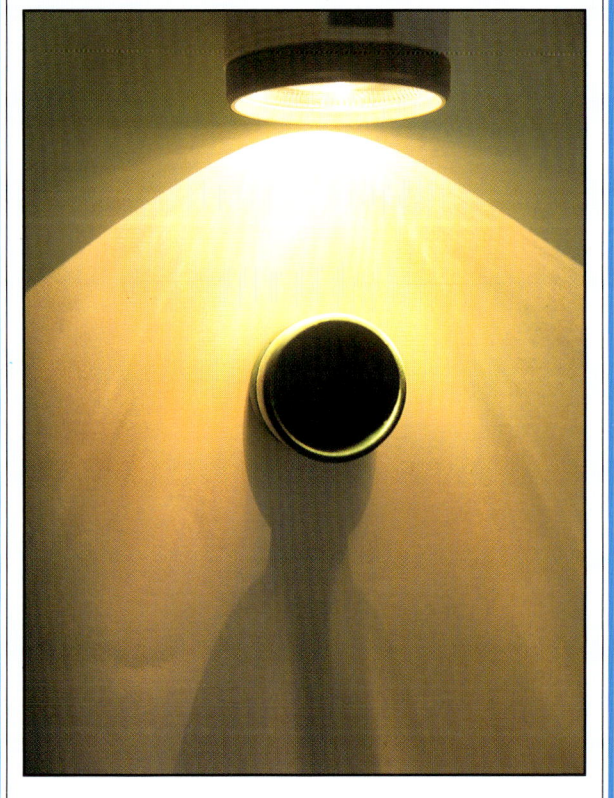

Thin umbra is inside the wide penumbra.

Why do shadows change length?

The size and shape of a shadow change with the size and position of the source of light. The length of the shadow you cast on the ground changes throughout the day. This is because the Sun is higher or lower in the sky at different times of the day. Your shadow is longer in the morning or evening, when the Sun is low in the sky. It is shorter at midday, when the Sun is high in the sky.

Long shadows form in the morning and evening.

Midday shadows are short.

See for yourself

You can use shadows to tell the time. As the Sun seems to change position during the day, the shadow it casts moves as well. On a sundial, the shadows point to hour markings. You can make your own, simple sundial using a stick and a piece of white card.

On a sunny day, lay the card on the ground and push the stick through the middle of it. Weight the corners of the card down to keep it flat. Mark the position of the shadow on the card every hour. Start early in the morning for the best results. On the next sunny day, replace your sundial in the same position and you will be able to tell the time.

Did you know

Sometimes the Moon is blocked out by the Earth's shadow. This is called a lunar eclipse. It happens when the Earth lies between the Moon and the Sun in a straight line.

Why is night dark?

The Sun cannot reach all parts of our Earth at the same time. This is why we are sometimes in darkness and at other times in light. The Earth and the other planets in our Solar System orbit, or travel around, the Sun. As the Earth travels around the Sun, it also spins on its axis. This is an imaginary line running down the middle of the Earth from the North Pole to the South Pole. The Earth takes one year to orbit the Sun once, and it takes 24 hours to spin round once on its axis.

The Sun shines on the side of the Earth facing it. Places on this side have daylight. No light reaches the other side, so places there are dark. As the Earth spins on its axis, the place where you live moves from light into darkness once every 24 hours. This gives you day and night.

? Did you know?

A day on Earth is 24 hours long. But a day on Venus lasts for 243 Earth days. This is the time it takes Venus to spin round once on its axis. On Jupiter, though, a day is just 9.9 Earth hours long.

? Did you know?

You cannot feel the Earth spinning on its axis because everything in the Earth, including you, is moving at the same speed.

As the Earth spins on its axis, different places face the Sun at different times. This gives us day and night.

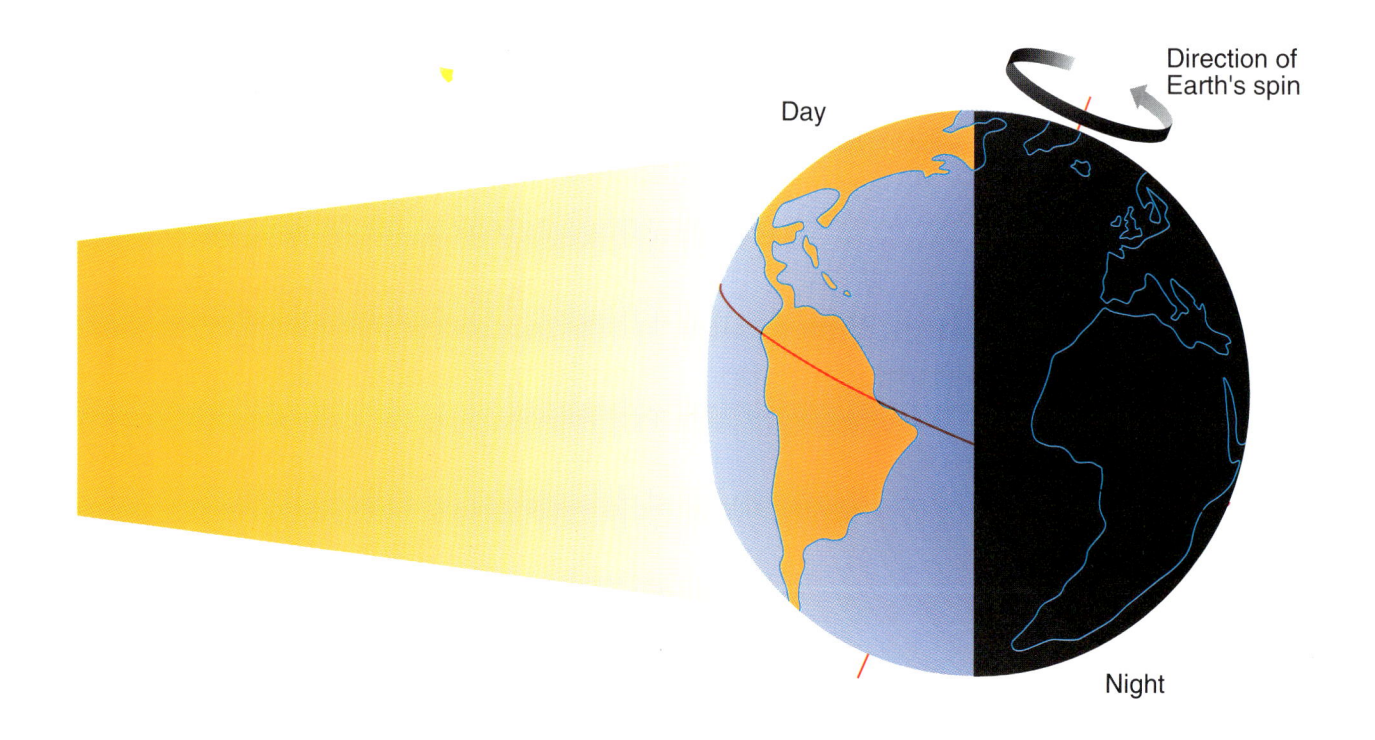

? Did you know?

The North Pole is light for 24 hours a day in June and July. It is known as the 'Land of the midnight Sun'. At the same time of year, the South Pole is in darkness for 24 hours each day. In December and January everything changes round. The South Pole has continuous daylight and the North Pole has continuous night.

Midnight in Antarctica and it's still light.

! See for yourself

Try this simple experiment to see how the Earth's spin gives us day and night. You will need a torch for the Sun. Use an apple or orange for the Earth and skewer it carefully with a stick or knitting needle so that you can hold it and move it around easily. Mark the **Equator** round the centre of the Earth. Hold up the stick, and turn the Earth anti-clockwise, tilting it on its axis. Ask a friend to shine the torch on the fruit. You will see how different parts of the Earth move into the light to give day, then out of the light to give night.

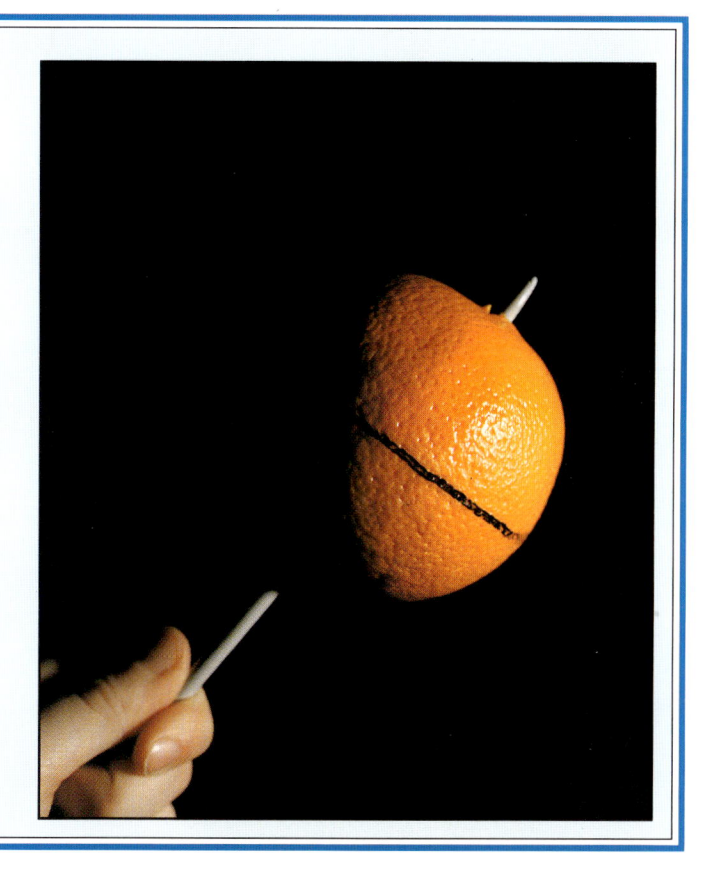

? Did you know?

The Earth spins in an anti-clockwise direction. As it spins, the Sun seems to move across the sky, rising in the east and setting in the west. In fact, the Sun does not move at all.

? Did you know?

In the **northern hemisphere**, summer begins on 21 June. This is the longest day of the year. Winter begins on 21 December. This is the shortest day of the year.

Why do we have summer and winter?

The seasons change as different parts of the Earth lean towards or away from the Sun. The Earth is tilted on its axis, which means that it leans slightly to one side, at an angle. As the Earth travels around the Sun, its tilt makes the Poles take turns in leaning towards the Sun and getting more heat and light. This is what causes the seasons.

When the North Pole leans towards the Sun, the northern hemisphere gets closer to the Sun and has summer. The days are warm and sunny.

Meanwhile, the **southern hemisphere** leans away from the Sun and has winter. The days are gloomy and cold. When the South Pole leans towards the Sun, the northern hemisphere has winter and the southern hemisphere has summer. In between winter and summer the hemispheres have spring or autumn.

Places near the Equator do not have seasons, though. They are never tilted away from the Sun, so they are always very hot.

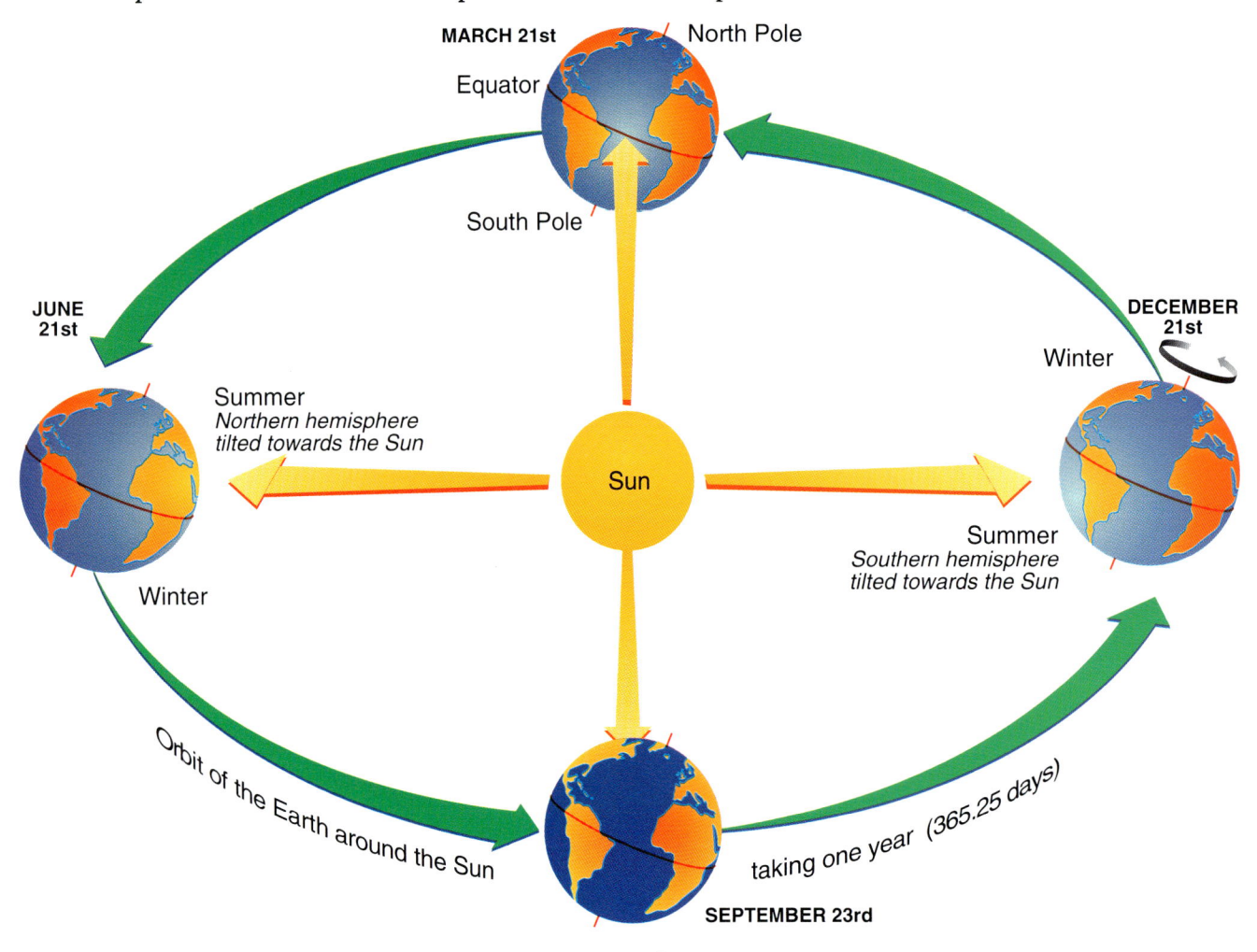

MARCH 21st — North Pole, Equator, South Pole

JUNE 21st — Summer *Northern hemisphere tilted towards the Sun* / Winter

Sun

DECEMBER 21st — Winter / Summer *Southern hemisphere tilted towards the Sun*

Orbit of the Earth around the Sun, taking one year (365.25 days)

SEPTEMBER 23rd

The seasons change as the Earth moves around the Sun.

What is a leap year?

A year is the length of time it takes for the Earth to travel once around the Sun. There are usually 365 days in a year, divided into 12 months. But the Earth does not travel around the Sun in exactly 365 days. It takes a bit longer than that – about 365.25 days. So, an extra day is added to February (as the 29th) every four years. This 366-day year is called a leap year and uses up the four extra quarter days. You can tell if a year is a leap year if it divides exactly by four. So, for example, 1990 was not a leap year because 1990 does not divide exactly by four. Can you work out when the next leap year will be?

> **? Did you know?**
>
> A year on Pluto lasts for 164.8 Earth years. This is how long Pluto takes to travel around the Sun.

> **? Did you know?**
>
> An Earth year is really 365.24219878 days long. To make calculations easier, we round it off to 365.25 days.

Above: A sunny summer's day.

Right: A snowy day in winter in the same place.

Why do puddles dry up in the Sun?

In warm weather, any puddles left by a shower of rain quickly dry up in the Sun and disappear. But where does the rain water go to when it disappears? The answer is that it evaporates. This means that the Sun's heat makes the liquid water turn into its invisible gas form, which is called water vapour. The **molecules** of water vapour then escape into the air and spread out.

Evaporation actually takes place all the time. The water molecules are constantly passing into the air. The puddle would eventually dry up of its own accord as long as there were no more showers. But on a warm day, the Sun heats the water and causes it to evaporate more quickly than it would otherwise.

There is always some water vapour in the air. It plays a very important part in the weather (see page 20). But warm air can hold more water vapour than cold air. This is why the water from the puddles passes easily into the air on a warm day.

! See for yourself

You can use a simple experiment to see how water evaporates in the Sun. Stand a small saucer of water on a sunny windowsill. How long does it take to dry up and disappear? Try the same experiment using a dark-coloured and a light-coloured saucer. The water in the dark saucer will heat up and evaporate more quickly than the water in the other saucer. The darker colour absorbs more heat than the lighter colour, which bounces a lot of it back into the air. This keeps the light-coloured saucer and its water, cooler.

The bed of a dried-up river in India.

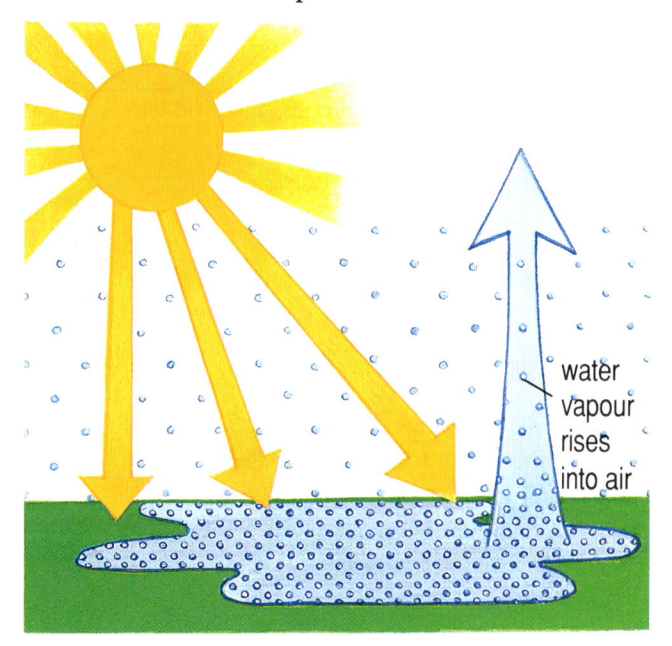

Water evaporates on a sunny day.

Why do we hang washing out to dry?

The best time to hang washing out to dry is on a sunny, windy day. The Sun dries the washing by evaporation, just as it dries up the puddle. The Sun's heat turns the droplets of water in the wet clothes into invisible water vapour, which vanishes into the air.

As the water molecules pass from the clothes into the air, they create a layer of 'wet' air around the clothes. If the air is very wet, the clothes will take a long time to dry. This is because the air is already **saturated** with water vapour, so it cannot absorb any more moisture from the wet clothes. The clothes will dry more quickly if the wind is blowing. This is because the wind carries the wet air away and replaces it with drier air, which can absorb moisture.

Washing dries by evaporation.

See for yourself

To see condensation at work, breathe out on to a cold surface such as a mirror or window pane. Your breath will cloud over the glass. After a while, you should be able to see tiny droplets of water trickling down the mirror or window.

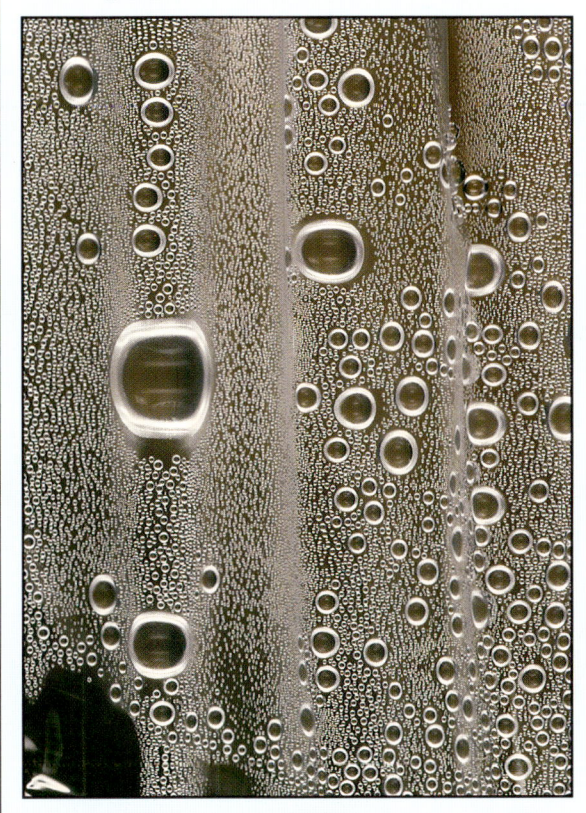

Condensation on a window.

Why can we see our breath on a cold day?

If water vapour cools down again, it turns back into liquid water (see page 20). This process is called condensation. When you breathe out on a cold day, does your breath make a white cloud? This is because of condensation. The air you breathe out contains some water vapour. When this comes into contact with the cold air, it cools down and turns into tiny droplets of water.

What makes it rain?

Rain forms inside clouds, particularly inside clouds which are dark and grey. Sometimes, hundreds of the tiny droplets of water inside a cloud collide with one another to form larger drops. When these drops are big enough, they fall from the cloud as rain. It takes over a thousand droplets to make a raindrop. Rain also forms if snow melts on its way down to Earth. Sleet is a mixture of rain and snow.

Raindrops are often thought to be shaped like teardrops. In fact, they look more like circles with the bottoms cut off. Raindrops are usually about as wide as the base of this letter 'b'.

A tropical downpour.

? Did you know?

The wettest place in the world is Tutunendo in Colombia, South America. It has an average of 11,770 millimetres of rain a year. This is enough to cover six people standing on top of each other's shoulders.

? Did you know?

The water on the Earth is used again and again. It moves around the world largely by evaporation and condensation (see pages 19 and 20). The Sun's heat evaporates water from the land, rivers and seas. It rises into the air as water vapour. As it rises, it condenses and forms clouds. Then rain or snow falls from the clouds, back on to the land and into the rivers and seas. No new water is ever made.

The water cycle happens all the time, reusing the Earth's water supply.

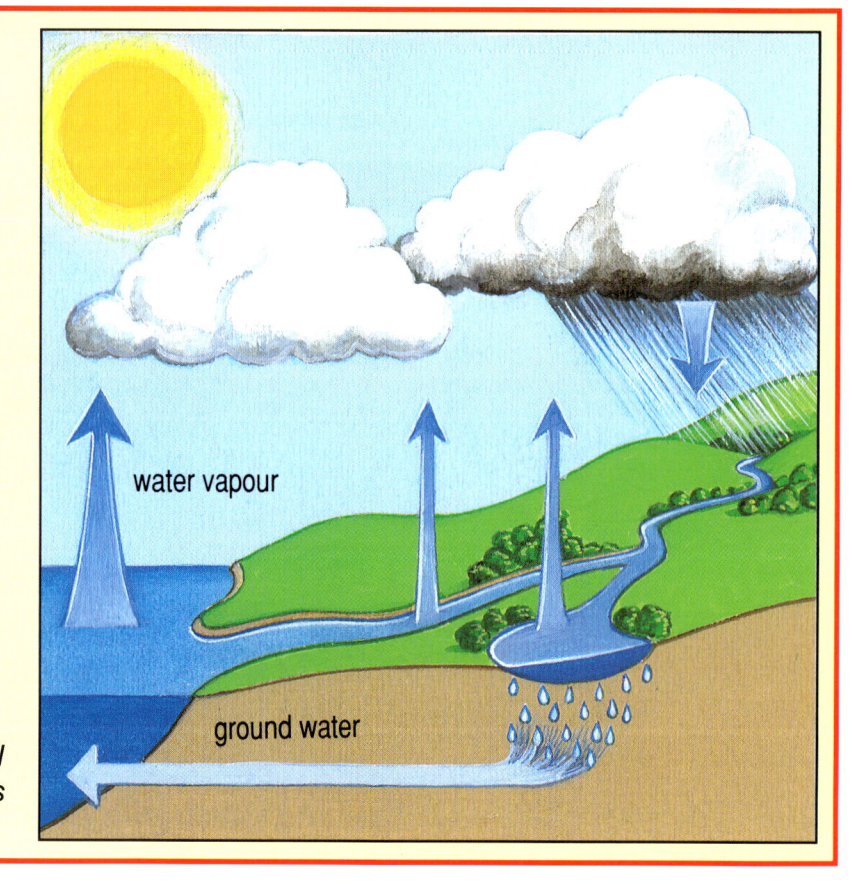

What are rainbows?

The light coming from the Sun is called white light. But it is made up of a mixture of different colours. The main colours in sunlight are red, orange, yellow, green, blue, indigo and violet. These are known as the colours of the spectrum. They are the colours you see in a rainbow.

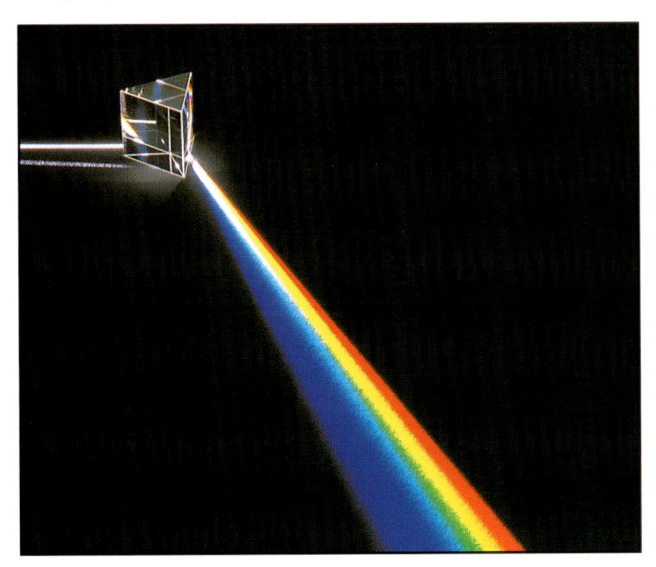

A prism splits white light into the colours of the spectrum.

If you shine white light through a triangular block of glass, it splits up into the colours of the spectrum. The block of glass is called a prism. As the light rays pass through the prism, they are bent, or refracted. Each colour bends a slightly different amount. This makes the colours fan out so you can see each one quite clearly.

When the Sun comes out during a shower of rain, the sunlight shines through the raindrops. They act like tiny prisms and split the sunlight up into its different colours. The colours form a rainbow in the sky. Red is always at the top and violet at the bottom. To see a rainbow, you must stand with your back to the Sun.

Why is the sky blue?

Blue is one of the colours that makes up white light. When the Sun is high in the sky, light has only a short distance to travel to reach Earth. But as it travels, it hits dust particles in the atmosphere. These particles scatter the light. Blue light scatters before any of the other colours in the spectrum, so it is the blue light that we can see. The other colours hit the Earth before they are scattered. After sunrise and before sunset, most of the sunlight passes straight through the gas molecules. But dust scatters the blue light all over the sky. This is why the sky looks blue.

But at dawn and dusk, when the Sun is low, light has to travel further, so other colours get scattered before they reach the Earth. This is why we get beautiful red and orange sunsets.

At sunrise and sunset, the sky is often a dramatic orange-red colour.

Why is Space black?

Space has no air at all. It is a vacuum. So white light can pass straight through it without being scattered. The Moon always has a black sky because it has no atmosphere to hold dust particles.

What is air made of?

Hot-air balloons are filled with a light gas, helium.

The air you breathe is made up of a mixture of different gases. About 78 per cent of the air is nitrogen. Some 21 per cent is oxygen. About 1 per cent of the air is made up of the gas, argon. There are also tiny amounts of carbon dioxide, helium, hydrogen, methane, neon, ozone, krypton, xenon and water vapour in the air.

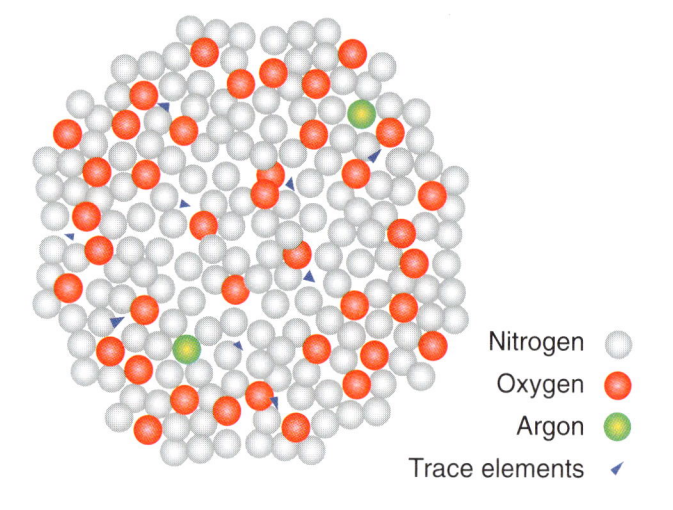

Nitrogen ○
Oxygen ●
Argon ●
Trace elements ◂

Air is made up of many different gases.

What is the atmosphere?

The atmosphere is a huge blanket of air which surrounds the Earth. It is divided into different layers, as you can see in the diagram below. We live in the layer closest to the ground. This is called the troposphere. It reaches about 16 kilometres up into the sky. This is also where our weather is made. The highest layer is the exosphere, where satellites orbit the Earth. It reaches a height of about 8,000 kilometres. Above it, there is

a satellite in the exosphere (500 – 8,000 km)

a space shuttle crossing into the thermosphere (80 – 500 km)

meteorites

the mesosphere (50 – 80 km)

Concorde and a weather balloon in the stratosphere (12 – 50 km)

passenger jet in the troposphere (0 – 12 km)

The layers of the atmosphere.

The atmosphere protects the Earth from the burning effects of the Sun's harmful ultra-violet rays. It also stops the Earth getting too cold, by preventing all of the Earth's heat from escaping into Space. The atmosphere is kept in place around the Earth by the Earth's gravity (see page 40). This stops the atmosphere from floating off into Space.

❓ Did you know?

Some 80 per cent of the air in the atmosphere is found in the troposphere. There is less and less air the higher up you go. In Space, there is no air at all.

Climbers run out of breath when they climb high up. Some even have to wear oxygen masks, although others try to climb to the top without them.

What is the ozone layer?

A gas called ozone is found high up in the Earth's atmosphere, and low down on the ground. At ground level, the ozone is man-made, mainly by gases from car exhaust fumes. These gases react in bright sunlight and change into ozone gas. It pollutes the air and can be poisonous to people and animals.

But high up, the ozone occurs naturally and helps to protect life on Earth. It forms a 'shield' around the Earth which stops the Sun's harmful ultra-violet (UV) rays from reaching us.

Since 1985, scientists have been worried that the amount of ozone gas in the layer is getting less and less. They have found patches of ozone which are so thin that they look like holes in the layer. These 'holes' drift and split up all the time, but a very large one has been found over the Antarctic. It is thought that man-made gases such as those in aerosol cans have thinned the ozone in this way.

Can you think what would happen if there was no ozone layer at all? The Sun's harmful rays would reach the Earth causing skin cancers and eye cataracts, and damaging plants. To stop the ozone from disappearing, we have to stop releasing damaging gases into the air.

The white area shows the hole in the ozone layer over Antarctica in October 1991.

What is lightning?

Hot, sticky weather and towering, black cumulonimbus clouds are sure signs that a thunderstorm is on its way. Thunderstorms can be very dramatic, with flashes of lightning, booming thunder, gusty winds and pouring rain. There may also be showers of hailstones (see page 24).

As a thundercloud grows, there is a lot of activity taking place inside it. Strong air currents bounce water droplets and pieces of ice up and down inside the cloud. These collide and rub against each other. The rubbing makes a force called an electrical charge.

The cloud is now charged with electricity. There are positive charges at the top of the cloud and negative charges at the bottom. The negative charges attract the positive charges and a giant spark of electricity jumps between them. You can see this spark as a flash of lightning. The lightning may also flash between the cloud and the ground.

A dramatic streak of lightning.

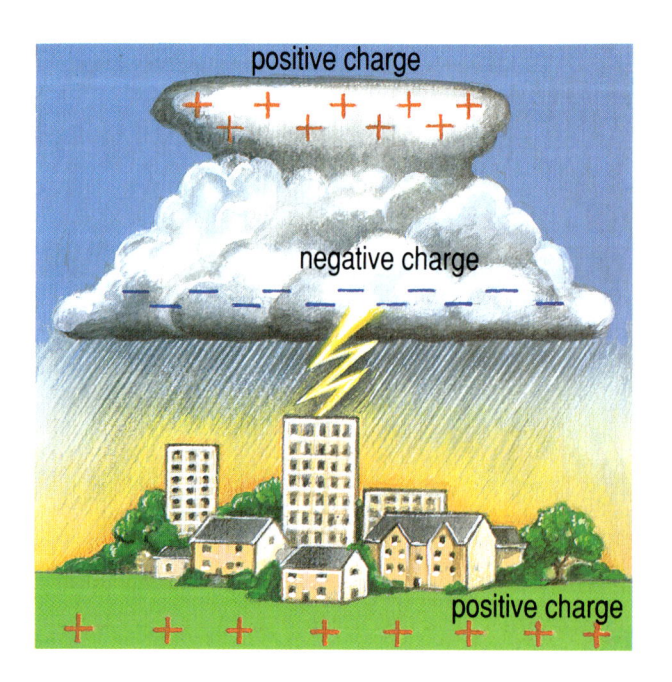

Lightning flashes within the cloud.

Lightning flashes to the ground.

> **! See for yourself**
>
> Lightning is a type of electricity, called static electricity. It is the same type of electricity that makes your clothes crackle when you take them off. If you undress in the dark, you can even see sparks coming from your clothes. Sometimes, static electricity can make your hair stand on end, or crackle when you comb it. To see how strong static electricity is, comb your hair with a plastic comb. Then use the comb to pick up some small pieces of torn-up paper.

> **? Did you know?**
>
> Thunderstorms are extremely powerful. If you could collect the energy from a single flash of lightning, it would be enough to light up a town for a year.

> **? Did you know?**
>
> It is very dangerous to shelter under a tree during a thunderstorm. Lightning always takes the shortest path to the ground. It could hit the tree on its way.
>
> *A tree trunk burned by lightning.*

Why does thunder boom?

As the lightning streaks through the cloud, it heats the air around it to about 30,000 °C. The air gets so hot that it expands very quickly indeed. This is what causes the loud, booming noise of thunder. The thunder happens at exactly the same time as the lightning. But you see the lightning first. This is because light travels through the air faster than sound.

> **! See for yourself**
>
> To find out how far away a thunderstorm is, count the number of seconds between the lightning and the thunder. Then divide the number of seconds by three. This will give the distance of the storm in kilometres.
>
> 1... 2 ... 3... 4... 5... 6...
>
> 6 divided by 3 = 2 kilometres

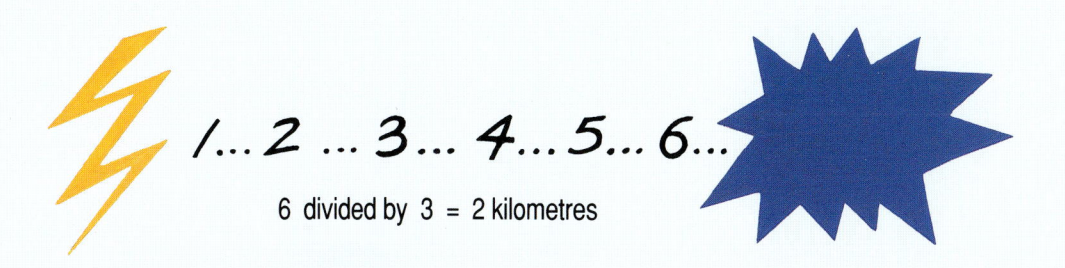

Why do leaves fall downwards?

If you throw a ball or a stone into the air, it always comes down again. It is pulled towards the Earth by the force of Earth's gravity. Gravity is an invisible force that pulls different objects towards each other. But the force of the pull depends on the size of the objects. The force of gravity becomes stronger as the objects get bigger. An object needs to be as huge as the Earth for its gravity to be very strong.

The Earth's gravity pulls everything down towards the centre of the Earth. It holds the atmosphere in place around the Earth (see page 7). It also holds you down on to the surface of the Earth. Otherwise, you would float off into Space. Gravity holds the Moon in place in its orbit around the Earth. It holds the planets in their orbit around the Sun. Gravity is also the reason why leaves fall downwards from the trees.

Objects have weight because the force of gravity pulls them downwards. The Moon's gravity is only a sixth as strong as the Earth's gravity. This means that when astronauts walk on the Moon, they weigh only a sixth of their weight on Earth.

> **? Did you know?**
>
> In the 17th century, the British scientist, Isaac Newton, was the first person to understand the force of gravity. Newton is said to have realized how gravity works after watching an apple fall from a tree.

The force of gravity makes leaves fall downwards.

Why do plant roots grow downwards?

A plant's roots anchor the plant in the ground and suck up water and minerals from the soil. The plant uses these to make its food. Roots do not grow downwards by accident. The cells at the ends of a root contain starch, which collects on one side of each cell as the roots are pulled by gravity. This tells the plant which way up it is and the way it should grow in order to find the things it needs. As water and minerals usually sink deep into the soil, a plant's roots therefore grow downwards in order to find them.

Gravity affects plants' roots.

? Did you know?

If a feather and a hammer are dropped from an aeroplane, gravity pulls them down at the same speed. So they should land together. Only air resistance stops the feather from landing at the same time (see page 38).

! See for yourself

All objects have a point at which their weight balances evenly. This is called their centre of gravity. Hold your palm out and try to balance a tray on it. When the tray is perfectly balanced, your palm will be under its centre of gravity.

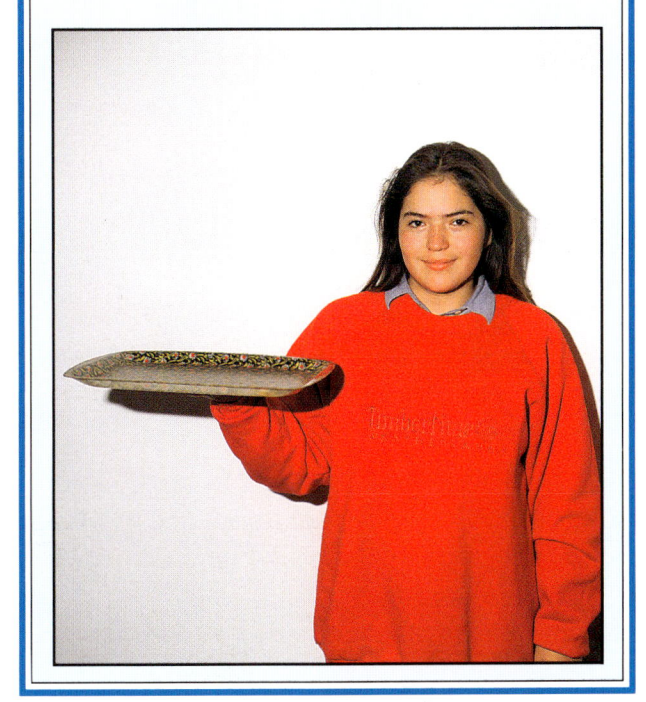

Why does rain fall faster than snow?

As an object falls through the air, the air slows it down. This is called air resistance. Some objects fall more quickly than others because they have smoother, more streamlined shapes. They do not meet as much air resistance as objects which have more irregular, spreading shapes. Raindrops have a more streamlined shape than snowflakes. This is why they fall more quickly through the air.

Sports cars and racing cars have sleek, streamlined shapes to help them cut cleanly through the air. Their design reduces air resistance, or drag, so that they can go faster.

Dragster racing cars are streamlined to make them go faster.

⚠ See for yourself

This simple experiment will help you see how an object's shape affects the speed at which it falls through the air. Find an A4-sized piece of paper. Let the paper fall and see how long it takes to reach the ground. Now take the same piece of paper and crumple it up into a ball. Drop it from the same height as before. It will fall much quicker because its shape is much more **compact**.

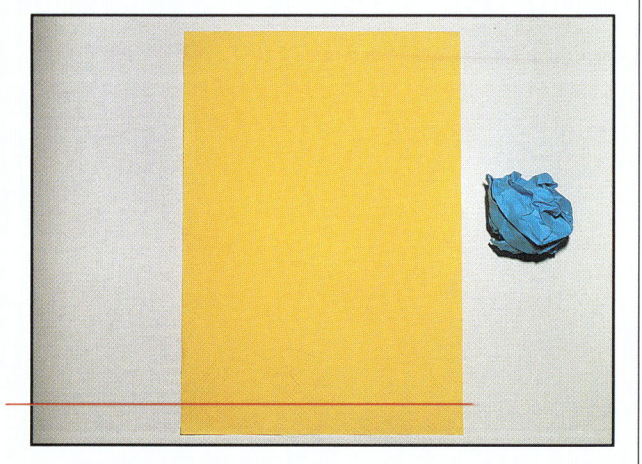

You can use many different shapes and sizes of paper.

How do parachutes work?

An open parachute has a wide, spreading shape. As it floats down through the air, a lot of air pushes against it, slowing it down and helping the parachutist to land safely. Without a parachute, a person would fall quickly through the air because there would be less resistance.

⚠ See for yourself

Make your own parachute out of a square handkerchief with a thread tied to each corner. Tie the threads together and attach them to different objects, such as a matchstick or a paper clip. Then see how long it takes to parachute to the ground from a set height. Now see how long it takes for the same object to fall without the parachute.

Above: A paraglider, like a parachutist, descends slowly because of air resistance.

Right: Hang-gliders glide on currents of air.

How far away are the stars?

Space itself is so incredibly huge that scientists have to use a special measurement to calculate distances within it. This measurement is called a light year, or the distance that light travels in one year. Light travels faster than any other known thing in the Universe, at 9.5 million million kilometres in a year. So one light year is equal to an amazing 9.5 million million kilometres.

The nearest star to Earth, after the Sun, is called Proxima Centauri. It is 4.25 light years away, or 40 million million kilometres. This means that the light you see coming from this star started its journey over four years ago.

If you could fly to Proxima Centauri in an ordinary aircraft, your journey would take over 5 million years.

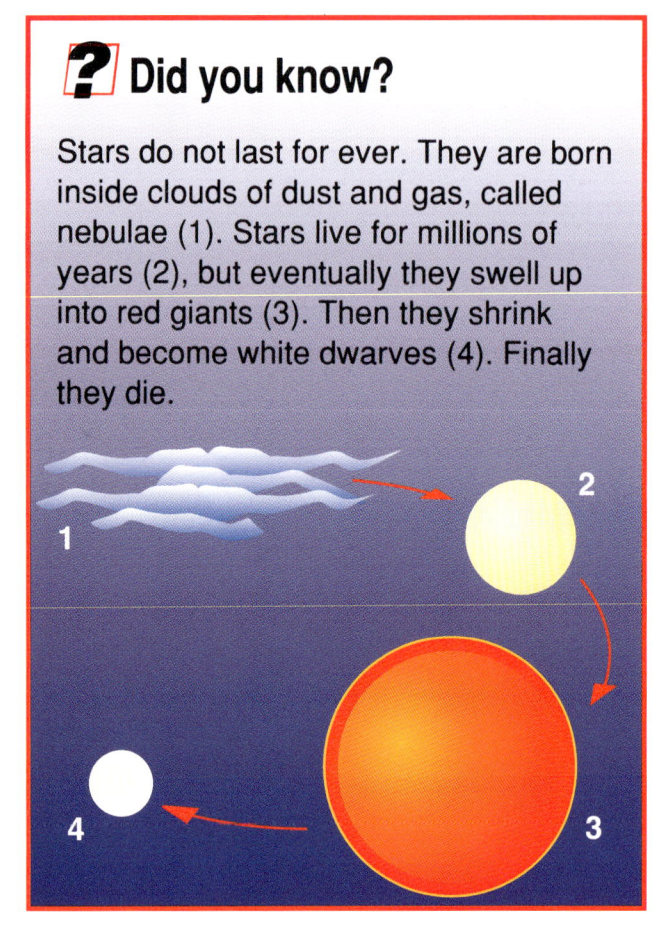

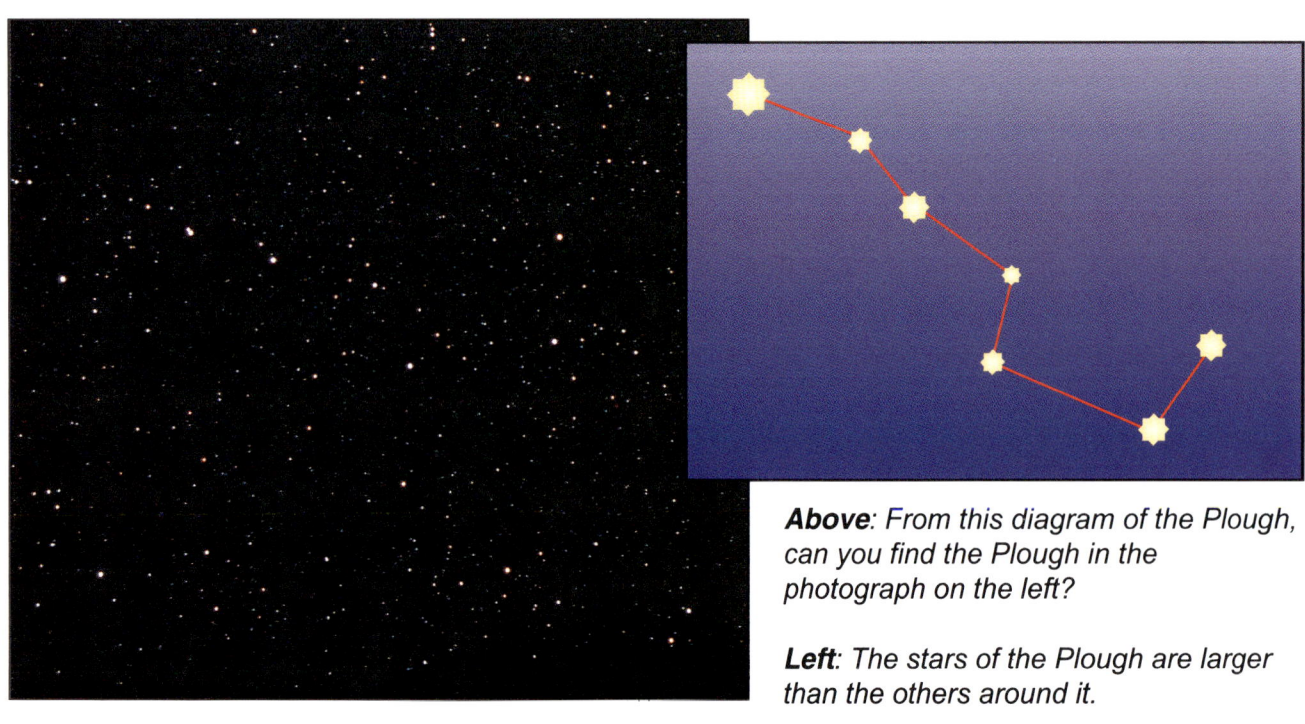

? Did you know?

Stars do not last for ever. They are born inside clouds of dust and gas, called nebulae (1). Stars live for millions of years (2), but eventually they swell up into red giants (3). Then they shrink and become white dwarves (4). Finally they die.

Above: From this diagram of the Plough, can you find the Plough in the photograph on the left?

Left: The stars of the Plough are larger than the others around it.

How many stars are there in Space?

There are millions and millions of stars in Space. But no one has ever counted them all. Our group of stars, or galaxy, is called the Milky Way. It contains about 20 million million stars, including our Sun. It is about 100,000 light years across. But the Milky Way is just one of about 100 million million galaxies in the Universe. If each of these contained as many stars as the Milky Way, it would mean that the Universe could hold 2,000 million, million, million stars!

! See for yourself

The Andromeda Galaxy is the furthest object in Space that you can see without using a telescope. It contains about 400 million million stars. It is about 2.25 million light years away. Can you work out how far that is in kilometres?

The Andromeda Galaxy.

Why do stars shine at night?

Stars are gigantic, glowing balls made up mainly of hydrogen gas. In the middle of the star, the gas is constantly changing into heat and light. This is how stars make their own light, and it is why they shine.

Stars shine all the time, not just at night. They are so far away, though, that their light is very dim. During the day, the stars' light is swamped by the light coming from the Sun, which is much closer to Earth. You can see the stars at night because there is no sunlight. The stars seem to twinkle because their light is scattered by the atmosphere. You can learn more about the atmosphere on page 26.

? Did you know?

The brightest star in the sky is called Sirius, the 'dog star'. It shines about 26 times brighter than the Sun.

? Did you know?

The planet Venus seems to shine as brightly as a star. Look out for it after sunset or before sunrise.

Planet Venus and the Moon.

Why does the Moon seem to change shape?

The Moon is the Earth's closest neighbour in Space, at a distance of 384,000 kilometres. It orbits the Earth once every 27.3 days. During this time, it appears to change shape from a thin, crescent shape to a full circle and then back to a crescent again. The Moon really stays the same shape all the time. But different amounts of it are lit by the Sun, so you see different shapes. Each shape shows a **phase** of the Moon.

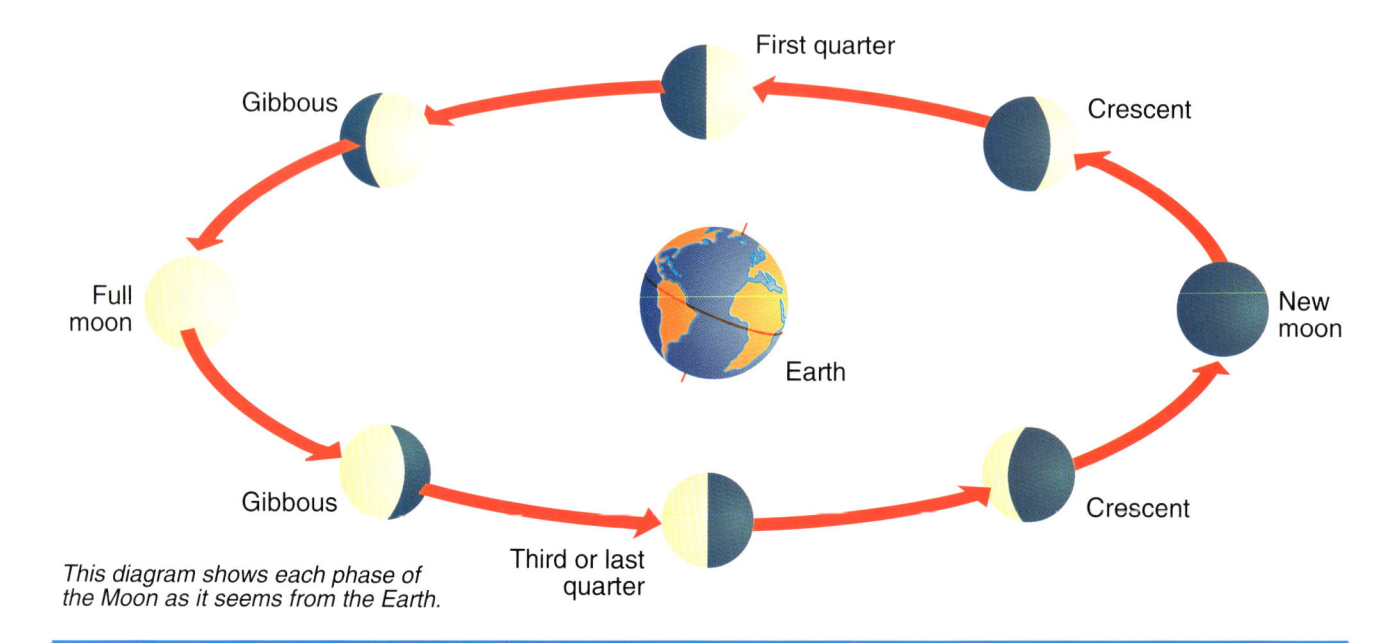

This diagram shows each phase of the Moon as it seems from the Earth.

❗ See for yourself

For this experiment, you will need the fruit and stick model from page 15 and a torch. The model is now the Moon, the torch is the Sun and the person holding the Moon is the Earth. Ask a friend to hold the torch and shine it at you. Now stand in the torch beam and hold the Moon straight up in front of you. Turn round in a circle, facing the same side of the Moon all the time. Can you see how the Moon waxes (grows bigger) and wanes (grows smaller) as it passes through its phases?

Which phase of the Moon is showing here?

> **? Did you know?**
>
> In July 1969, Neil Armstrong became the first person to set foot on the Moon. He was part of the American Apollo 11 Moon mission.
>
> *Neil Armstrong – the first person on the Moon.*

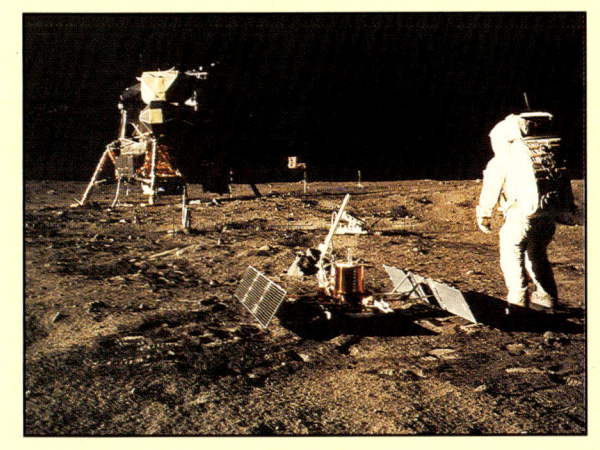

What is the dark side of the Moon?

The Moon takes 27.3 days to circle the Earth. It also takes 27.3 days to spin once on its axis. This means that the Sun only lights up one side of the Moon so that, from Earth, we always see the same side of the Moon. We can never see the far side, or dark side, of the Moon from any part of the Earth.

In October 1959, the Russian Space probe 'Luna 3' flew behind the Moon and took photographs of the dark side. This was the first time that the dark side of the Moon had ever been taken.

> **? Did you know**
>
> The biggest crater on the Moon is called 'Bailly'. It covers the area twice the size of the country, Belgium.

What are the dark patches on the Moon?

On a clear night, you can easily see the dark patches on the Moon's surface. They make a pattern which sometimes look like a face. This is what started the story of the 'Man in the Moon'. The dark patches are seas. But they are not full of sea-water. They are great plains of **lava** which flowed from inside the Moon million of years ago. When the lava flowed out, it was red hot, liquid rock. As it reached the surface, it cooled and became solid. The seas on the Moon have wonderful names, such as the 'Sea of Serenity', the 'Ocean of Storms' and 'Bay of Rainbows'.

The surface of the Moon is also pitted with craters. These formed when meteorites (Space rocks) crashed into the Moon.

A crater on the dark side of the Moon.

> **? Did you know?**
>
> It is totally silent on the Moon. This is because there is no air to carry sounds from place to place.

See for Yourself! Outdoor Science Quiz

Now that you have read this chapter, you could test yourself with these questions.

Questions
1. How hot is the surface of the Sun?
2. How many minutes does it take the heat from the Sun to reach Earth?
   a) 2   b) 8.5   c) 16   d) 24.5   e) 50
3. What is the Sun's energy called?
4. What are solar cells used for?
5. What is the name of an object which allows no light to pass through it?
6. What is a lunar eclipse?
7. How long is a day on planet Jupiter?
8. In what direction does the Earth spin?
9. What causes the changing of the seasons?
10. How can you tell if a year is a leap year?
11. How long does a year last on the planet Pluto?
12. Where does rain form?
13. Which type of gas makes up 78 per cent of the air we breathe?
14. What is the difference between ozone gas found at ground level and ozone gas found high in the Earth's atmosphere?
15. During a thunderstorm, why do you see the lightning before you hear the thunder?
16. What is the name given to the invisible force that pulls objects towards each other?
17. What is the name given to the Earth's group of stars?
18. Why does the Moon seem to change shape?
19. How long does it take the Moon to circle the Earth?
20. Why is the Moon totally silent?

Answers
Look back to find the answers on these pages.

Question	Page	Question	Page	Question	Page	Question	Page
1	158	6	163	11	167	16	176
2	159	7	164	12	170	17	181
3	161	8	165	13	172	18	182
4	161	9	166	14	173	19	183
5	162	10	167	15	175	20	183

Glossary

absorbs soaks in, like a sponge soaking in water

absorbed soaked up; taken in

adapted when an animal has changed over a long period of time to suit a certain way of life or living conditions.

acidic sharp and sour, like lemon juice; some acids can burn you

alveoli (alveolus) air sacs in the lungs

appliance a useful piece of equipment

atmosphere the layer of gases that surrounds the Earth

average a number or measurement that is not the greatest or the smallest, but is the mid-point between the two

bleached made lighter in colour

blood vessels tiny thread-like tubes which carry blood around the body

body tissue the kinds of material that we are made of

bonds connections; links

carbon a natural substance that is made from plant matter and is found in rock; there are many forms of carbon, from coal to diamonds

cell the smallest living thing; the building block from which all living things are made

chemical reaction any change within a substance which alters its chemicals; or a change that makes it into a different substance

climate the normal pattern of temperature and rainfall in a particular part of the world

colonies large groups that live together

compact tightly packed together

concentrated a very strong substance; when there is a lot of a certain substance mixed with very little water

condensed changed from water vapour into water, for example, when the vapour in a cloud changes into raindrops

currents water flowing in a certain direction

cycle a series of changes that keeps repeating itself

dappled spotted or blotched with patches of different colour

decreases gets less

digested when food has been broken down into small enough pieces to be absorbed into the bloodstream.

digestive juices juices inside an animal or plant which help to break down food into parts that the animal or plant can use

dissolve when a substance breaks up in water so that the substance can no longer be seen, such as when you mix a spoonful of salt into a glass of water

distorts when the normal shape of something changes

environments the rocks, buildings, trees and other plants among which a plant grow

enzymes chemicals made by living cells which can break down food into nutrients

Equator an imaginary line that passes right around the Earth at its fattest point, between the North and South Poles, dividing the Earth into two halves

evaporate when liquids are heated and the water in them turns into vapour in the air

evolved when an animal has changed or developed over many thousands of years, so that it has a better chance of survival

extinct describes a living thing that has died out completely

fibres fine threads

focus to make the edges of shapes clear and sharp so that the shapes can be seen easily

focused when the edges of shapes are clearly seen and do not look blurred

fossils the remains of prehistoric plants and animals which have turned to stone

fronds leaves, especially ferns and palms

glands pockets of special fluids, or liquids, in different parts of a body; the glands release the fluids, which have special jobs to do in the body

gravity a force that pulls on something solid

hibernate to hide away and sleep during harsh weather such as a very cold season or a very dry season; an animal's body slows down so that it does not use up too much energy

image a picture or likeness of something

insulates protects, usually against the cold or the heat

interprets explains

lava hot, liquid rock that flows out of volcanoes

lens a clear material through which light can pass, and which can bend the rays of light

lenses the parts of an eye which help it to focus

microscopic something that can only be seen in detail with the help of a microscope

molecules tiny pieces of matter with which all substances are made

nectar a sweet, sticky food for many insects. It is found deep inside flowers

nerve a tiny, very thin thread, along which messages are sent both from the body to the brain, and from the brain to the body

northern hemisphere the northern half of the Earth above the Equator

nourishing foods containing a lot of goodness, which keeps animals and plants healthy

nutrients minerals, vitamins and other good things in food: they help animals and plants to grow and stay healthy

orbiting following a certain path around a planet or the Sun, such as the Moon going round the Earth or the Earth going round the Sun

phase a certain stage that is reached

pigment colouring

potting compost a special mixture of soil and broken-down, rotted plant and animal matter; it is good for the healthy growth of flowers and vegetables that are planted in it

prey animals which are killed and eaten by other animals

prise to force open with a lever

projected thrown onto

protein the body's building or repair material

react to respond or change as a result of coming into contact with something different

reactions changes that are sparked off by something

regurgitate when food which has already been chewed and swallowed is brought back into the mouth from the stomach

reflected bounced back

resources raw materials, such as trees and metal ores, from which other things are made

saturated completely soaked

sensor something that can detect, or feel, different conditions, such as rough or smooth, hot or cold, soft or hard, etc.

southern hemisphere the southern half on the Earth below the Equator

species groups, or types, of plants and animals

spores special single cells that can reproduce, or make new plants, on their own, without needing any other cells

starch energy-giving foodstuff found in rice, potatoes, spaghetti, bread and so on

stun to knock out, or paralyze, so that an animal's body cannot move

summits the tops of mountains

supple something that is soft and can change its shape

taut tight and straight

transparent completely clear

vapour the gas form of a liquid

vibrates moves backwards and forwards very quickly

vibration moving backwards and forwards very fast

waste products things that cannot be used

water vapour water in the air in the form of an invisible gas

Index

Achilles tendon, 12
Aestivation, 53
Air, 172-173
Air pollution, 160, 173
Air pressure, 59
Air resistance, 177-179
Algae, 68, 69, 71, 92, 93
Alveoli, 16, 17
Amphibians, 38, 54-55
Angel Falls, 117
Ants, 43
Appendix, 21, 23
Arachnids, 39, 46
Arteries, 14
Atmosphere, 159, 171, 172, 173, 176
Atoms, 128, 129, 136

Baking Powder, 152
Balance, 29
Bark, 84-85
Batteries, 137, 139
Bee-orchids, 77
Bees, 42, 43
Big Bang, 99
Birds, 38, 41. 58-59
Birds-of-prey, 41
Blood, 14, 15, 16
Boiling, 130
Bones, 8, 10 - 11
Brain, 12, 20, 28-29, 33
Bread, 152-153
Breathing, 18-19
Bulbs (electric), 139
Butterflies, 43, 44, 45

Cacti, 90, 91
Camels, 60-61
Capillaries, 14
Capillary action, 135
Carbon, 144
Carbon Dioxide, 152
Cartilage, 10
Caterpillars, 44-45
Cells, 8-9, 16
Centripetal force, 148, 149
Chemical reactions, 150, 151

Chlorophyll, 70
Chloroplasts, 70
Chromium, 151
Clay, 144
Clouds, 170, 174
Coffee, 131, 132
Cold-blooded animals, 39
Colours, 48, 55
Compasses, 145
Condensation, 130, 169, 170
Conduction, 159
Cones, 69, 93
Conifers, 69
Continents, 100, 101
Convection, 159
Cork, 85
Coughing, 18
Crystals, 109
Crustaceans, 39
Cuttings, 69

Deltas, 116
Density, 19
Deserts, 120-121
Detergents, 134 - 135
Diamonds, 109, 144
Diaphragm, 16, 19
Diatoms, 68
Digestion, 21, 22, 23
Dinoflagellates, 88
Dinosaurs, 39
Dissolving, 131, 132, 133, 135
Dragonflies, 40, 45
Dunes, 121

Ears, 28-29
Earth,
  Age of, 98
  Crust of, 100, 102. 104, 106
  Inside the, 100
  Mantle of, 100
  Measurements of, 99
  Plates of, 100, 102, 104
Earth's Axis, 164-166
Earth's spin, 164-165

Earthquakes, 104-105
Eclipse, lunar, 163
Electricity, 136-139, 140, 146, 160, 174-175
  Circuit, 138-139
  Dangers of, 139
  Static, 136, 137, 175
Electrons, 136
Elephants, 63
Ectotherms, 39
Endotherms, 39
Energy, 20, 160
Enzymes, 22
Erosion, 103, 114
Estuaries, 116
Evaporation, 130, 168, 169, 170
Eyes, 26-27, 40, 41

Feathers, 58-59
Ferns, 68
Fibres, 135
Fire, 150, 151
Fish, 38, 48-53
Fizzy Drinks, 133
Flat-fish, 48
Flowers, 76-77, 81
  Biggest, 77
  Smallest, 77
Food, 20-21, 22, 23
Forces, 148
Fossil Fuels, 113
Fossils, 112-113
Freezing, 130, 131
Friction, 144, 148, 151
Fridges, 131
Frogs, 54-55
Fulcrum, 146-147
Fungi, 69, 86, 87
Fungus, 36-37

Galaxies, 158, 181
Gemstones, 109
Generator (electric), 138
Genes, 27
Germination, 78, 79
Germs, 18

Geysers, 107
Giant Sequoia, 81
Gills, 50
Giraffes, 40
Glass, 129
Gold, 110
Graphite, 144
Grasshoppers, 45
Gravity, 74, 99, 148, 173, 176-177
Growth,
   Fastest, 80
   Slowest, 81, 89

Hammer throwers, 33
Heart, 8, 14-15
Heat, 159
   Ways of travelling, 159
Herbs, 81
Hibernation, 53
Hiccuping, 19
Honey, 42-43
Honeyguides, 77
Honeypot ants, 43
Horsetails, 68
Hunger, 20

Ice, 128, 130, 131
Ice skating, 131
Insects, 39, 40
Invertebrates, 39
Islands, 101

Joints, 10, 11

Kettle (electric), 136, 137, 138

Lakes, 116
   Ox-bow, 116
Lava, 106, 107
Leap years, 167
Leaves, 70-71, 89
Lenticels, 84
Levers, 146, 147
Lichens, 69, 89, 93
Ligaments, 10
Light, 142, 143, 159, 162, 171
Light years, 180

Lightning, 136, 174, 175
Liverworts, 68
Load, 146-147
Locusts, 45
Lung-fish, 53
Lungs, 16-17

Magnetism, 145, 148
Mammals, 38
Mangroves, 75
Matter, states of, 128, 130
Meanders, 116
Melanin, 27
Melting, 130
Metals, 110-111
Metamorphosis, 44-45
Midnight Sun, 165
Milky Way, 158, 181
Minerals, 108-109, 110, 112
Mirages, 121
Mirrors, 142, 143
Molecules, 128, 129, 130, 131, 132, 133, 168, 169, 171
Molluscs, 39
Moon, 171, 182-183
   Craters, 183
   Dark side of the, 183
   Phases of the, 182
   Seas, 183
Moray eels, 52
Mosses, 68
Moths, 41
Mould, 153
Moulting, 45, 57
Mountains, 102-103
   Block, 102
   Fold, 102
   Under-sea, 119
Mount Everest, 103
Mucus, 18, 30
Mud-skippers, 51
Muscles, 8, 10, 12-13

Nails, 8
Navigation, 41
Nectar, 42, 43
Nerves, 24, 26, 30, 33
Night, 164, 165

Nose, 38
Nutcrackers, 146
Nutrients, 14, 20

Oceans, 118-119
Oil, 134, 135
Orchids, 75, 77
Ores, 18-19
Oxygen, 70, 71, 73, 128, 129, 150, 151
Ozone layer, 173

Pangaea, 100
Panthalassa, 101
Panting, 17
Parasites, 83
Pencils, 144
Peristalsis, 21
Petals, 77
Photocopiers, 137
Photosynthesis, 70-71, 72-73, 82, 93
Planets, 99
Plants, 177
   Carnivorous, 82-83
   Desert, 90-91
   Flowering, 68-69
Plugs, 137, 138
Poisonous, 86
Pollen, 76, 77
Pollination, 42, 76-77, 78, 83
Pulse rate, 15

Radiation, 159
Rain, 114, 122, 170, 171, 178
Rainbows, 171
Rainforests, 122 - 123
Recycling, 111
Reflection, 142, 143
Respiration, 72-73
Ring of Fire, 105
River Nile, 115
Rivers, 114- 115, 116, 117
Rocks, 98, 106, 108-109
   Igneous, 108
   Metamorphic, 108
   Sedimentary, 108, 113
Roller coaster, 149

Roots, 74-75
   Ariel, 75
   Buttress, 75
   Stilt, 75
Rust, 151

Salt, 132
Scissors, 147
Seaquakes, 13
Seas, 98, 118-119
Seasons, 171, 166-167
Seaweed, 68, 92, 93
Sediment, 114-115, 116
Seeds, 78-79, 91
   Biggest, 79
   Smallest, 79
Self-defence, 86-89
Senses, 26
Shadows, 162, 163
   Penumbra, 162
   Umbra, 162
Sharks, 49
Silicon, 129
Silks, 46, 47
Skeleton, 10-11
Skin, 8, 33
Sky, colour of, 171
Sleet, 170
Smell, 30-31, 32
Snakes, 56-57

Sneezing, 18
Snow, 170, 178
Solar system, 99
Solutions, 132
Sound, 140, 141
Space, 159, 171, 173, 176, 180-181
Spiders, 46-47
Spin dryers, 148
Spinal Cord, 24
Spores, 68
Squid, 41
Stars, 180-181
Stone plants, 89
Sugar, 131, 132
Sun, 158-159, 160-161, 164-165, 173, 182
   Distance from Earth, 158
   Heat and light, 159, 171
   Solar power, 160-161
   Temperature, 158
Sundial, 163
Sunrise, 171
Sunset, 171
Sweating, 33
Swim-bladders, 49
Synovial fluid, 10

Tadpoles, 54-55
Taste Buds, 32

Telephones, 140, 141
Tendons, 12
Thunder, 174-175
Thunderstorms, 174-175
Tissue, 8
Toads, 54
Tongue, 32
Towels, 135
Trees, 68, 69, 74
Tsunamis, 105

Valleys,
   under-sea, 119
Vertebrates, 38
Viscosity, 129
Volcanoes, 98, 102, 106, 107

Warm-blooded animals, 39
Water, 171
Water cycle, 171
Water vapour, 98, 128, 130
Waterfalls, 117
Webs, 46, 47
Whales, 38

Years, 167
Yeast, 36, 37